Crossed Lives—Crossed Purposes

Crossed Lives—Crossed Purposes

Why Thomas Jefferson Failed and William Wilberforce Persisted in Leading an End to Slavery

RAY BLUNT

RESOURCE *Publications* · Eugene, Oregon

CROSSED LIVES—CROSSED PURPOSES
Why Thomas Jefferson Failed and William Wilberforce Persisted
in Leading an End to Slavery

Copyright © 2012 Ray Blunt. All rights reserved. Except for brief quotations in critical publications or reviews, no part of this book may be reproduced in any manner without prior written permission from the publisher. Write: Permissions, Wipf and Stock Publishers, 199 W. 8th Ave., Suite 3, Eugene, OR 97401.

Resource Publications
An Imprint of Wipf and Stock Publishers
199 W. 8th Ave., Suite 3
Eugene, OR 97401
www.wipfandstock.com

ISBN 13: 978-1-61097-571-1
Manufactured in the U.S.A.

All scripture quotations, unless otherwise indicated, are taken from the Holy Bible, New International Version®, NIV®. Copyright ©1973, 1978, 1984 by Biblica, Inc.™ Used by permission of Zondervan. All rights reserved worldwide.

William Wilberforce by John Russell, Ref. 759, ©National Portrait Gallery, London

William Wilberforce by John Richmond, Ref. 4997, ©National Portrait Gallery, London

William Wilberforce by Charles Howard Hodges, Ref. D37512; published by John Rising; ©National Portrait Gallery, London

Heroes of the Slave Trade Abolition, Ref. d9338, ©National Portrait Gallery, London

John Newton by John Russell, The Church Missionary Society and The John Newton Project, London.

Portrait of James Madison by Gilbert Stuart, District of Columbia, 1804, accession #1945-23, image #TC 1992-23, *The Colonial Williamsburg Foundation. Gift of Mrs. George S. Robins.*

Portrait of James Monroe by John Vanderlyn, District of Columbia, 1816, accession #1946-80, image #TC 91-77, *The Colonial Williamsburg Foundation.*

Thomas Jefferson by Gilbert Stuart, District of Columbia, 1805, accession #1945-22, image #DS 92-17, *The Colonial Williamsburg Foundation. Acquisition funded by John D. Rockefeller, Jr.*

George Wythe by William H. Crossman, New York, NY, 1927, accession #1938-226, image#KC13c, *The Colonial Williamsburg Foundation. Gift of the Vestry of Bruton Parish.*

Stowage of the British Slave Ship Brookes under the regulated slave trade act of 1788, Library of Congress.

Abraham Lincoln, photograph taken by Alexander Gardner, 10 April 1865, The Granger Collection, New York

Thomas Jefferson, Writing the Declaration of Independence, Howard Pyle, 1898, The Granger Collection, New York

The ideas regarding the comparisons of the mentors, community and worldviews of these two men, first appeared in the C.S. Lewis Institute *Knowing and Doing Journal* in 2004 as a three-part series. I appreciate their willingness to allow me to use many of the embryonic thoughts that were expressed there as the seedbed for this book.

*The nations have heard of your shame,
and the earth is full of your cry of distress.*

—Jeremiah 46:12

For all of those millions of human beings who died or who endured the Middle Passage and the tragedy of a lifetime of slavery—our brothers and sisters who were created equal with us—and for those who heard their cries.

And for Rachel, Joshua, and Jacob Luckenbaugh; Carissa and Audrey Blunt; and all the other amazing students at Ad Fontes Academy: the next generation of servant leaders. Keep persisting until you are across the finish line—Hebrews 12:1-2.

Contents

Foreword by Steven Garber xi
Preface xv
Acknowledgments xvii
Introduction xxiii

1   The Holy and the Unholy / 1
2   The Beginning of a Scientist / 14
3   The Making of an Enthusiast / 25
4   The Virginians / 37
5   The Saints / 62
6   A New Dawn in America, 1789–1808 / 86
7   The Long Obedience in England, 1789–1808 / 111
8   A Fitting Epitaph / 129
9   One Task Remains / 147

   Interregnum / 168

10 The Conundrum of Optimism / 173
11 The Puzzle of Persistence / 200
12 Lessons and Legacies / 220

Epilogue, Wilberforce, Jefferson, and the End of the Story / 239
Appendix, Comparative Life Timelines / 248
Bibliography / 251
Index 255

Foreword

Nobody is against empathy. Nonetheless, it's insufficient. These days empathy has become a shortcut. It has become a way to experience delicious moral emotions without confronting the weaknesses in our nature that prevent us from actually acting upon them. It has become a way to experience the illusion of moral progress without having to do the nasty work of making moral judgments. In a culture that is inarticulate about moral categories and touchy about giving offense, teaching empathy is a safe way for schools and other institutions to seem virtuous without risking controversy or hurting anybody's feelings.[1]

SOME YEARS AGO I had a remarkable conversation with the woman who initiated the very first effort to take up the problem of human trafficking in the city of Washington. A project of Harvard's Kennedy School of Government, her vision attracted the best and brightest graduates of America's universities, mostly young women. The combination of Harvard, human rights, and Washington was very appealing. We talked for quite a while, and finally she said this to me: "Inevitably these young women walk down the hall to my office, knock on the door, and ask if they can talk with me. By now I know what they are going to say, because it is always the same. After thanking me for the job, and affirming the importance of the work, they say, 'But I just wonder why it is that we think we have the right to say to people in Cambodia that human trafficking is wrong.' I just wish that I had access to a kind of young person who believed in basic right and wrong in the universe."

Reading Brooks recently, I remembered her words, wondering what he would make of her lament. Would he see an incarnation of his argument in her experience? Would it be one more example of "the limits of empathy"?

Very simply he says, "Nobody is against empathy. Nonetheless, it's insufficient." He argues that empathy does not necessarily lead to moral

---

1. Brooks, "The Limits of Empathy," A25.

action; that one can "feel" for someone or something, but not have the courage or desire to address the issue because of its personal cost. He concluded his essay with these words:

> People who actually perform pro-social action don't only feel for those who are suffering, they feel compelled to act by a sense of duty. Their lives are structured by sacred codes. Think of anybody you admire. They probably have some talent for fellow-feeling, but it is overshadowed by their sense of obligation to some religious, military, social or philosophic code. They would feel a sense of shame or guilt if they didn't live up to the code. The code tells them when they deserve public admiration or dishonor. The code helps them evaluate other people's feelings, not just share them.... The code isn't just a set of rules. It's a source of identity. It's pursued with joy.[2]

After a few more questions, the anti-trafficking program director said this, "Watching the human rights debates here in Washington, one thing is clear. Everyone's passionate, everyone cares. But mostly, over time, everyone gets burned out. They just get tired, because it is so very hard. The only ones who keep at it are those with a religious commitment; they seem to have deeper reasons for why it all matters." At the time she had no religious commitments herself, other than a belief in enlightened secularism. It was an afternoon and a conversation that I will never forget.

Ray Blunt has spent the years of his life asking good questions about the good life. From the Air Force Academy to the Pentagon, through years of service giving leadership in the public sector, he has forged a deeply wrought vision for things that matter.

When I first met him, he was teaching in what I called "Daniel-schools," institutions and programs that exist to develop the next generation of leaders—just as the school for young leaders in the Babylonian empire once drew in the young exiled Jew, Daniel. In our day they are called the Council for Excellence in Government (now the Partnership for Public Service) and the Federal Executive Institute, and Ray was a prized faculty member.

Over breakfast at a local diner, I asked, "So what do you do?" He told me that he had recently taken a group of young leaders from various branches of the federal government to Williamsburg where they

---

2. Ibid.

spent several days learning about the nature of leadership. One evening they had an audience with Thomas Jefferson—or at least the colonial Williamsburg version—and among questions that were asked, one had to do with Jefferson and his slaves. Only able to speak as Jefferson himself would have, the man answered that in fact one of his first acts as a young politician in the House of Burgesses was a bill for the abolition of slavery. Yes, he had been against slavery.

That night Ray went back to his room and took up a book that told the story of William Wilberforce. The more he read, the more intrigued he was. The two men, Jefferson and Wilberforce, had lived about the same time, had the same social and class backgrounds, had very similar educations, and had both taken up slavery as a politically contentious issue early in their careers. What was deeply different about them was the way their visions of vocation unfolded, and what that meant for their societies and the world.

Jefferson, to put it simply, did not persist in his passion. A brilliant political philosopher and an eloquent writer, he often offered words that stirred his own generation and that continue to do so generations later, but sadly his words did not become flesh. While notions of dignity and freedom threaded their way through his documents and speeches, he kept his slaves and defended the right of slavery throughout his political career. Again, simply, Wilberforce is still the "hero for humanity" because his passions persisted, and they became his life, changing not only his own nation but they continue to echo across history two hundred years later.

As Ray returned to his students the next day, he brought Wilberforce with him—and that decision is the genesis of this book. The days that followed turned into years, and Ray began a disciplined and deep reading program, wanting to learn all that he could about these two men. First it was mostly biography, namely, what is the story? who were they? what were they like? where did they come from? what did they believe? But that biographical background became the foundation on which another set of questions grew. And those questions grew into this book, *Crossed Lives, Crossed Purposes*.

Ray asks: "Why did William Wilberforce persist and why did Thomas Jefferson not? Why was Wilberforce able to lead a global, colonial, class-conscious monarchy to end slavery—the nation vilified as the great tyrant by America? Why would the monarchy, England, show its slaves mercy and grace? Why did Thomas Jefferson fail to lead an end to slavery in the world's first truly democratic republic, founded as it was on the religious and philosophical impulses of the freedom and equality of humanity that he wrote of so memorably in words that still ring compellingly across the globe?"

The questions matter. Not only for our understanding of history, but also for our understanding of our own moment. As the incisive British poet Steve Turner puts it, "History repeats itself. Has to. Nobody listens." [3]

Brooks presses his point on the pages of *The New York Times*, wondering about the meaning of empathy. No one is against it—and yet. The director of the human trafficking program in Washington, DC, is grateful for the passionate young women who care about injustice—and yet. If we have ears to hear history, learning from the gifted public teacher and servant that Ray Blunt is, we will learn that Jefferson can only take us so far, that there were limits to his empathy. But better, we will learn that Wilberforce coherently connected his conviction that slavery was unjust with a deepening vocation that gave him vision and passion that lasted a lifetime—and that eventually brought about the abolition of slavery.

While it might be best to sit quietly at Ray's feet, hearing him tell this tale, readers will find that *Crossed Lives, Crossed Purposes* is his labor of love—especially a love for those who will take up the responsibility of leadership in the next generation. That is why he lives, and that is why he has written this book.

Steven Garber
The Washington Institute
Falls Church, Virginia

---

3. Turner, "History Lessons," in *Nice and Nasty,* 6.

Preface

THE TELLING OF THIS story, as Steve Garber recounts in the Foreword, did indeed begin in the then capital of the most important state in the American colonies: Williamsburg, Virginia. It was there among students and young leaders that the task of this story began to take *me* up rather than the other way around. That's the way it is with stories. Ten years later, I finally feel I am at least closer to understanding the paradox of leadership, character, and purpose in a life story well lived and how nations are transformed by those who lead sacrificially.

The process of understanding, however, was not simply one of research, reflection, and writing; it was one of living into this story with many other students and young leaders over the years and in conversations with people far wiser than I. It comes to fruition at a time when many of us are wondering, "Where have all the leaders gone?" As a student of leadership and of history, I can honestly answer, "I do not know, not precisely." What I do know approaching my three score years and ten is that once there was a time when great leaders emerged to face with courage and persistence the moral challenge to raise the banner of hope for freedom and human worth. Good societies, however flawed, emerged from their acts. Though badly tattered, that banner does still call to us. So, too, do the stories of two men and two nations as true examples of how seemingly impossible barriers can be overcome by those willing to serve first rather than be served. I hope by the end you will feel the same.

Ray Blunt, Mt. Vernon, Virginia
All Saints Day, November 1, 2011

Acknowledgments

TRUE CONFESSION: I'VE NEVER quite understood the point of lengthy acknowledgments in books. Like perhaps many readers I have often and dutifully worked my way through the acknowledgments pages simply to know the authors a bit better—who were their friends, what kind of family did they have, what kind of writing retreat was made available to them to produce such a work? It has always felt to me like I owed it to the authors. But I usually have this vague feeling that it's a bit of a reach to be handing out thanks to people who helped in writing a book. This is not the Academy Awards or American Idol, for Pete's sake! It's a book, and thousands come out every year, making it a pretty humdrum event. Then I wrote a book. Or rather I began to write a book well over seven years ago at the behest of a couple of friends (who will be credited shortly, of course) who lured me into something of which I had no idea lay ahead. It was a quest that began to occupy a small shelf in my brain, gradually growing larger and larger so that when it finally, thankfully, drew to a close (some say the part *after* the writing is the hard part—oh my), I find myself wanting to say "thank you" and actually and finally—albeit belatedly—"getting it." It would have been impossible without all of these fine people. So here it goes.

Tom Tarrants was the first one to put a bug in my ear about a book when I thought a three-part article for his C. S. Lewis Institute's *Knowing and Doing* journal was entirely sufficient. His quiet affirmation at least made me wonder if this was to be part of my vocation, and his inquiries every once in a while kept me thinking.

But it took a second friend, my colleague, tutor, and a mentor to hundreds of others besides myself, who was the final inspiration—Steve Garber, on whom I took revenge by asking him to write the Foreword. He made me think harder that perhaps I ought to be listening to this call to write. As I was helping him begin The Washington Institute a few years ago now, we had two heroes for our role models who were both public servants—Wilberforce and George Washington. They became the touchstones for our work together these past six years. Steve and I have some unusual connections to these two men.

My family lives on a small tract that is part of Washington's former River Farm, and The Washington Institute is housed within The Falls Church, where Washington served on the Vestry and Steve currently serves as revered teacher. It is Washington's character that towers over the place we have been planted. But it was Wilberforce's example of persistent, faithful living within the culture and confines of the capital city of the world of the eighteenth and nineteenth centuries that energizes us both in our callings here in Washington, D.C. He helped Steve and me to see that our work in *this* nation's capital helping others in their public vocations could bear fruit. Public service was actually possible, it seemed, according to the lessons of history anyway, and making headway in an era of political stalemate and personal enmity was not some pipedream: Wilberforce had done it before.

But, I owe Steve more thanks than simply for his encouragement and vision in this enterprise. His thinking and mine intertwine so much now that I hope I have acknowledged it in all the right places. One of the biggest contributions he made to this project was the three-part framework of mentors, community, and worldview that allows all of us to better understand the nature of the persistence of Wilberforce and Jefferson in a new light. His now classic *Fabric of Faithfulness*[4] lies behind every page.

Then there were those patient readers who politely worked their way through the early drafts, giving me gentle and often not so subtle feedback that took this manuscript through about a dozen complete edits and revisions (so who's counting?), making it far better than when I thought I was finally done a few years back. One is inclined to press this task upon friends and family who will not abandon you despite it all. Thanks go to, in no particular order, D. J. Smith, younger friend, IT expert, and Washington Institute board member, who gave me the idea on how to begin at the end and several other keen insights as well. Sheryl Henderson Blunt, my daughter-in-law, a world-class wife and mom, is also Senior Writer for *Christianity Today*. She did some of the initial heavy lifting by doing the edits that taught me I had so much to learn. I hope I did improve it just a bit, Sheryl. Lots of salient comments came as well from our daughter Robin—classical school teacher, learn-

---

4. Garber, *Fabric of Faithfulness*.

ing disability therapist, and another world-class mom and wife. She read through several chapters in different versions and, if for nothing else, I thank her for the advice to dispense with the "yawp!" Robin, I hold no hard feelings, and the book is none the worse for it. Matt, our son, also weighed in with good candor and helpful insights as befits a guy who has been on over thirty years of backpacking trips with his dad. It was perhaps his typically straight-from-the-shoulder comment, "Dad, it seems like you're trying too hard to make it sound like a book," that helped me to find my voice in the midst of pretentiousness.

Don Jacobson, a brilliant, gifted young leader at the State Department, and founder of the GovLeaders.org website, has been a voice of encouragement for years and gave me a forum to test some of these ideas. He patiently read through every chapter and offered historical and practical insights that made this a far more accurate text. Paul Aganski, now *Dr.* A. I might add, also went through the early drafts and is a fellow lover of Wilberforce who wanted even more pages than I could produce. His ebullience and unremitting encouragement rank him among those rare people who kept me going. Tyler Martin, gifted young friend of our granddaughter, Rachel, also slogged through every chapter and offered insights that the younger generation I am trying hardest to reach would find useful. Anne Cregger Patterson, dear friend, colleague at The Washington Institute, and a mentor of mentors, unfailingly offered encouragement, prayers, and helpful commentary at every step. She is the original "Energizer Bunny," making everyone around her the better for it. Finally, my very late-in-life mentor and colleague at Gordon–Conwell Seminary, Haddon Robinson, read an early draft and guided me toward cleaning up my writing act. He also made the first pitch to another publisher on my behalf. His life has been an example of how one finishes well and persists in one's calling. He has shown that it *is* possible. I hope to follow him.

Along the way, I found out that the publishing industry has been changing rapidly and not for the benefit of new writers. By God's grace, for that surely is what it was, I had two people come alongside me—both of whom had to sacrifice valuable time to do so—and helped me learn and persist. First was Byron Borger, proprietor with his wife, Beth, of perhaps the most amazing bookstore in America, Hearts and Minds Books in York, Pennsylvania. Byron's blog demonstrates that he is likely among the best-read people on this continent. He is also a great encourager. His early reading of the manuscript, his belief that this was a publishable book, his helpful ideas along the way, and his consistent advice to be patient and wait on the Lord for a good traditional publisher acted much like John Newton did for Wilberforce—it kept me in the game. Then there was Miranda Gardner, a young woman I have never met, who did what no editor seemingly ever does these days—she took the time to champion my book and then to offer unsolicited advice on where to go for publication and how to do it. At two different publishing houses she pitched the book, and although ultimately this manuscript did not "fit," she pointed me toward a strategy that paid off. Without her I'd still be writing inquiries and proposals.

I also want to acknowledge that in any enterprise, however modest a book may be, praying people make a difference. I don't know precisely how it works, but I do know it's true. My walking buddy of Friday afternoons, Fred Clapp, patiently heard my laments week after week and kept praying and encouraging, and then finally celebrating with me. Fred, you deserve good things for your faithfulness. My son-in-law, colleague, and boss in classical education, Dean Luckenbaugh, was also among the persistent ones asking about the project and ensuring I knew he was with me. A good son and brother is he. My little sis, Jan Sherman, and my brother-in-law Doug, a frequently published author, also came alongside. I also remember good friends like Beau Boulter, Bill Haley, Doug Jenkins, Lindsay Hutter, Bill Krulak, Nancy Ziegler, all the dear members of our small group, and others who asked about this book and told me they would pray. (Here's where I get into trouble—always; please put your name here if you prayed, even once, and I left you out; God knows anyway.)

I'd also be remiss not to add my old roommate at the Air Force Academy, Todd Jagerson, whose travails we discovered mirrored mine in publishing his manuscript of the life of our "leather helmet" generation. We spent many hours on the phone in deep conversations about our books and life and faith with more yet to come. Few felt and expressed the joy he did when the publisher accepted the book, and that is a true friend. Todd, I'll rejoice with you when you get the nod for your book contract.

I do not want to neglect two men who run partnership publishing houses, a niche between self-publishing and traditional. Mike Janiczek of Advantage Books and Bill Carmichael of Deep River Books both believed in this manuscript and offered some very good alternatives had Wipf & Stock not come along. They talked me patiently through the publication process, offered practical advice, and gently pitched their alternatives. They definitely helped me to understand the changing book industry. In other conditions they would have been a good fit. Winning the contest Deep River offered was also a big boost of confidence for me to keep going, and Bill was gracious to advise me that I should go the traditional route if it came along.

This parallel comparison of Wilberforce and Jefferson began as an illustration for leadership courses I began teaching over ten years ago. I used the material in seminars, seminary and graduate programs, conferences, and private conversations. I lost count long ago of how many people have given me their own take on what they have learned from these two stories. Certainly my students and colleagues in the Excellence in Government Fellows, the Federal Executive Institute, The Falls Church, and the Gordon-Conwell Theological Seminary Doctor of Ministry Program gave me insights I would have sorely lacked. But that's how learning happens—in dialogue, among a group or community, in reflection as one sharpens another. It now takes a much keener edge to cut through myths about leaders, life, and character. I also owe a vote of thanks to Terry Stokesbary at the Murdoch Trust, who used the three articles I wrote as a basis for leadership development programs they regularly sponsor. It was an unbidden confirmation that perhaps this story had a place of usefulness. So, for all those folks who taught me while I was ostensibly teaching them, you have my thanks, most recently my students at Ad Fontes Academy. I hope it does not disappoint.

That this was an unfinished work, even after all of the many rewrites, soon became evident. I would thank my editor for showing me the previously undiscovered gaps that remained. Phil Beard, a man I have never met, took on this project with great diligence and care and labored with me through the editing process. He and I have worked back and forth electronically, and he provided a great grace to me. Thanks so much, Phil, for running these last steps alongside.

Of course this book would not have been published without the trust that Wipf & Stock placed in an unknown author. Christian Amondson, the Assistant Managing Editor, has been the point man and wise helper all along the last phase of this journey.

However, the person to whom I owe the very most in these last years, and through all our years together, is my wife, B. J. She has probably read and reread more chapters than anyone and still kept her sense of humor and sanity—and her sharp edge of honest critique. She punctured my pompous language and severed my rabbit trails better than anyone else. Her encouragement to get to the point and to cut out the extraneous language made this far, far better than I could have managed alone. But alone I was not, particularly not in the aftermath of the many times I faltered and had doubts. She simply would not let me turn aside to self-publish and helped me to see that if I did not persist, I would be letting William Wilberforce down—and her. A man finally learns who his best adviser is this side of heaven and the one who makes him complete. This is the woman I want to "grow old along with me . . ." and to finish well with. Thanks, sweetie.

Finally, as I learned even more deeply in writing this book, a call on a man's life, once heard, does not come without responsibility. By God's grace, I have seen my call now for over twenty years as being to help grow the next generation of servant leaders. My sense has been that this is his enterprise, not mine, and often I've had to pause and ask for help as my own capacities were but a weak and faltering reed. If this book helps a young leader learn the importance of purpose and persistence in a vocation, or if this helps an older person turn aside to help those coming behind and finish well, then give thanks where it is due as I have tried to do. For the places where this work falls short, know that is of my own doing and that those places mark well that until the finish line I need to continue to learn, above all to be an apprentice of the One who freely made me his own and who will be there at the end when I break the tape and cross over. Soli Deo Gloria.

Introduction

The ultimate question for a responsible man to ask is . . . how the coming generation is to live. It is only from this question, with its responsibility towards history, that fruitful solutions come, even if for the time being they are very humiliating. In short, it is much easier to see a thing through from the point of view of abstract principle than from that of concrete responsibility. The rising generation will always instinctively discern which of these we make the basis of our actions, for it is their own future that is at stake.

—Dietrich Bonhoeffer, "After Ten Years"

STORIES

Lives are stories. They begin. They experience crises and resolutions, then they end well—we hope. Once we become aware of our mortality, we nurse a vague unease about it all. As far as we can comprehend, among all of God's creation, humans alone know that they will die, that the story has an end. And that changes everything.

For one, it is a sad and terrible ending to die with regrets. We know this, and none of us wants to contemplate the scene. Rather, we want to do our best, to finish well, and to leave a legacy that says we were here on earth for some good purpose. While most of our ongoing life stories have chapters of bad choices intermixed with the joys and triumphs for which we are thankful, if we aware of our shortening time, we might want to take some action. Perhaps we would make amends, seek forgiveness, or at least make an intentional choice that will allow our life stories to end "happily ever after." For this reason, we do not want to leave such important repair work until the very end. We want a heritage for our children that says the world is at least slightly better than when our story began. Even if we believe there is yet an eternal story, we still want a good ending to this life under the sun.

We are also a people who love stories because we sense that there is a greater story in which we are involved—a story with final meaning to it all because it takes a redemptive turn at a place in time. Some believe this is so because God is a storytelling God who tells us this greater story.[5] Thus we gradually come to know that those choices made and not made are determinative for how our story works its way out and then ends hopefully tied to the one, larger story. Wherever we are in its writing, our own story matters and it matters now.

With the rear-view mirror that history affords us, we find that what is true for us as people is true for nations as well. To study the past is to see with modern eyes that our forebears sometimes made blind, immoral, or simply foolish choices that led to bad endings. Dietrich Bonhoeffer's courageous charge[6] to his generation concerning their responsibility to the next was a fierce burden few took up in the run up to World War II. We do not want to repeat the errors of our ancestors, nor should we discount the difficulty of courageous action to right the course of history.

Herein lies a paradox, for in learning the lessons of history, we will discover that we in the West have our own unique blind spots, our own overlooked errors that will bear down on our children and our children's children. Isn't it just possible that future generations will look back, as we do now, and say we missed *our* moment in time? Bonhoeffer agonized over that very burden even as he faced the cauldron of the Nazi killing machine. That should give us pause as this story set over two centuries ago begins. As we will see in the following pages, actions that shape a culture come at a personal cost, often that of a life.

This is a tale of two lives, two stories, which reverberated with costly commitments to change their time. By the end we will wish one story had turned out differently.

A PARALLEL STORY

This is all true. Its telling is that of critical moments when one generation was on the brink of either—to use the already hackneyed phrase—"kicking the can down the road" or at last coming to grips with one of the most prolonged immoral acts of man against man in history. It was a time crying out for leadership, just as ours is today. In a comparatively

---

5. See Ryken, *Realms of Gold*, for a fuller discussion of this insight. I am also indebted to Janice Faulkner Hendrickson, colleague and teacher of literature and rhetoric extraordinaire, for pointing this out to me.

6. Bonhoeffer, "After Ten Years," 20.

brief fifty-year period bracketing the eighteenth and nineteenth centuries, the actions of two men who never met had deep implications not only for their day but also for ours. This generation continues to reap both the good and the bad that they left behind them. We will take up the narrative of the fitful and uneven end of that terrible human scourge—slavery, African kidnap-transport slavery—in which both men played an irreplaceable role. Transport slavery was an oppression of the most bestial variety yet devised by man against other men, an undiluted evil.

In this narration of its ending, the story will be told in two parallel parts, on two continents, and focus primarily on two men. When the story concludes, you may find, as I have in telling it, that it was not the way it was supposed to end. On the other hand, you may also find, as many have, that it is an unlikely hero's tale played out in our mother country, England, and wonder why this was so there and not here in England's American colony. When the final chapter closes on these two lives lived in the same era, you will discover more ironies and deeper impacts than you might have expected, containing important lessons for us all in our time of crisis. Or at least this is the way it has been for me as I have learned the story and now tell it to you.

I first began to use the double story of Thomas Jefferson and William Wilberforce as a simple case study—an illustration in teaching both the younger and older generations about the personal responsibility that adulthood and leadership requires. I wanted to think out loud with varying audiences about how the power of a purpose and our life's calling shape us as we seek to engage the trials of our times, how the deepest ideas and beliefs we hold have consequences that reach far beyond our brains and hearts. I also wanted to try to answer certain questions that began to form more clearly as we have talked together over some years now. The three questions that came into focus go to the heart of each of us and well beyond the issue of slavery's solution alone:

- How does one form or discover a life purpose that is worthy of giving oneself to until the end?
- What lessons can one learn for living such a purposeful and good life that persists, overcomes great obstacles, and brings about profound change for the good of people?
- How does one finish their story well, leaving a good legacy behind for the next generation?

This inquiry required me to dig deeper into my own understanding in order to find answers, especially if I was to continue the exploration with others—in large measure the next generation of leaders. My purpose became focused on going further into this unique coincidence to unearth some answers for the coming generations and for the leaders of today and tomorrow. I continued to learn from others by telling this interwoven story and discussing it over and over again. As I found, we learn better in community than through individual introspection.

In answering the three questions we have posed, I believe the heart of this deeper story can be extracted from the tales of each man: the at once tragic course of the beginning and the fitful, heroic ending of slavery in the Western Christian world and of the leaders who were stewards—for good and for ill—of its long delayed demise. Although it can be told as a single story, it is best told not as sociology or history but as biography, not of one life but of two that intertwine. When these two life stories are seen side by side, they cause us to wrestle more deeply with these three questions for ourselves, as the course of their lives shows us. The outline is deceptively prosaic, yet the parallels are completely unique.

Thomas Jefferson and William Wilberforce grew up in America and England during the same eighteenth century era. They had strikingly similar backgrounds as youths, experiencing a common, early hardship when both their fathers died. Each then attended a distinguished university, came into an inheritance at the age of twenty-one, then entered the same career—politics. Against the grain of their times, their vocations began by courageously challenging slavery's hold on their nation's economies and the blind, hypocritical beliefs about human nature that marked their generation. This common, intractable moral issue would cause deep struggles for each man during their life as well as for their native countries over the decades they lived in—and well beyond. These two men would rise to become internationally respected leaders and remain over the course of their long lives at the epicenter of the great international contest over slavery and over the question of freedom itself. They would both wrestle in the death grip of their opponents where morality and pragmatism would viciously contend on the field of legislation and political will.

Both men arrived at the end of life having used their time on earth well. They both rose to the heights of their professions, still publicly declaring their abhorrence of slavery and their love of liberty. The cause was never far from their doorstep. By their last years, each had taken many difficult and courageous risks, suffered from fierce opposition, experienced great personal hardships, and nearly turned aside from his course in life on more than one occasion. Yet, guided by visionary purposes and aided by able mentors and colleagues, they remained deeply committed to one important though vastly different belief about tyranny all their lives. Jefferson and Wilberforce would be seen by posterity as exemplars of their age and of their distinct modes of belief—the opposing worldviews each embraced—the emerging Enlightenment philosophy of Jefferson and the much older, practical Christian theology of Wilberforce. At the end of the day, each man was lionized by his native country and by the world. Subsequently both had monuments erected in their honor marking them as among the "greats." And yet . . . their lives, seen together, provide us with troubling perplexities as well as abiding lessons: this I have seen play out repeatedly as the story was discussed, whether in small, informal groups or in executive seminars; whether in classrooms with serious doctoral students or earnest, young high school students; often in simple, personal conversations.

Despite the enduring individual honor Jefferson and Wilberforce enjoy even now, one of these men succeeded in resolving the all-surpassing cause that bedeviled his moment in time while the other failed, tragically—this you likely already know. One man failed to persist toward his early vision of emancipation, finally turning aside as he mounted the main political stage in a leading role; the other man, against the odds, would live to see his life's work and his vision for freedom vindicated at the very end. Our conundrum is that the common trajectory of their early lives diverged ever more pointedly the longer they lived, as the cause each man embraced with so much hope and courage as young leaders ended in severe contradiction. Ultimately their common beginnings saw them come to live their mature years at crossed purposes, leaving two differing legacies behind.

If they had eyes to see from their final place of rest, both would have witnessed half a million African men, women, and children greet their liberation with joy in 1834 in the West Indies and beyond. But they would also have seen more than six hundred thousand lives extinguished in a bloody civil war fought from 1861–1865 to bring an end to the dominion of fear and ignorance in America. The legacy of these two men lives on in our own day. So, too, do the lessons of their stories.

Once we see this simple yet troubling framework of their lives, the question naturally arises: why? Why did both young men courageously embrace a common but unlikely and unpopular cause? Why did William Wilberforce persist and why did Thomas Jefferson not? Why was Wilberforce able to lead a global, colonial, class-conscious monarchy to end slavery—the nation vilified as the great tyrant by America? Why indeed would the monarchy, England, show its slaves mercy and grace? Why did Thomas Jefferson fail to lead an end to slavery in the world's first truly democratic republic, founded as it was on the religious and philosophical impulses of the freedom and equality of humanity that he wrote of so memorably in words that still ring compellingly across the globe?

This is a paradox I had never really thought about until these two men entered into my awareness, but I have come to believe that in their stories lie badly needed lessons for us today—as individuals, as leaders of many, as students beginning a vocation, as elders nearing the end while seeking to mentor those coming after. Our time on earth calls for these answers—with great urgency—for all generations.

If you are in high school or college, you may be reading this story as a means of understanding your calling and how to sustain it as life unfolds. As such, you may be seeking to understand how one's worldview and beliefs shape choices and actions, and how one is prepared for leadership or for a life of service as a vocation.

If you are a leader or someone more mature in life's experiences, I hope you will find in these pages some encouragement to keep on the difficult path or to take seriously your role of mentoring. In helping to resolve the conundrums of our own era, these insights from history may cause you to reflect upon the legacy of your life and changes you might make.

I do not come to this task as a trained historian. My calling is to play some small part in raising up a generation of leaders who serve others and in encouraging today's leaders to prepare and bring along those who come behind. Through this remarkable story, many of us can gain new insight about how we can take up *and then persist in our commitments* (for persistence is what it takes) to confront the great tasks of our time, whether in our neighborhoods, our cities, our nations, or the world. The scope of such choices varies greatly, but the principles for leading and for living responsibly in accomplishing our purposes in our life stories are very much the same as theirs was in their time. These principles also become part of that great unfolding story.

For those who might want to reflect more deeply on the lessons of this story in a classroom, in a small group, or simply in personal reflection, a few questions are provided at the end of each chapter for this purpose. Looking ahead, chapters 1–9 tell the life stories of Jefferson and Wilberforce. An effort to understand why each man took a different path at midlife is presented in chapters 10 and 11. A discussion of the larger lessons and suggested answers to our three deeper questions comprise the final chapter.

I would still encourage you to do your own thinking about these lessons and also about how you would answer these questions for yourself. Especially if you are using this in a leadership course, a class, or personal development, then by all means see if your conclusions mesh with those of others who have heard these stories as they reflected on their own leadership challenges.

One final observation: each of us, regardless of our age, has our own unrecognized opportunities to do at least one thing differently before the end of our time. We can and should plunder the past to discover wisdom for today. We might even write a different ending, whether we are just beginning our story, living at the peak of our energies and responsibilities, or are nearing or past the threescore years and ten. I hope we will learn in these pages that we are each responsible to act with purpose, courage, persistence, and an awareness of the fleeting nature of our time. As a young man, that was what Dietrich Bonhoeffer was about.

As we turn now to their story, we can only guess at the final thoughts of these two men as they took stock of their years on earth and what it all had meant as the last page was turned.

We begin at a quiet and holy moment.

1

The Holy and the Unholy

The past is but the beginning of a beginning and all that is and has been is but the twilight of the dawn.

—H. G. Wells, The Discovery of the Future

DEATH IS A HOLY time. It is a time unlike any other, a time when someone who is alive slips away and passes in but a moment from this life to another. The ancients considered the dying to be both pilgrims and prophets, going where we have not yet been, seeing what we cannot yet see. As much as we try to discern meaning from these times, we can only observe the final seconds from this side of the divide. We do so quietly and in awe.

So it was on the night of July 3, 1826, as Dr. Robley Dunglinson, a doctor and a friend kept watch with his longtime patient.[1] Yet it was not for death that they looked, not right then; rather, they were intent on a clock that sat in the room keeping silent vigil over the hours. As the minute hand moved slowly past midnight, they each had a moment of quiet satisfaction: it was July 4. The race was run.

This was the day the dying man was seemingly waiting for, holding tenaciously onto life as only the dying can. In less than twelve hours, Thomas Jefferson slipped from this earth as the nation celebrated the joyous fiftieth anniversary of the decision set forth in the great document he had penned so long ago. His most famous words marked the birth of a new nation: a nation resembling none before it. Though Jefferson did not survive the day, his words were as alive as the day he wrote them— and far more celebrated.

1. Malone, *Jefferson and His Time*, 497.

CROSSED LIVES—CROSSED PURPOSES

Presiding over the festivities that day was the president, John Quincy Adams, son of the man who gave Jefferson his writing assignment those long years ago, John Adams. In a coincidence that John Quincy later termed "the hand of God," his father was to succumb only hours after Jefferson. His last words were, "Jefferson survives." And so he does. The great purpose he was given by Adams in writing the Declaration of Independence coincided with his increasingly crystallized purpose in life: to end tyranny and, in the bargain, help forge a good society of freedom. The voice he gave to that cause has yet to be stilled either here or around the globe. The freedom of man ever since is rarely spoken of without reference to his memorable phrases.

In his last known letter, written just ten days before his death, Jefferson sent his regrets, as had John Adams, that due to ill health he could not accept an invitation to be present in Washington to observe the fiftieth anniversary celebrations. In this letter, he reiterated both his beliefs about the rights of man that had long been at the core of his life and his long hatred of the tyranny exercised by governments and religions, truths illuminated by the rise of science he had championed in his lifetime:

> May it be to the world, what I believe it will be (to some parts sooner, to others later, but finally to all) the signal of arousing men to burst the chains under which monkish ignorance and superstition has persuaded to bind themselves, and to assume the blessings of security and self government. That form which we have substituted restores the free rights of man. The general spread of the light of science has already laid open to every view the palpable truth, that the mass of mankind has not been born with saddles on their backs, nor a favored few booted and spurred, ready to ride them legitimately, by the grace of God. These are the grounds of hope for others. For ourselves, let the annual return of this day forever refresh our recollections of these rights, and an undiminished devotion to them.[2]

While he died content that the new nation survived, proud of the beacon of freedom it had lit, he also knew that the slaves he sought to free early on in his vocation now numbered over three million souls. This was more than triple their numbers in 1776.

---

2. Koch and Peden, *Life and Selected Writings of Thomas Jefferson*, 729–30.

A SECOND ENDING

Seven years later across the Atlantic Ocean, in the country toward which Jefferson long held antipathy, another holy moment occurred as another aged hero, William Wilberforce, now a frail old man, also hovered near death. He, too, was waiting—not for the passing of the hands of a clock but for the passage of a bill in Parliament. On another hot July day, the 22nd, word came to him that the bill had passed its second reading and success was now assured. The Abolition of Slavery Act was a certainty. Though a celebration was not held until it became effective one year later, by this law England became the first nation in history to outlaw slavery. This little man, now blind and wasted, had begun it all forty-six years before. He had seen it through to the end of his time on earth.

As each man lived out his waning hours an ocean and six years apart, the earthly stories of their long battles against tyranny ended. At their end, one man lived in a nation where his eloquent words of freedom and equality were belied by a freedom only for masters, not for their slaves. The other lived his last days in the nation from which America had separated, yet it was here, ironically, where all men were actually free indeed. Though Wilberforce and Jefferson occupied a common era, each subject to many of the same vagaries of life under the sun, their youthful, lofty purposes of ending slavery and establishing a good society had diverged by the time of their deaths. To understand why is to go back to the beginning. It is in the parallel stories of their two lives that answers begin to emerge. They both began life in an era that was anything but holy.

THE UNHOLY TRIANGLE

In the beginning there was a triangle—an unholy triangle—a three-sided journey by ship that for more than four centuries brought unsurpassed wealth to millions, beginning with Catholic Spain's first steps in 1517. If the love of money is the root of all sorts of evil, then greed for vast sums can only provoke something monstrous. Indeed it did. From the sixteenth century to the very end of the nineteenth century, the unholy triangle held economic and political sway over the Christian European nations and their American colonies, aided and abetted by Muslim slave traders and animist African kidnappers—all who profited from this joint rape of humanity. Slavery became the irreplaceable centerpiece for national economic prosperity for the colonial powers. It fueled the capacity to wage war, opened distant lands to agriculture and mining, and provided the opportunity to spread the wealth well beyond a privileged few. In its widening wake, slavery brought forth a growing number of apologists and supporters who shared in its largesse. Such support crossed traditional class lines and was perplexingly undergirded by a religious and practical rationale that blinded moral choice for all but a few. Above all, the unholy triangle and its outworking altered the theological and philosophical understanding of what it meant to be a human being brought forth on earth by a Creator. Jefferson merely wrote of this "self-evident" idea, which had long been in the wind of religious faith but was so rarely brought to walk the earth among peoples of differing classes, let alone races.

The scheme of transport slavery itself made eminent economic sense. The numbers told the tale. The first leg began in Europe, notably in England, the largest sea-going nation in the world. From there, trading goods and metal currency from Europe were loaded aboard ships that sailed south to Africa, where an exchange was made for a second cargo of superior value to those more than willing to pay in the currency of human beings. The second leg set sail to the Americas: the Indies and North and South America—the infamous "Middle Passage." There the human cargo was offloaded and sold locally, enriching the trade brokers and those who purchased these misbegotten people. In exchange, agricultural and mining products brought forth by the blood and sweat of African slaves were loaded for the third leg back to Europe to be sold there. Each leg of the journey was profitable to many at the apex of the triangle and, in the bargain, this profitable route helped to open up what the European nations erroneously called the New World. What *actually* opened up was an ever-expanding industry trading in flesh and human sweat used to enrich these same colonial powers. It was a perfect example of one lesson culled from Adam Smith's 1776 economics blockbuster, *The Wealth of Nations*. Here Smith showed that the new laws of mercantilist economics could be used in an international trading system to bring accumulations of wealth produced by an "invisible hand" of self-interest we now call market capitalism.

Adam Smith never meant to imply that human beings were trading goods; yet they became the key to the genius of the unholy triangle. Their "production" was unlike anything yet seen on earth for its heartless efficiency. It required a facile untruth, a blinding of the moral eye, that allowed people to be considered as chattel—private property—governed by historic laws of such ownership. The captured slaves, the unfortunate men, women, and children alike, traveled as mere cargo, trussed and laid out as close as logs might be aboard the ships that traversed the Middle Passage. Perhaps half died en route to the coast of Africa or in the holding tanks before they even boarded the ships for the Indies where further horrors awaited them. At least another 20 percent died during the voyage of three or more weeks; often one half died if the weather was bad and delayed the voyage.

First branded for identification, they were then chained in row upon smothering row laid below in the hold of the ship with almost no movement possible. Here the human cargo was subject to disease, the foulness of human waste mixed with draughts of blood, and dead and dying bodies all around them. The women were routinely raped in front of their horrified husbands and children by drunken and debauched sailors. It was a hell on earth. Where they were going they knew not; perhaps it was better that way. Ahead, for the survivors, there were beatings, unending toil in heat and rain, separation from family, and an early, often welcome death.

This African Diaspora forcibly displaced masses of human beings to the New World and dwarfed anything yet known by history. Ten million? Fifteen million? Twenty million? There is no completely reliable source and little agreement because record keeping was spotty. It was a drawn-out genocide that rivals any of our time, yet the descendants of the survivors of that killing passage can be found today in both poverty and achievement, with few ever returning to their homeland.

TWO CRIES

Yet history, much like nature, has its way of balancing extremes of injustice. If the evil of man rises up to become a stench in the nostrils of all that is just, then a good somehow is eventually raised up as well. And so two births a few years apart marked an inauspicious beginning response to the cries of the oppressed in the midst of the relentless grinding onward of the shiploads of humans as "the trade" flourished. Two new, frail beginnings of life, two cries that would ultimately signal the demise of a monster, entered the world stage as so many before them. Yet these two babes had a mission it seems.

Born on two sides of the Atlantic, upon whose waters the slave trade flourished, these two tiny newborns would have ears to hear what others had so long ignored. The crushing of the Triangle is an unprecedented lesson from history that saw slavery abolished and nations and cultures transformed for the good of mankind in little more than the space of their lifetimes. Ultimately, multitudes of the lower classes were also touched beyond those of the African slaves themselves. In addition, many were raised up who would do what was just and, to some extent, redeem the past as a selfish culture was transformed. This is a good story in the end—particularly for those who would aspire to live lives of a purpose in serving others; for those who care about the world and its course; and for those who would lead and learn to lead—by serving.

MUCH IN COMMON

Every person begins his or her calling in a unique set of circumstances. So, too, did Thomas Jefferson and William Wilberforce. They would become linked, not only in their endings, but also in the common purposes of their lifework in the journey of their lives, and finally in their legacies. Although they never met or communicated directly, they were destined to become great leaders, deeply implicated in shattering the unholy triangle and in changing their nations' cultures. Yet these changes were accomplished in vastly different ways and ultimately for purposes that were in conflict. So we take up one "why" we must explore—why were their early common purposes so divergent by their end?

In the beginning, what they had in common was remarkable. To begin, they shared a common era, and they entered life in very similar ways. Thomas Jefferson was born on April 13, 1743; William Wilberforce, just 16 years later, on August 24, 1759. Each came from famous bloodlines when such things mattered far more than today. They shared a privileged family background, a distinguished heritage, and the high expectations that such a heritage brought. Both were raised in what can best be described as nominal Anglican beliefs. Similarly, they experienced the same tragedy in boyhood when each lost his father while the son was still very young.

YOUNG TOM

Jefferson's father died when Tom was 14. Though Peter Jefferson was not an educated man, he was quite prosperous and successful. The owner of two tobacco plantations, Shadwell and Tuckahoe, he also married well. His wife, Jane, was a Randolph, a daughter of Virginia's renowned first family. This descent from the Randolphs gave young Tom Jefferson a pedigree stretching back to the ancient histories of England and Scotland. It also set him on a road that began with a good life of books, horses, and growing skills in the outdoor activities and pursuits of a large landholder's son.

At his death, Peter Jefferson left his young scion land and property; the most valuable of all his property—so declared by the Commonwealth of Virginia—was his slaves. Jefferson's father also left something Tom came to value even more than wealth in later life. Peter Jefferson insisted that his son receive a classical education in the poetry, philosophy, and drama of ancient Greece and Rome. The ultimate result was that Thomas Jefferson became a recognized scientist in a new age, later becoming president of the American Philosophical Society for eighteen years. His own words poignantly, perhaps belatedly, describe the impact of his father's bequest:

I thank him on my knees, him who directed my early education, for having put into my possession this rich source of delight; and I would not exchange it for anything which I could then have acquired . . .[3]

For two years young Master Jefferson studied under a classical scholar and clergyman, Rev. William Maury, and at the age of seventeen, this tall, bookish, red-haired lover of the outdoors entered The College of William and Mary in Williamsburg, Virginia. He was well prepared by his classical education under Maury and by his already prodigious habits of fifteen hours of daily study. Jefferson seems not to have taken to Maury as a person, or at least in his autobiography he gave him scant credit for his early education. Yet what the teenage Jefferson began to learn under Maury continued at William and Mary and opened to him a lifetime of scholarship, an unequaled wealth of books, and a classical way of thought that he spoke of and practiced to the very end.

Jefferson as a young man was already becoming devoted to great and universal ideas fed by the love of learning across a wide variety of

---

3. Ibid., xvi.

subjects, old and new. He went on to assemble the largest private library in America—twice, as fire consumed his first library collection. At twenty-one he came of age. He inherited the felicitous place he would return to over the course of a public career filled with setbacks and conflicts. This would become his beloved Monticello, set in the hills overlooking Charlottesville, and kept in production and repair by the slaves he inherited and those he later purchased to work the land and produce his wealth. Jefferson would always view himself, romantically, as a yeoman farmer. In reality, he and his peers were more English country gentlemen in their way of life, although self-deception seemingly kept this realization from Jefferson's awareness.

His father's death also left behind a young man yet to be fully formed, searching for guidance. It was not until he entered The College of William and Mary that he would find the mentors he so much lacked in his father's absence. One of these older mentors he later described as doing more to shape his approach to thought and open his vista on life than anyone or anything: William Small. Another would become the father he did not have—a law tutor, business partner, and colleague in his calling, the mentor to a generation, George Wythe.

YOUNG BILLY

An ocean away, William Wilberforce had a similarly privileged upbringing in England, in the port city of Hull where his father and grandfather were wealthy merchants who profited from the lucrative Baltic trade under the protection of the world's greatest navy. Yet Hull, while producing great wealth as the fourth English port, was also the only port that did not take part in the slave trade. This providential distinction later became crucial for young William in his chosen vocation of politics, allowing him the ability to focus much of his attention on abolition. It would not have been remotely possible to pursue this course had he represented any other port city.[4]

Like Jefferson, his lineage was superior. The Wilberforce family name could be traced back to the twelfth century and Henry II. It was his namesake, his grandfather William, who became a powerful force in his time and in his grandson's life. Twice mayor of Hull, the grandfather

---

4. Metaxas, *Amazing Grace*, 2.

was known as "Alderman" from then on, likely giving some impetus to the younger William in his decision to stand for Parliament.

Whereas Jefferson was a tall and robust boy who loved the outdoors, Wilberforce was small and frail, prone to sickness all his life, and possessed of poor eyesight. Nevertheless, he had a brilliant mind and a luminous personality that made an early impression on adults. He also had an unusual compassion and thoughtfulness for others, even as a youth. One anecdote about him survives from his early days when he quietly came into the sick room of a visitor at his parents' home and asked earnestly about his recovery. For this bright, compassionate, and sensitive young boy, people, rather than place or learning, would prove to have the most profound influence upon his life.

At a younger age than Jefferson, little William also experienced the wrenching death of his father, Robert, when he was only nine. In many ways his father's death, like that of Jefferson's father, set the stage for the man William would become. Like Jefferson, he would find himself independently wealthy at the age of maturity, which opened the door to a political career but also put him under the beneficent sway of other men. Because his mother, Elizabeth, became quite ill shortly after her husband was buried, young William was sent to live in London with his aunt and uncle, Hannah and William Wilberforce, firstborn son of the Alderman. It was these brief two years away from home spent in the daily company of Aunt Hannah and Uncle William that would become another key influence in Wilberforce's life. He would later say of them, "I loved them as if they had been my parents."[5] Most importantly, under their care Wilberforce was taught and influenced by their family beliefs and by their relatives and friends in London. Within that fondly remembered London circle Wilberforce would meet the man who called him Billy and became his lifelong mentor: the converted slave ship captain, John Newton.

What made Wilberforce's aunt and uncle somewhat odd among the reigning English society was that they were recent evangelical converts to Methodism. Their conversion resulted from the preaching of their close friend, George Whitefield, who spearheaded a spiritual revival of the upper classes first in England and then later in America. John Wesley, later a correspondent with Wilberforce and a contemporary of Whitfield's, was simultaneously having great influence in England among the work-

---

5. Ibid., 6.

ing classes. To be a Methodist in the eighteenth century was to be given the derisive term "enthusiast"—a religious stance despised by the staid Church of England's more nominal members. Among the majority in the state-supported church were most of the ruling elders of England. The obvious Methodist influence that began to show in young William as he embraced this new faith severely alarmed his mother and grandfather back in Hull. So, despite his tearful protests, he was hurried home to learn to be a proper English gentleman.

The desired comportment of such a distinguished member of humanity was to be seen as nominally religious, genteel in dissipations, and certainly untouched by any such religious "enthusiasm." This move back home would gradually erode his newfound faith, as a careless love of gaming and drinking accompanied by casual scholarship became deeply embedded in the boy by the time he entered prestigious Cambridge University. Here he indulged himself with his friends in more of the same as he spent his wealth enthusiastically and his time thoughtlessly.

THEIR TIMES

Thus these two young men, growing up thousands of miles apart, were similarly and singularly blessed despite the loss of their fathers at an early age. They were privileged, well connected, certain of being wealthy as young men, destined for a first-class education, and influenced by exceptional mentors. At the time they were ready to be launched onto the stage of life, they possessed none of the religious fervor that was beginning to quietly agitate in both countries to recognize the cause of the slaves and the needs of the poor in the remote corners of society.

Yet by the time they had entered their political vocations and taken their first, tentative steps, each in a different way would, at a precocious age, forever change the way we look at freedom and humanity—and slavery. Their journeys, though diverging more and more as time went on, would take them both to world prominence as leaders. They were to become linked inextricably in their purposes as each would help to transform their times and the culture of their birthplaces. As children of their times, they were shaped by them, while simultaneously reacting (as do many young men) against them. Shortly after completing their education, both were on the brink of taking up the causes that would be the legacies of their lives. The story behind their singular, unprecedented acts lies a bit ahead of them.

Not unlike our age, the home countries of both Jefferson and Wilberforce faced threats to national survival. While it was a time of slavery, it was most notably a time of war, uncertainty, and a growing fear of revolution that was bubbling on the Continent of Europe and in America. Theirs was also a time of the threat of military conquest—England vying with France and America facing England, with all three countries posturing for support against their antagonists. This unsettled scenario created a situation in which the failure of the slave-driven economies was tantamount to a national security threat.

It was also an age of ferment from the Enlightenment thought that fed the undercurrent of revolution. For England, in particular, the ideas and the examples of the French and American revolutions, fueled by ideas of freedom and individual rights, loomed as a frightening specter for the monarchy and the state church. Occasional slave uprisings in the West Indies only heightened that fear. Instability was not to be courted, nor was anything that smacked of change to be tolerated, lest it weaken England's historical foundations. Wilberforce was destined to contend with lifelong resistance to the threat of altering his country's dependence on slavery. Perhaps even more so, he would be challenged to transform the upper class's dedication to the still waters of their self-serving habits of the heart.

Americans, throughout most of Jefferson's lifetime, would strike out for freedom from what they saw as the political and economic tyranny of England, first opposing economic inequities and later declaring their independence entirely. Often the writings of patriots of that era were characterized, ironically, by arguments that England was turning its American colony into an island of slaves. After independence, it was England's bullying on the high seas that would again briefly lead to war. Jefferson's America would also face military threats from France and then Spain. Within, there were the growing passions of regional contention between the states of the manufacturing North and the agrarian South. These differing perspectives became inflamed by the gradual outlawing of slavery in the North as it industrialized and grew wealthy. With a burgeoning plantation economy in the South, ever more slaves were required as the landholdings expanded deeper into the southern states, then into the opening of the West as the soil became depleted by large-scale tobacco farming. As the thirteen original colonies became one growing nation, this issue alone—to be slave or free—threatened the very capacity of a United States to hold together from the time of its founding onward. Jefferson would be in the eye of this regional storm for over fifty years and would have much to say—and not say.

In both countries, any alteration to the benefits of slavery was seen as a seemingly unsupportable threat, not only to prosperity but also to national security and stability. Nor was there any serious impetus from the church early on that would lead either country to seek the moral direction leading to abolition. Such religious impetus came mainly from the fringes of religion, not the established, prosperous church.

The passions against abolition ran high in both England and America even as anxieties do today when the national security is threatened or significant, unsettling change is proposed. For both young men who chose a common career—politics—the road to success was not likely to be paved with advocating on behalf of eliminating slavery. Yet, as budding politicians, that is precisely what each man did, and each suffered a predictable and early defeat at the hands of the slave interests and their elders.

By the end, as their nationally prominent political careers advanced to maturity in the last quarter of the eighteenth and the first quarter of the nineteenth century, both men continued in one way or the other to be linked to slavery's end—for good and for ill. By the close of their lives, both would find a nation far different than the one they were born into. Wilberforce and Jefferson were to become as influential as any single person of their era in effecting significant changes to the political and moral culture of England and America, respectively. They would carry out their cause in vastly different ways, ultimately working at surprisingly crossed purposes. We now turn to how that all began to happen.

One explanation for the initial trajectory in each man's life was that both men were shaped early in the crucible of suffering—the loss of their fathers. The hole that such a loss left in these young boys was soon to be filled by men who can only be described as exceptional, men who remain unsung but who shaped the destinies of England and America in ways we can only now appreciate.

But Jefferson and Wilberforce also entered life at a fortuitous time when change was in the air and ideas formed the grist of an upheaval that had yet to run its course. Human freedom from the tyranny of monarchs and the distorted inward-looking notions of religion were galvanized by the new philosophical discourse encouraged by the Enlightenment, resulting in fundamental challenges to moribund religion. It was the contention of these ideas that fueled controversies about governance and long-held assumptions about the nature of humanity. This is the crucible in which the first sparks for change were struck. Wilberforce and Jefferson fanned those flames into a blaze in very different ways. It was not to be extinguished by their deaths.

KNOWING AND DOING

1. If you look back over the course of your early life, what two or three events—seeming blessings or curses at the time—have shaped the course of your life so far?

2. How can you encourage someone coming after you that what we first see as a hardship can become something for good later on?

3. If revolution, slavery, and transformation of a dissolute culture were major ethical and moral challenges during the eighteenth and nineteenth centuries, what do you see as the greatest moral and ethical challenges facing the twenty-first century?

4. What might be one way that you or your colleagues, family, or friends could take one step forward to help resolve a great (or small) moral or ethical issue of our day?

2

The Making of a Scientist

> *... and the prince sat down as Mentor took the floor, Odysseus'*
> *friend-in-arms to whom the king, sailing off to Troy, committed his*
> *household, ordering one and all to obey the old man*
> *and he would keep things steadfast and secure.*[1]

UNEXPECTED, OFTEN DIFFICULT CHANGES occur in the lives of young boys when they lose their fathers. The absence of a role model, guide, teacher, and older friend can be devastating. If that void is not filled, even in boys of inherited privilege, they may become unguided or idle adult men prone to a life of leisure and pleasure, if not dissolution. That outcome would not have been unusual in the life of either Wilberforce or Jefferson, but there was a common grace for them both—mentors of great character and wisdom came alongside. Even the most devoted mother cannot entirely fill the void when the father is gone. Yet both Wilberforce and Jefferson emerged from their youth, not with crippling wounds, but with certain strengths and a fixed determination. What providence gave to each was a few older men who joined them on their bumpy roads at the right time. They were exceptional mentors; men who embodied those components of character, wisdom, virtue, and commitment to action that helped to mold their young protégés, as can best be seen in retrospect. These guides and advisers were not there for a few casual conversations, rather they long participated in shaping each man's life purpose and, more importantly, embodied what ultimately became each man's worldview: the lens through which they perceived truth and reality, made critical choices, and lived out their lives to the end. It is an old and honored role dating back at least to the ancient Greeks.

---

1. Homer, *The Odyssey*, Robert Fagles, trans., 100.

THE MYTH OF TELEMACHUS

The role of a "father figure" or mentor is elevated beginning with the great *Odyssey* of Homer, a tale Jefferson and Wilberforce were certainly well familiar with. Likely they read it in the original Greek as young boys. As it is told, Odysseus, King of Ithaca, was reluctant to go off to war against Troy. He had the future of his country's well-being to consider. Should Odysseus lose his life gloriously in battle, his son, Telemachus, the crown prince of Ithaca, would succeed him. (Telemachus was about the age of Wilberforce and Jefferson when their fathers died). Ahead lay the most important years for Telemachus's development in becoming a wise, powerful, and good king. While Odysseus had in Penelope a marvelous wife he dearly loved, he knew that she possessed neither the flint-hard wisdom a king would need to defend and rule the country nor the experience necessary to cope with the many tests of discernment that come to a king from those who would deceive him. His solution was to put young Telemachus's upbringing into the hands of a wise, older man who would be able to teach the boy all the skills he would need to lead Ithaca. Odysseus knew just the man to do it. In this, he was not disappointed. Upon Odysseus's return after twenty years of wars and wanderings, he found Telemachus was a man in full. The old man had done his job well. His name? Mentor.

Since that time long ago, the role of an older person who helps to shape the life and character of a younger person has been that of a mentor. Jefferson and Wilberforce shared the singular gift of extraordinary mentors early in life and even later: men who gave much of themselves to these rising young leaders, providing the gifts of both wisdom and time. They played a critical and often unrecognized role for these two young men who would later stride onto the world stage. Neither of them sought out these mentors and father figures, but they were irreplaceable in the end.

HE "FIXED THE DESTINIES OF MY LIFE"

As he entered The College of William and Mary in 1760, seventeen-year-old Thomas Jefferson could not have known that he would soon acquire the friendship of three older men who would influence him for a lifetime, particularly in his way of thinking and the choices he made of a career.

The first man was William Small, Jefferson's philosophy and mathematics professor. Small was in America for a time, having arrived from his native Scotland where he was already well renowned. He was the only non-clergy person on the faculty of the Virginia school; more importantly for this story, he was also one of the earliest and foremost Scottish Enlightenment scholars in America. The second man who helped to influence the young Jefferson was a friend of Small's, Francis Fauquier, and the British Governor of Virginia. Fauquier, although a British appointee, held surprisingly strong views on the limited role of a central government and the need to curtail state-sponsored religion—issues Jefferson later took for his own. Finally, there was the prominent attorney, judge, and politician, George Wythe, a man who would influence Jefferson not only as his early mentor at William and Mary, but also as his law tutor, business partner, and lifelong colleague and friend. Wythe was respected for his character and his probity and was among the few men of prominence in Virginia who believed slavery was morally wrong.

What bound the three men together was their love of good conversation and their advocacy for the new Enlightenment philosophy that had arrived from the Continent. These ideas were either replacing or altering in many ways traditional religious explanations of the world. This new philosophy captured the fertile mind of young Thomas Jefferson such that he would go on to become its greatest proponent and exemplar in his later years.

Small thought so much of his young student's sharp mind and depth of learning that he drew him into this august circle, setting the stage for all that came afterward for Jefferson. For Professor Small to sponsor a somewhat callow student to join such a distinguished circle is a testimony to his prescience about Jefferson, but it also underscored Jefferson's capacity to contribute intellectually to the group. If nothing else, Rev. Maury's preparation of young Thomas (as noted in chapter 1) and Jefferson's own diligent attention to a wide-scale reading program opened up for him an opportunity that few if any young people experience at such an age or even in a lifetime.

These four men formed a somewhat European-style salon throughout Jefferson's two university years, although their relationships later continued in other ways. The three older men made the teenage Jefferson the clear beneficiary of their distinguished company and held wide-ranging conversations on the great political and philosophical questions of the day. As he looked back later in life, Jefferson considered these conversations in Williamsburg to be the key part of his early education, far more so than his studies at college. These informal tutoring sessions sharpened Jefferson's personal philosophy and grasp of national issues as he began to move toward exploring how these ideas would come to bear in the new world that was emerging in America. As Jefferson would later write in his autobiography:

> It was my great good fortune, and what probably fixed the destinies of my life that Dr. Wm. Small of Scotland was then professor of Mathematics, a man profound in most of the useful branches of science, with a happy talent of communication, correct and gentlemanly manners and an enlarged and liberal mind. He, most happily for me, became soon attached to me and made me his daily companion when not engaged in the school; and from his conversation I got my first views of the expansion of science and of the system of things in which we are placed.[2]

Although Small left William and Mary after six years in 1764, his influence on his young protégé continued indirectly. As a visiting professor, he had begun a society in Williamsburg to encourage the growth of science in the colony of Virginia through a forum for ongoing discussion of the newly emerging Enlightenment philosophy and the many scientific findings emanating from Europe. Upon Small's return to Scotland, the society was subsequently chaired by Jefferson's former salon partner and sometime mentor, Governor Fauquier, who continued to play an indirect role in Jefferson's education through this society. As a member, young Jefferson was greatly influenced to further his scientific pursuits as his legal education and maturity continued under Wythe's tutoring. It also gave him a forum for testing his advanced learning with wiser men and provided him an extraordinary opportunity for keeping abreast of the latest exciting advances in science.

OPTIMISM EMBODIED

Small's greatest impact on Jefferson was likely that of kindling his lifelong passion for science and the supremacy of rational thought over supernatural revelation and providential guidance. These ideas, prominent Enlightenment tenets, greatly influenced the man Jefferson would become. Another facet of Enlightenment thinking he readily imbibed

2. Koch and Peden, *The Life and Writings of Thomas Jefferson*, 4.

was an optimism regarding man's intellectual and moral progress which would be guaranteed primarily through the twin engines of education and scientific discovery. To facilitate this inexorable progress, a beneficent political system was required that freed people from tyranny and shed the encumbrances to personal conscience that state-supported religion induced. Moral progress was seen by Enlightenment thinkers as linked to widespread education enhanced by political restraint and human freedom. This would become the critical insight gained in Jefferson's unfolding understanding of how to ultimately redress not only slavery but also all forms of tyranny.

The seedbed for the emergence of the Enlightenment had been the ravages of the seemingly endless religious wars of the previous centuries. They had decimated Europe and the Middle East, leading to national and moral exhaustion. War weariness along with the enthusiasm of the Renaissance and the subsequent emergence of striking scientific findings gave rise to a search for philosophical alternatives to religion—alternatives that produced cooler, more rational approaches to shaping the world and less passionate responses than seen in the wars that swept through and nearly destroyed Europe. This was the fuel for Descartes's quest to find meaning in life beyond religious dogma while still holding to God's existence as the prime mover of human thought. Later, with Locke's philosophy of balanced governance and Newton's breakthroughs in understanding the operations of the universe, a new philosophy and worldview were born. This worldview would be fully embraced by the young Jefferson and many of the American founders as a means of understanding the way of reordering the old monarchial power structures. In this worldview they were joined by much of Europe, particularly on the Continent.

Thus, while Jefferson was serving in France in the 1780s, the French version of the Enlightenment philosophy helped him to continue to form his view of the role and the limits of government, including the importance of individual rights in thought and action free from tyranny, be it by government or religion. This became, in later years, what developed into political Jeffersonianism, the guiding philosophy of the Democratic Republican party of which more will emerge later in the story. But, for Jefferson, it all began with Small, Fauquier, and Wythe in Williamsburg. His mentors could only have had an inkling of the role Jefferson would play in the founding of a new nation. Little could they have foreseen that he would give such memorable voice to mankind's quest for universal liberty, religious freedom, and representative democratic governance. The ideas first formed during his early tutelage would express to the world the reasons the colonies were constrained to break from Britain's iron grasp and then help to form a new vision for the structure of a good society

A SECOND FATHER

Thomas Jefferson graduated from William and Mary with highest honors after two years of study. To his delight, George Wythe remained keenly influential in his life, helping more than anyone to fill the hole that Peter Jefferson's death had left. Wythe invited Jefferson to read law with him and then to be his business partner. Later, Jefferson as Virginia's governor returned the favor by appointing Wythe as America's first law professor at William and Mary in 1779.

It was common at that time to read for the law for a year, memorizing case law and precedent; however, Jefferson and Wythe read together, as was Wythe's practice, for the unusual tenure of five years. In these studies, Wythe took a unique approach that drew so many students of that generation to him. His teaching methods would likely unsettle today's law school faculties. Using a tutorial approach, Wythe had his students read the classics together and then discuss and debate them, applying the principles discovered to historical and current events as well as to daily life. Above all he wanted his students to learn how to think and to apply the virtues and philosophical insights of antiquity to the vexing problems of the day. He required of his charges sound research, writing, public speaking, analytical thinking, and fully thought out answers to probing questions.

Wythe further believed that they should gain experience by observing the practice of their future profession in the legislative councils of the House of Burgesses where he served and by attending court trials where he often was the presiding judge. His goal was to give them a mature understanding of what they were being prepared for, knowledge that bridged theory and practice. His own creative and singular view was that his role was more than simply a teacher and mentor preparing law students for the bar. He had a larger view—that they were also preparing for public leadership. Hence, his task was also to focus on giving them experiential opportunities and lessons that would form their character even more than their intellect in being readied to serve their peers.[3]

3. "Building Statesmen," George Wythe College Website.

George Wythe, Jefferson's Mentor, Law Partner, and Colleague

Wythe not only mentored the future president, he also was to have as future protégés John Marshall, later the chief justice (who also became Jefferson's nemesis when president); James Monroe, another future president and Jefferson's protégé and colleague; and Henry Clay, who became Speaker of the House and one of the most brilliant legislators in the history of the Congress. Many other future representatives and senators also studied with Professor Wythe. He would become known as mentor to an entire generation of great men and political leaders.

Jefferson, late in life, would say of him, as did so many others, that he was like a second father: "Mr. Wythe continued to be my faithful and beloved mentor in youth, and my most affectionate friend through life. In 1767 he led me into the practice of law at the bar of the General court, at which I continued until the Revolution shut up the courts of justice."[4]

George Wythe was also a respected legislator as a member of the House of Burgesses and later was appointed to the Continental Congress that signed the *Declaration of Independence* and to the Congress that drafted the Constitution. His example had a powerful effect on young Jefferson's choice of career, particularly on his habits of reading and thinking, which helped to form his mind and character. Seemingly, Wythe's vast library also gave Jefferson an example that spurred him toward the rising bibliophile's extensive purchases, which would contribute to leaving his heirs a bankrupted estate. That would not have been Wythe's intent as a man of frugal instincts.

Above all, George Wythe was known as a man of great integrity; not only a mentor, legislator, attorney, and jurist who helped grow a generation of future leaders, but also a man whose profound impact on the formation of the new nation and its first generation has been vastly underestimated by history. His deep humility—he most often worked behind the scenes—has left a quiet but inestimable imprint. Not unlike the deeply hidden organs of the body, his influence would perhaps best be appreciated when it was missing, as it was by Jefferson later in life.

After Wythe's premature death by poisoning in 1806, Jefferson contributed to his biography, closing his reflective narrative with this laudatory description of the man who shaped him so profoundly:

> No man has ever left behind him a character more venerated than George Wythe. His virtue was of the purest tint; his integrity inflexible, and his justice exact; of warm patriotism, and, devoted as he was to liberty, and the natural and equal rights of man, he might truly be called the Cato of his country without the avarice of the Roman; for a more disinterested person never lived.... In his philosophy he was firm, and neither troubling, nor perhaps trusting, any one with his religious creed, he left the world to the conclusion, that that religion must be good which could produce a life of such exemplary virtue.[5]

---

4. Koch and Peden, "Autobiography of Thomas Jefferson," 5.
5. Ibid., "Notes on the Biography of George Wythe," 182–83.

Before his tragic end, Wythe, as an early supporter of ending slavery, likely was the person who most stimulated Jefferson's Enlightenment worldview toward his early focus on the rights of man.

THE VIRGINIA PLANTERS

The largesse of time and energy that a renowned man such as Wythe heaped upon the young Jefferson was an example of a system that had existed in Virginia since the seventeenth century. The wealthy planters who dominated colonial interests with their British governors believed that skillful leadership and governing were keys to protect their great estates from excessive incursions by England. Intellectual and social gifts were prized political skills, as was the identification of the next generation of those who would take up politics. Spotting and nurturing youthful talent was a practice well embedded by the time Thomas Jefferson was gaining maturity, and as one of its beneficiaries he would rise rapidly to the top of the class of his generation. Later, James Madison would enter the House of Burgesses at the age of nineteen as a result of similar talent spotting, subsequently becoming a protégé of Jefferson's. At about the same time, in 1780 Jefferson selected James Monroe to read law, and thus began Monroe's rise through his mentor's sponsorship much as Jefferson had risen through Wythe's. Both Madison and Monroe would of course later become Jefferson's trusted colleagues as the cycle of Virginia leadership recruitment and development continued. Wythe had begun a process with the young Jefferson that would lead to two dozen unbroken years of American presidency from this lineage.

A BOLD ACT

In 1769, in his first year as a representative in The House of Burgesses from Albemarle County, Thomas Jefferson somewhat shockingly caused a measure to be introduced that would give all slaveholders in Virginia the right to free their slaves. He did so under the approving gaze of his mentor, law partner, and now political colleague, George Wythe, who likely urged this precocious initiative by Jefferson.[6] It was an early mark displaying Jefferson's beliefs about tyranny and his willingness to take on a cause that few would back. Characteristically, Jefferson did not offer the bill as its main sponsor (a fact he skips over in his autobiography)

---

6. Chadwick, *I Am Murdered*, 110.

but had his cousin do so while he signed on in support. Nevertheless, the authorship was known, and it went down to a predictable and sound defeat of the young man's ideals. Even then, Jefferson would ascribe the result not to the land-holding plantation owners, who were the main group among the delegates, but rather, somewhat hypocritically, he blamed the British occupation for corrupting the colonists. As long as they ruled, he averred, the British tyrants held even men's minds in their sway, making them too timid and subservient to England's policies. In particular, Jefferson charged, the British facilitated the use of slaves in all their colonies for swelling their national coffers—certainly a true statement.[7] Despite defeat, his course was seemingly set, his colors struck on the great, unspoken moral issue of the day. How Jefferson reacted to this early defeat would be a telling crucible in his life.

Across the Atlantic, William Wilberforce was following a similar course in his career and was himself about to come under the tutelage of a very odd but critical mentor.

We see already in Jefferson the young politician the strong influence that his early mentors had wielded in his life. Small probably shaped Jefferson's ideas the most profoundly as he absorbed the Enlightenment philosophy of the rights of man with relish in his classes and in those deeply serious conversations Small organized in the Williamsburg salon. Jefferson's commitment to learn, immersing himself in the classics and the science of the day, and his emerging break with the "superstitious" strictures of religion, both were tenets that Small and his colleagues exposed him to that kindled his passions. Certainly Fauquier helped continue Jefferson's advancement in the philosophical society. Yet it was more likely Wythe, the yearned-for substitute father, who tutored Jefferson in applying his love of the classics to the challenges of governance and revolution. As Wythe sponsored him at the bar, gave freely of his companionship, and then worked alongside Jefferson in his early legal ventures, it was this friendship and example that seemingly was the most important influence on who Jefferson became. His choice of a political career and then taking that first tentative but courageous legislative step to end slavery were the early marks of Wythe on his young law partner. George Wythe

---

7. Koch and Peden, "Autobiography of Thomas Jefferson," 5.

was the exemplar for Jefferson of the man he might become: a man of unquestioned moral integrity and deep learning: one holding an abiding antipathy toward the tyranny of one man over another.

The fingerprints of Jefferson's three mentors would be detectable in one way or the other long after their departure from the earth. In many ways, Thomas Jefferson was their legacy to the world. Such is the role of mentors.

KNOWING AND DOING

1. In what other ways can you imagine that Jefferson's three mentors might have shaped the early course of his life, bearing fruit later on?

2. If you are of an age to begin seeking a mentor, what are the qualities you would look for in character, in competence, and in temperament?

3. If you are of an age to be a mentor, is there a young person in your acquaintance whom you might begin to informally meet with to see if you can serve in some way? What qualities will you look for?

4. Our time has been described by many observers as one in which the younger generation is hungering for good mentors. Why do you think there is such a dearth of willing mentors for the next generation? Is there a possible remedy?

5. Do you think there is a difference in how young men and young women are mentored and in who should be their mentors? Is it harder for young women to find a mentor as some would claim?

3

The Making of an Enthusiast

The Lord has given me many friends, but there is room in my heart for them all. And methinks as much room for you, as if you were the only one. Short as our acquaintance has been, there are few, if any, whom I can more cordially address in the words of Horace than yourself—'Our minds with this exception gay, that you, our friend, were far away.'[1]

As a young boy of nine, William Wilberforce fell in with a despised group of "Enthusiasts," a term with few positive implications for the proper upbringing of an upper-class young gentleman in eighteenth-century England. These were hardly thugs or gamblers, but early Methodists whose unusual religious enthusiasm contrasted sharply with the sedate faith of English society. Yet, in the category of key turning points in Wilberforce's life, surely membership in this group ranks highly. It was the tragic death of young Wilberforce's father which set in motion a series of consequences that would mark him later for both disdain and admiration.

With his mother's decline in health soon after the funeral, he was sent to live for a time in the home of his aunt and uncle, Hannah and Robert Wilberforce. Little did he—or anyone else—know that this brief period's influence would shape his legacy to the world. For while living with them in London, not only was William thoroughly moved toward a serious, impassioned faith at the early age of ten—hence the title he gained, "Enthusiast"—he also made several other acquaintances in this small group who would later loom large in molding his mature convictions.

---

1. Rouse, ed., unpublished letter from John Newton to William Wilberforce, undated, 1786. Latin Quotations is from Horace's Epistles, 1.10.50:

William Wilberforce at Age Ten in London

Two men in particular became key mentors to the young Wilberforce during those two years—men who would, like Small, Fauquier, and Wythe for Jefferson, become an unquestioned influence on the man and leader Wilberforce would become. One of these men was John Thornton, a friend of his uncle and his aunt's half-brother, and like them a convert under George Whitefield's preaching.

Thornton was one of the wealthiest men in England, but he was determined to live simply, using his wealth to do what he referred to as his "Church work." One task was teaching young William a lesson in life he never forgot. It was an object lesson that required Wilberforce to act on his newfound beliefs. Thornton gave the boy a large sum of money and instructed him to use it to alleviate the needs of the poor—however he saw fit. For a well-to-do upper-class boy, soon to enter society, exposure to the poverty of the lower classes was hardly a normal part of one's education as a gentleman; in fact, it was to be avoided. Yet it was through this early, unorthodox lesson that William's caring heart was first nurtured to respond to the needs of others. Thornton helped him remove the blinders that wealth and indifference encouraged, even as Wythe showed Jefferson the great halls of power and what it took to influence men in government. The impression on Wilberforce was an indelible one that would motivate him time and time again as an adult, ultimately with tragic results for his own finances.

Wilberforce took up dozens of causes for the poor in England over the course of his life and sponsored an unprecedented outpouring of social legislation that marked the Victorian era. The roots of his efforts can be traced in some real measure to John Thornton's personal example and lessons. This early encounter would not be the end of Thornton's influence on Wilberforce, directly or indirectly, as he grew into manhood.

AN AMAZING MENTOR

John Thornton also connected young "Billy" Wilberforce to a number of leading Methodist "Enthusiasts," including not only George Whitefield but also the rough-cut preacher, John Newton. At that time, Newton was the rector of the rural Olney parish, financially supported in that role by Thornton. More important to young Wilberforce, Newton was a colorful, delightful storyteller, a former ship's captain, and a converted slave trader. Today we know him primarily as the author of "Amazing Grace," but he made a far greater impact on his era than with that one, great ubiquitous hymn.

The contemporary view of Wilberforce's relationship with John Newton has been somewhat influenced by the 2007 film, *Amazing Grace*, in which Newton is portrayed as a guilt-ridden, nearly blind old monk, doing penance by recording his past sins for the world to read. In reality, he was a powerful, energetic force for change and for the faith when Wilberforce first encountered him as a boy and then later when he reconnected after Wilberforce became a British member of Parliament (MP). But, as Jonathan Aitken, a more recent MP, observed, "to understand what really made Wilberforce tick, a far better starting point [than the film] is his long relationship with Newton, much of it greatly illuminated by hitherto unpublished letters and diaries."[2] If William Small "fixed the destinies" of Jefferson's life, Newton possibly did even more so for Wilberforce. Because of the old preacher's continuing influence during much of Wilberforce's lifetime, and his own regretted past, he undoubtedly did more than anyone to firmly set Wilberforce along his life's trajectory, keeping him persistent despite numerous disheartening setbacks. It is no exaggeration—without Newton as a mentor there would not have been a Wilberforce.

Like Wilberforce's aunt and uncle, Newton was childless, but in the two years Wilberforce spent in London, Newton and the boy he came to call his "son" spent a good deal of time together. Newton was known to stop by the Wilberforce house frequently to preach "parlor sermons," often an exposition of a portion of John Bunyan's great allegory, *Pilgrim's Progress*. Equally vivid in Wilberforce's memory was his first exposure to the horrors of slavery as the old slave captain told him tales of the sea, sadly confessing his own shameful role in "the trade" and the horrors of the Middle Passage. This providential friendship between the young boy and the much older preacher and former slave trader was to bear fruit in ways neither of them would ever have imagined.

THE GREAT CHANGE

Upon Wilberforce's forced return to Hull, his mother and grandfather began to redirect his youthful religious wandering, as they deemed it, endeavoring to guide him on a correct path toward upper-class propriety. They determined to expose him to the rounds of parties, theater, gaming, and other distractions common to their class and to the young gentlemen of that era. Later, Wilberforce would see these common practices of his family and peers as a product of their watered-down Anglican faith. But as a teenager, he slowly began to lose his zealous beliefs, as many do in these years, and went down the all too common path of his day—and ours.

His life journey then took him to Cambridge University where at age seventeen he continued to fine-tune his careless lifestyle. He would later

---

2. Aitken, "Newton, Wilberforce, and the Spirituality of Abolition," March 12, 2007.

see this time as wasted, a period which he later described: Recreation is its chief business. Watering places, field sports, card playing (never failing cards), the theater—all contribute their aid. Amusements multiply, combined and varied, "to fill the void of a listless and languid life."[3]

After his time at Cambridge, where he was hardly the distinguished scholar that Jefferson was at William and Mary, Wilberforce stood for election to Parliament from Hull at the ripe age of twenty-one. What led him to that choice of career is not certain, but two factors likely influenced him: his grandfather's example in politics and his close friendship with William Pitt, fellow student at Cambridge and son of the prime minister. Pitt would take his classmate and fellow conspirator to watch the great debates in Parliament, much like Wythe with Jefferson, and later would dissect the arguments with his friend. Pitt, like his father, was destined to be prime minister of England and had an early passion for politics that engaged Wilberforce's imagination more than any other career choice. By graduation, Wilberforce had come into his large inheritance, which was an essential requirement for entering English politics in the late eighteenth century. Lavish entertainment was the expected norm in return for votes, requiring aspiring MPs to have a goodly sum of money at their disposal. Such a beneficial inheritance and Pitt's encouragement made Wilberforce's career choice much easier. His grandfather's sterling reputation as the Alderman also gave Wilberforce the name recognition of the family line. Thus William Wilberforce began in politics, much like Jefferson, as an MP elected from his hometown of Hull. This inauspicious beginning did not predict the impact this young, high-living bachelor and MP would have on England and the world. That portent was hardly obvious then.

Unlike Jefferson, Wilberforce did not initially engage the world of politics with true seriousness or even preparation. His honest description of those early years in Parliament was less than promising of a significant career: "The first years I was in Parliament I did nothing—nothing to any purpose,"[4] thus continuing his Cambridge way of life. The gaming, the profligate spending of his inherited money, and the late nights of singing (he had a beautiful voice) in his five gentlemen's clubs all gave evidence of a young man whose ambition was for hedonism, like

---

3. Wilberforce, *Real Christianity*, 54.
4. Ibid.

most of his peers. It would have been seen as an unremarkable life in the London of the 1780s—unless you were John Newton.

Newton had not lost track of Wilberforce but had followed his career from afar, even using him as a repeated sermon illustration of how a good life could go off track: "The strongest and most promising views of this sort [Christian conviction] I ever met with were in the case of Mr. Wilberforce when he was a boy. . . . But now they seem entirely worn off, not a trace left behind, except a deportment comparatively decent and moral in a young man of a large fortune."[5] Newton spoke these words in his wealthy London parish of St. Mary's Woolnoth where he had moved, again by Thornton's patronage. Wilberforce was now not only in Parliament but also within the orbit once again of the Rev. John Newton.

For Wilberforce's part, the subject of Newton's sermon illustration was finding that his early faith and his conscience were beginning to challenge his bachelor, man-about-town ways. Questions began to plague his mind, and he became restless with his idle life. While on a tour of the continent when Parliament was out of session, Wilberforce and his chosen companion, Isaac Milner, gingerly began to discuss the questions that pricked his conscience, keeping him awake with the doubts he had about Christianity and his eternal destiny. What he did not know was that Milner, a brilliant scholar and a jovial man, was also a Christian "Enthusiast." Wilberforce knew him only as physically enormous, highly intelligent, and a conversation companion with an enormous laugh and great sense of humor.

It was on the second of these continental excursions with Milner that Wilberforce was led to make a crucial break with his past, recommitting himself to his earlier Christian faith. As he had gone back over this old, happier ground, he found that he was now able to turn away from his idle pastimes with a new strength and enthusiasm for a life of faith, one in which his conscience was now at peace. But this posed another problem that soon beset him with worry.

Wilberforce knew full well that this turn of his life would come at a price: to be a religious enthusiast was political suicide. He felt he had to step down. In making this decision, however, he feared the reaction of Pitt, his close friend and promoter, who by now had ascended to the office of prime minister and had enlisted Wilberforce as a key ally.

---

5. Turner, *Amazing Grace*, 95.

Surprisingly, Pitt was not perplexed in the least by Wilberforce's change, and argued for him to remain in politics. At only twenty-four years of age, Pitt needed his friend as a colleague in the political wars that lay ahead for the two young upstarts. But for Wilberforce, the only course that seemed open to him now was the ministry; politics and religion simply did not mix in eighteenth-century England—certainly not the serious religious views that Wilberforce now held. And, he knew he would be a man almost alone in Parliament. Finally, Wilberforce came to the conclusion that as a professing Christian who had undergone what he referred to as his "great change," he could not possibly remain in the sordid world of politics. His course seemed obvious to him.

Nevertheless, he wanted to be sure so he sought out his old childhood pastor for counsel even though he had not spoken to John Newton for years. He felt Newton would likely confirm his decision and end any remaining dilemmas. But, as evidence of his still unsettled mind, he did not want to be seen publicly visiting with a known Enthusiast like Newton. This would be a gross political *faux pas*, one for which he would pay a steep price. This fear exposed his torn heart over remaining or quitting, and it had to be resolved. Wilberforce's diary explains the thinking behind his ultimate decision. The turning point came with a note he sent to the old preacher requesting the secret meeting and the subsequent conversation that would alter his life for good:

> After walking about the Square once or twice before I could persuade myself, I called upon old Newton—was much affected in conversing with him—something very pleasing and unaffected in him. He told me he always had hopes and confidence that God would sometime bring me to Him. . . . When I came away I found my mind in a calm tranquil state more humbled and looking more devoutly up to God.[6]

---

6. Aitken, *John Newton*, 303.

John Newton, Mentor to Wilberforce and Many of His Generation

This was to be life-changing, for although he went to Newton with the purpose of receiving confirmation to enter the ministry, he was counseled just the opposite. Confounding him, Newton told Wilberforce that his calling was to remain right where he was, not follow in Newton's steps. The government needed godly leaders during these difficult times; his friend Pitt particularly needed him, and Newton made it clear that Wilberforce's calling to politics was not a *lesser* choice. This was an unusual piece of advice by a clergyman of that day. This understanding of his vocation would become the centerpiece of Wilberforce's work for the next forty years and would soon lead him directly to a clearer understanding of his calling.

TWO GREAT OBJECTS

After his great change and his decision to remain in politics, Wilberforce naturally joined St. Mary's parish and attended Newton's worship services twice each week, on Wednesdays and Sundays. He also began to meet regularly with his pastor and to correspond often. His old mentor's primary focus was on teaching Wilberforce a better understanding of the Gospel and the consequent implications of the Gospel as a call to action, not simply neat theological ideas partitioned off for Sundays. As Newton energetically wrote in a letter to the young MP in 1786, "Great subjects to discuss, great plans to promote, great prospects to contemplate will always be at hand. Thus employed, our hours, when we meet, will pass away like minutes."[7]

Newton also drew in others for conversations on political calling, men such as John Thornton and John Venn, vicar at Clapham. Their purpose was to explore together the nexus of the realms of Christian faith and politics as they intersected at the ground level of life. Newton also introduced Wilberforce to some of the early abolitionists whose faith fueled their political passions. These new friends would become Wilberforce's closest and most loyal supporters. As a result of conversations within this group, the subject of slavery began to be more and more at the forefront of their agenda and drew their minds together to focus on a single, great cause.

It was thus in 1787 that Wilberforce's life purpose was coming into focus, much as Jefferson was beginning to see that ending political and religious tyranny was his. As Wilberforce wrote in his journal, he now began to see that his specific mission was set forth in "two great objects"—to abolish slavery in all of Britain's colonies and to reform the manners and morals of England. Against horrendous odds, that breathtaking vision remained his focus for the rest of his days. It may be but an unusual coincidence, but Jonathan Aitken, Newton's biographer, discovered that the night Wilberforce wrote this passage in his journal followed a long period of counsel with Newton on the morning of the very same day. It

---

7. Rouse, unpublished letters between Newton and Wilberforce, March 21, 1886.

seems highly likely that as Wilberforce's mentor, Newton helped him to clarify his "north star" and to tie together the abolition of slavery with the transformation of a greedy, nominally religious, and self-centered English culture, oblivious to the needs of the poor near and far.[8]

ANOTHER BOLD ACT

Not long afterward, in 1787, Wilberforce, like Jefferson in 1769, took his bold step as a young MP and formally announced his intent to introduce a bill to abolish the slave trade in all of the British colonies. There is some debate about why Wilberforce took such a rash action so early in his career and with so little experience, but Newton's influence, somewhat like Wythe's on Jefferson, likely led him to act on his new beliefs. A coterie of abolitionists who became his core team also was instrumental. But Pitt, too, received credit as Wilberforce later recalled an intense conversation with the young prime minister under a huge, ancient oak tree. It was here that Pitt urged him to be the one to take up the cause of the slaves and end the slave trade.

Despite his passion and belief in the moral rightness of the cause, Wilberforce predictably suffered the same fate as Jefferson when he took on the slave interests in America. Although believing that the evidence of the moral depravity of "the trade" was obvious, and convinced that he had the necessary votes in his pocket, Wilberforce found to his disappointment that the measure never had a chance. He realized he had likely mistaken sympathy for support, a neophyte's error. Although the bill did not fail outright, it was sent to legislative limbo—for further documentation and study. How he would react to such public failure in the wake of this crucial moment will show much about Wilberforce as the leader of a supposedly "doomed" cause. Yet it was providential that for the next twenty years Newton would remain to walk with him in the dark moments of discouragement and ultimately the joyous times of success.

Apparently sometime during the almost yearly legislative setbacks that lay ahead, Newton purposed to write to Wilberforce quarterly to encourage him and to remind him of his vocation:

> I must not forget my promise of waiting upon you quarterly, with a token of my respect and love, as long as I am able. Indeed for

---

8. Aitken, *John Newton*, 310.

some time past I have thought, perhaps this may be the last letter I shall write to Mr. Wilberforce; and my reason for thinking so, should strike me more forcibly every returning quarter. For now at least (though my health continues firm) I may well account myself an Old Man. . . . Our departments are very different. The concerns of my general and particular calling, happily coincide. If I am wise and watchful, my employments in the pulpit and out of it, have a tendency to strengthen each other. It is otherwise with you; much of your time is necessarily spent in connections and converse with those, who can give you little direct assistance or comfort in your spiritual walk. But the grace which is needful for me, is sufficient for you likewise. And perhaps what you are daily forced to see and hear, may by an antiperistasis,[9] brace up your mind, and make you more sensibly thankful to him who has caused you to differ from them, and has called out of the miserable darkness of this world, into the marvellous light of his Gospel. So it is observed that the fire burns brightest in a severe frost.[10]

To the end of his days on earth, John Newton was William Wilberforce's stalwart mentor, friend, pastor, and intercessor. If one wonders at the phenomenon that was the work of Wilberforce, a good place to start would be with the man who considered him the son he never had.

As a mentor, Newton had an early influence that led to the religious conversion of young William; his later influence would be even more telling for Wilberforce's life's work. First, Newton helped Wilberforce see that his vocation was politics, not the church, and he helped Wilberforce frame the wider implications of that decision to remain. Second, over the next two decades, Newton helped Wilberforce gain a deeper understanding of the odious operations of the slave trade and its economic grip on society. Wilberforce as a result developed profound empathy for those who suffered after being captured and transported along the Middle Passage.

---

9. "Antiperistasis" is a general term for various processes, real or contrived, in which one quality heightens the force of another, opposing quality. Historically, this explanation was applied to numerous phenomena, from the interaction of quicklime with cold water to the origin of thunder and lightning. Peripatetic philosophers, those followers of Aristotle, made extensive use of the principle of antiperistasis.

10. Rouse, unpublished letter dated March 30, 1796.

Finally, Newton would help Wilberforce build the evidence that would dismantle, once and for all, the Unholy Triangle. Without Newton's influence and encouragement, Wilberforce probably would not have persisted. Indeed, Newton's greatest impact on the world was in the shaping of Wilberforce's career and character over many years, step by difficult step. "Unsung hero" is an overwrought appellation; in Newton's case the shoe fits well, as it does for George Wythe's influence on Jefferson.

Where and how Jefferson and Wilberforce applied these early lessons of their failures and the lessons from their mentors is the next compelling and unique chapter of their stories, as their lives and commitments began to diverge even while their careers advanced. Drawn into their circles of influence, both supporters and opponents would grow up around them as they began their rise to the national and then the international scene. These groups were every bit as important as their mentors in shaping Jefferson and Wilberforce and in helping them continue on their course.

KNOWING AND DOING

1. How would you compare the influence of Wythe and Newton? How was their influence on their protégés alike? How was it different?

2. Why do you think Wilberforce and Newton never had any contact from the time Wilberforce returned to Hull to the time of his existential crisis, despite his father-son relationship with Newton for two years in London?

3. Why did Wilberforce conclude that if he was serious about his faith, then he had to become a minister?

4. Are some vocations more spiritual than others and more important in God's eyes?

5. What are some ways young people can find their true vocation when doubts creep in about their choices or they simply do not know what direction to take?

4

The Virginians

The inescapable conclusion of this investigation is that the political philosophy known simply as "Jeffersonian" is actually an amalgam of ideas, which owes very much to James Madison.

—Adrienne Koch, *Jefferson and Madison*

MANY OF US HAVE likely found by now that our youthful eyes could not see the horizons we arrived at later in life. Thus the admonition many of us receive in our youth—"You can't put an old head on young shoulders"—takes on new meaning the older we grow. In the same way, we cannot view the past, in this case the last half of the eighteenth century, through our twenty-first-century eyes with true clarity. It is quite difficult for us to fully understand the blindness of that past age about the meaning of being a man or a woman, or the controversies over human equality. The terrible oppression of kidnapping, transporting, and cruelly exploiting poor Africans did not gather the protests of outrage that our era would raise. Jefferson and Wilberforce were certainly rarities in their time to speak out publicly, let alone seek to legislate this scourge away. At this point in our story, we find them standing almost alone after their first attempts as young men to end slavery in their countries. For Jefferson it was in 1769 that he first stood apart; for Wilberforce it would be nearly twenty years later when his own intent was announced to Parliament. The result was the same: an older generation slapped down the young Turks. Each tasted defeat at the hands of his elders. The firmly established economic and societal interests that led to moral obtuseness in the Virginia House of Burgesses was mirrored in the English legislature. Their political benefactors were not unlike the powerful lobbying influence that moneyed interest groups leverage today. The politicians and commercial interests of Jefferson's and Wilberforce's day simply reflected the beliefs and ethos of their time in firmly opposing any changes to slavery and to the valuable trade from which so many benefited. It was hardly even discussable publicly, and it certainly was not seen as anything against nature. Indeed, nature revealed that some were meant to rule and some to serve. This common biblical and moral interpretation appeared to support that noxious idea in most pulpits, tea houses, and pubs—if the subject was even broached.

Although both young men had seen the issue as a moral one, the notion that slavery was indeed an issue of human justice was not yet in the consciousness of most political leaders in the eighteenth century. Neither the new Enlightenment belief in the rights of man nor the historical Judeo-Christian belief that all mankind was created in the image of God had penetrated the culture in America or England. Instead, the political opponents that each young man encountered simply expressed the *real economique* and *real politique* of their times, which accorded with their constituents' beliefs. It should not have been surprising that the young politicians' proposals for abolition fell on deaf ears. It would be decades before their antagonists would have ears to hear.

As the counterargument went, it was simply a matter of the nature of Africans; they were destined to be ruled by others—*for their own betterment*. In the bargain, they would live a life superior to that offered by the jungles while also serving the national interests of civilized nations populated by peoples who were destined to rule. When the Bible was cited for support, the allusion ran to the fate of Noah's son, Ham, who was prophesied as becoming the servant of his brothers for sins against his father. With this worldview and the harsh economic practicalities, the demise of slavery in England and in America would come neither easily nor quickly: this was the message both political neophytes heard in response to their first, idealistic efforts.

In their twenties, their entire careers lay ahead, and both of them were faced with the same challenge—would they pursue their early beliefs or would they take a more pragmatic course and tactically withdraw from the battlefield in favor of career advancement? It's the kind of decision young people have faced in every century—idealism versus pragmatism. In the crucible of failure, most who seek to make changes to the established order find they cannot go forward alone for very long.

It seemed likely that great feats lay ahead for both young men, but in no sense would they accomplish them simply because they were nascent "great men." In persevering in their commitments and in pursuing their vocations, both of them would profit from the collaboration and support of others in reconciling the lifelong tensions between their beliefs and their vocational success. Jefferson and Wilberforce were to be shaped and certainly sustained as leaders not only by caring mentors who already had entered their lives but also by those who gathered around them as they advanced. But whether they would continue to be joined by others in the battle against slavery was quite another matter in these early days.

A look into their communities—consisting of colleagues, supporters, and friends—helps to explain further *who* they became as mature men and leaders as well as *how* and *why* they did what they did in the important years following their initial failures. The nature of these communities will also help to answer the central questions we have raised about whether they would persist. In short, the loneliness of the leader, the so-called self-made man, is seen here to be a somewhat facile assumption that does not stand up to close scrutiny in most cases—these included.

LEADING BEHIND THE SCENES

After his ignominious defeat in his quixotic attempt to abolish slavery, Jefferson continued to pursue his dual career as a legislator in the House of Burgesses and as a lawyer, gaining a reputation for being a "committee man," a term that in his day described a person possessed of powerful written persuasiveness and articulation, someone more comfortable working behind the scenes and alone. This role suited Jefferson's temperament and gifts very well and, though young, he quickly excelled. Despite being quite tall for his day, about six feet, two inches, with a commandingly austere presence, he preferred not to be at the front of a matter, despite what his physical presence would suggest. Instead, he preferred to avoid visible, public roles—a trait that would never completely disappear, even as president. Perhaps this was due in part to his surprisingly thin and high-pitched voice, which engendered in him a reluctance to speak publicly. In short, his platform skills were not impressive.

Jefferson's most powerful gifts were those of vivid, written expression and a disciplined, curious, and creative mind combined with superior organizational skills. When these gifts were juxtaposed with his hatred of personal conflict and the disapproval of his peers, there emerged a unique leadership style as he reached his thirties and climbed the ladder of Virginia law and political circles. Also to his benefit in his dual vocations, in private conversation he was widely known as charming and self-effacing; one-on-one he was winsome and highly effective, in contrast to his reluctant public persona.

As a classically educated scholar, emerging Enlightenment advocate, and lover of all things scientific, Jefferson found the inspirational source for his ideas in the great philosophers and historians, some ancient but especially those more recent—Bacon, Locke, and Descartes among them. He began to discover that his power lay in using their ideas enfolded into his more expressive language. His passionate and even dogmatic and idealistic belief in their emerging philosophies and worldviews shaped both his approach to his political thought and his collegial work. It was the power of the expression of these new ideals wrapped with grace into his persuasive rhetoric and optimistic vision that appealed to so many among his ever-enlarging group of followers.

This committee man was clearly most effective working behind the scenes to influence the debates by force of private argument and skillful writing. He would excel in drafting legislation for his native Virginia and for the Continental Congress, but his more enduring fame lay ahead in penning the single document by which we remember him. In many ways, his early success using this quiet, patient, serving approach established him in the House of Burgesses as a force for liberty that spread beyond Virginia's borders. These early lessons as a young legislator under Wythe's tutelage would come to inform his later time in higher office as a man who strongly influenced others, yet was often careful not to leave fingerprints. His biographers agree that neither his weaknesses in public speaking nor his sensitivity to criticism sullied his great but publicly humble political ambitions for very long.

As a budding politician steadily gaining notice in Virginia, Jefferson began to attract a cadre of followers and supporters to help elevate his star and to extend his revolutionary ideas about liberty from the tyranny of England. Later, as his role expanded, he gave voice to the governing of a new nation when the yoke of England was overthrown. Above all, however, he was a Virginian. His fellow plantation owners were his most central community, his "country."[1] They were the ones who put him forward in these early years as a rising leader. These landed neighbors became the people he most trusted as his colleagues and the group from which his protégés emerged. More than any others, they would act to help shape the choices he would make—and those he would decline to make—as he progressed inexorably toward the national stage.

PRIDE OF AUTHORSHIP

It was only a relatively short time before Jefferson's precocious ability to write persuasive, passionate prose and to mount powerful arguments gained him national recognition in the colonies. Particularly noteworthy was his early polemic against British tyranny: *A Summary View of the Rights of British America.* He wrote this document in 1774 as counsel to the Virginia delegation to the first Continental Congress . Although his Old Dominion colleagues refused to adopt his recommendations because they found the young man's language too harsh and confrontational toward their British rulers, subsequent printings of this argument earned Jefferson wider favor in America, especially in New England. In and around Boston, the confrontations with Britain were already far more intransigent than those in the South.[2] Perhaps the most memorable language in this early document that touched his contemporaries, especially John Adams, was Jefferson's closing argument directed to King George himself, taking a liberty of language and forthrightness unheard of by a subject of the king:

> That these are our grievances which we have thus laid before his majesty, with that freedom of language and sentiment which become a free people claiming their rights, as derived from the laws of nature, and not as the gift of their chief magistrate: Let those flatter who fear; it is not an American art. To give praise which is not due might be well from the venal, but would ill beseem those who are asserting the rights of human nature. They will therefore say, kings are the servants, not the proprietors of the people. Open your breast, sire, to liberal and expanded thought. Let not the name of George the third be a blot in the page of history. .

  1. Robert E. Lee would later voice the same expression when asked by Lincoln to head the federal Army: "I cannot raise my hand against my birthplace, my home, my children." He reluctantly turned down the president. Cited in *The History Place*, July 18, 2011.
  2. Koch and Peden, *The Life and Selected Writings of Thomas Jefferson*, 290.

> .. The great principles of right and wrong are legible to every reader; to pursue them requires not the art of many counselors. The whole art of government consists in the art of being honest. Only aim to do your duty, and mankind will give you the credit where you fail. No longer persevere in sacrificing the rights of one part of the empire to the inordinate desires of another; but deal out to all equal and impartial right. Let no act be passed by any one legislature which may infringe on the rights and liberties of another.[3]

Jefferson not only lays the problem for the impasse between America and England squarely at the feet of the king, but he also invokes the natural rights of man as his support, lecturing the king on the tenets of a good government and asserting the principle that one legislature cannot rule another—a glimpse of where his thoughts would lead twenty years later when the federal–states issues first began to fray the early comity of the new nation. But now his direct appeal to the king would foreshadow the document for which we best know him.

Thus it was not surprising that a still youngish Jefferson was appointed to be among the four Virginia representatives (which included George Wythe as the leader of the delegation) to the Continental Congress in 1776. Their purpose was to consider the possible response to British incursions on the liberties of the American colonies. Once there, the young delegate found he already had gained John Adams' attention.

As a crusty, experienced Massachusetts patriot, Adams had read *A Summary View* with great approval and not only already knew Jefferson's reputation and abilities as a committee man but also appreciated his philosophy of liberty as it squared with his own. Although later they would come to different conclusions about how to govern, at this time it was a relationship of mutual admiration providing a needed boost for this young protégé of Adams. As the drafting committee Chair charged with writing the reasons for separation, Adams wisely chose Jefferson not only for his skill but also as a man less contentious than himself and a valued Virginian voice. That Jefferson, not Adams, came to pen the terms for the thirteen colonies to declare independence from England— The Declaration of Independence as it came to be called—seemed innocuous. Yet it was this event that would prove to be the key leading to Jefferson's spectacular rise over the next twenty-five years, culminating

---

3. Peterson, *Thomas Jefferson*, 121.

in the highest office in the land. At the time, however, it was viewed by the leaders neither as a singular assignment for the young man nor as apt to be of any historic value that would accrue to a single individual. All the signatories instantly became traitors—a far more ominous decision than who wrote it or who were the editors. Adams would much later come to rue the date when his star began to be eclipsed by Jefferson's.

For this writing project, Jefferson borrowed heavily from source material contained in previous documents, a not uncommon technique at the time because attribution was not considered important. Then, after a brief couple of days' work, Jefferson submitted a draft to the committee (which also included Benjamin Franklin) where it was edited and then sent to the Congress. After several further edits were made, it was ready for the fateful signatures. But it was the process that Jefferson would later recall as he sat watching in silence as more than eighty editorial changes were made, including the addition of two new paragraphs and the deletion of his powerful closing argument.

On the one hand, it is fair to say that The Declaration of Independence was not an individual achievement, certainly not in its entirety, for it contained ideas and even wording from previously written documents (particularly those from George Mason) as well as thoughts and expressions from many in the Congress that were the product of delicate negotiations.Nevertheless, the flowing language and the overall framework for the argument are pure Jefferson. Because it is difficult to publicly recognize a committee, let alone a body of legislators, Jefferson rightly remains for us the embodiment of America's most important document and our core beliefs. It was this for which he was duly recognized well before his life's end. It was not, however, without footnote.

Although Jefferson rarely spoke up in defense of his draft at the time of the editorial debate, Franklin, seated next to him, could sense his anger and frustration and tried to calm him with humor. Nevertheless, long afterward it became apparent that he remained somewhat embittered concerning the emending process, which he felt savaged his prose and carefully crafted arguments. His autobiography, written near the end of his life in 1821, was his major effort to set the record straight once and for all—both as to his authorship and as to the disadvantageous changes others made to its expression. In particular, he was piqued about the deletion of what he intended to be the ringing, concluding charge against the king—that he had foisted slavery upon a moral people and then restricted their right to legislatively abolish the practice. Wythe, the head of the Virginia delegation,[4] may have encouraged Jefferson to include this charge as the stellar conclusion. Jefferson particularly objected to this deletion, citing it in his defense of authorship as a telling deletion:

> He has waged cruel war against human nature itself, violating its most sacred rights of life & liberty in the persons of a distant people who never offended him, captivating & carrying them into slavery in another hemisphere, or to incur miserable death in their transportation thither. This piratical warfare, the opprobrium of *infidel* powers, is the warfare of the CHRISTIAN king of Great Britain. Determined to keep open a market where MEN should be bought & sold, he has prostituted his negative for suppressing every legislative attempt to prohibit or to restrain this execrable commerce.[5]

This argument, of course, was a somewhat one-sided and exaggerated case against the British crown. Virginia's plantation owners and those colonists of the deeper South were also enthusiastic supporters of this seemingly inexhaustible source of labor. In continuing the litany of the king's crimes, Jefferson wrote in his draft that the king had encouraged the slaves to take up arms on the side of the oppressor nation, England, who would reward them with freedom if they did so. In fact, this was true, although the "encouragement" was not much more than an offer of freedom, which several thousand slaves accepted in return for joining the fight. Subsequently, many did settle in England after the war, where they realized their hope of freedom but continued to live, for the most part, in poverty.

In a later about-face, Jefferson would attribute the deletion of this passage on slavery to both northern and southern states' regional interests and personal self-interest. First, Jefferson cited the objections of Georgia and South Carolina, "who had never attempted to restrain the importation of slaves, and who, on the contrary still wished to continue it." Second, he blamed the North, too, for economic selfishness: "Our northern brethren also, I believe, felt a little tender under these censures; for though their people had very few slaves themselves, yet they had been pretty considerable carriers of them to others."[6]

4. Chadwick, 110.
5. *Papers of Thomas Jefferson.*
6. Koch and Peden, "The Autobiography of Thomas Jefferson," 21.

What Jefferson did not, and likely could not, comment upon was that he himself was one of those southern slaveholders (and quiet traders), an incongruity he did not dwell upon. Hence the argument he had drafted for abolishing slavery was not as neat as he would attempt to make it later. Nevertheless, in 1776 he had not given up on changing men's minds on the issue of slavery. His own private doubts about the moral decision seemed buried in his psyche. His public avoidance of this great question would not come until ten years later amidst another setback.

THE VIRGINIA CONNECTION

Thomas Jefferson Drafting The Declaration of Independence

In the aftermath of penning the Declaration, Jefferson was viewed as the rising star in Virginia and the likely successor to Washington as *primus inter pares*. The general was to be absent in the North for the next eight years commanding America's combined colonial troops. But for Jefferson, this elevation did not come without a price—a steep price both personal and professional, and one he would come to rue.

Elected to the Virginia House of Delegates in 1776, he was given responsibility for drafting the revision of Virginia laws after the decision for independence. This was a prodigious task, and he applied himself with great, meticulous diligence teamed with his mentor and now colleague, George Wythe. Jefferson's two personal priorities were introduced as bills to the House—the Statute for Religious Freedom in 1777, and the Bill for the More General Diffusion of Knowledge in 1778. Religion and education were to be important issues throughout his life. At this time, he seems to have decided, at least for now, that any further legislative efforts on behalf of slavery's abolition in Virginia were fruitless. He took no action to propose an end to slavery either in committee or in the plenary meetings except to draft a provision to allow individual choice. Should *others* call for it, he had the mechanism ready. He apparently concluded that for himself the most important focus he could provide for the emerging nation was to eliminate any vestige of the British tyranny of conscience by ending state support for the Anglican Church. He also became a strong advocate for advancing the knowledge and education of the people to prepare them for the new era of full liberty and freedom in the dawning age of science and reason.

We see here the first indicator that Jefferson's view of the most serious form of tyranny was likely beginning to shift from that of slavery to religion. Religion became, after monarchial oppression (by England and later by the Federalists), the despotism he would come to oppose above all others. In Jefferson's working out of this issue, religion bound the conscience, thus state funding for any one church was tantamount to telling free men what they must believe. In his view, honed through hours of discussion in the Williamsburg salon, the moral progress of humanity could come only by advancing the knowledge of the people. It was education not religion that would act to restrain monarchial tendencies by raising up intellectually equipped legislators who, by dint of reason, would be morally inclined to protect the people. For Jefferson, this set of beliefs gradually became the only possible course by which slavery might one day cease to exist. A new, more educated generation would ultimately come to see its duty to end the moral blot of owning other human beings and exploiting their labor by force. Whether this was simply Jefferson's rationalization or a deeply held belief, the rest of the story itself will have to reveal but its outlines can already be seen.

It is worth noting at this point that Wilberforce also saw education as a critical component in changing minds about slavery—but education and firm political and moral action were required to operate in tandem if results were to follow. They would not leave it to a vague hope in man's moral progress.

But before Jefferson had to confront slavery again, he came very near—as Wilberforce later would for different reasons—to abandoning his career in public service. He was about to be accused of the most heinous of failures that a leader and a Virginia gentleman could be charged with, and it nearly sent him into permanent retirement.

IGNOMINY AND GRIEF

Jefferson received the blow that nearly unhinged him during his role as wartime governor of Virginia, which he had assumed in 1778. In 1781 the British army was advancing on the seat of Virginia's government, forcing Jefferson to flee for his life along with the legislature. First heading west to Charlottesville, they were then driven further into the mountains in Staunton, where he sought to consolidate the state government. It was then that the accusation of treason was lodged.

Jefferson's political enemies charged that he had abandoned his post for eight days once arriving in Staunton, returning home while his successor as governor was being selected and installed. Not only was the word "coward" widely and publicly proclaimed to his lasting embarrassment, but a formal charge was also drawn up against him. This indictment was subsequently dropped, but not before Jefferson suffered what he plaintively described as "a wound on my spirit that will only be healed by the all-healing grave."[7]

The sad denouement of this ignominy was the untimely and grievous death the very next year of Jefferson's dearly beloved wife, Martha. They had been married a mere ten years, yet in that time they had watched three children die along with Jefferson's mother. Now left alone, he had

---

7. Ellis, *American Sphinx*, 78.

two little girls to care for, Mary and Martha, ages four and ten, and a newborn baby, Lucy Elizabeth—while dealing with a cavernous hole in his heart. Little Lucy Elizabeth would not survive two more years.

On top of his public shaming, the loss of his wife left him deeply depressed and withdrawn for months. After weeks spent in seclusion, he finally took two long, solitary rides in the countryside, returning exhausted but beginning the road back to the life ahead. He was to remain unmarried for the rest of his life to honor the deathbed request of Martha, who sought to protect her young daughters from a stepmother. That pledge possibly led to another embarrassing chapter much later in his life.

The weight of both these events—the public humiliation followed closely by the death of Martha—left Jefferson determined, not for the last time, to withdraw entirely from public life to cultivate his dreams of private peace as a plantation owner, sage, and scientist. As he wrote somewhat cynically to James Monroe in 1782, if public service was thrust upon a man, it was tantamount to slavery and a violation of human rights. In his experience, he confessed, public service had given him nothing but prolonged private misery.[8]

Yet in time this stark view seemed to fade and Jefferson's calling to public service recrystallized. His sense of responsibility to those Virginians who would have him serve began to call to him once again, but it was a different man who answered that call. Unrealized ambition may also have played a part in his response, although Jefferson's motives have never been open to public scrutiny. What can be seen is that he continued to experience the push and pull of the desire for public service contending with his yearning for privacy. He would never fully resolve this personal dilemma, entering into the political fray only to withdraw at least three more times before his final "retirement." And so for most of the next two years Jefferson continued to build his beloved Monticello—a lifelong construction project that was never quite finished. And perhaps this was his intention. As he immersed himself in architectural drawings and supervised the plantation operations, he slowly began to heal from his grief and public humiliation before he tentatively took up the public gauntlet once again.

By 1783, his determination to remain sequestered sated, he again heeded the call to the responsibility—and the consequent opprobrium—

---

8. Koch and Peden, *The Life and Selected Writings of Thomas Jefferson*, 364.

of office. He accepted election to the Continental Congress, and a year later he was appointed by the newly formed government to become the economic trade commissioner, and later minister, to France. While he was in France, he was to take his final public stance against slavery as the tension between his belief about its need for redress and his sense of his promising future arrived at a crossroads. It was also in France that Jefferson began to assemble the coalition that would both serve him and shape him in the many long years ahead.

FRENCH LESSONS

Joseph Ellis describes Jefferson's supporting staff (what we might call a team today) in France as operating something akin to how he organized the plantation work at Monticello in the form of concentric circles. It all began with an inner circle whose purpose was the management of the household and day-to-day affairs; Jefferson of course was at the center. The second ring was formed to deal with political and diplomatic affairs in France. This cadre included William Short, a William and Mary graduate, as Jefferson's personal secretary, a role that extended far beyond that of administrative tasks as Meriwether Lewis his personal secretary in the White House would find. The third tier was comprised of his protégés and colleagues, James Monroe and James Madison, living back in Virginia and Philadelphia, respectively. They would become his eyes and ears and sometimes his hands in America.

To Madison fell the task since his mentor was in France, of apprising and consulting with Jefferson on matters in Congress where he served. Madison, perhaps more than any other man, drafted much of the new Constitution and with Alexander Hamilton, acted as its most articulate public defender. Madison is also the source of most of the insight from the closed deliberations about the Constitution, for leaks were few and his notes were by far the most fulsome for future historians. Monroe was to do much of the drafting work in shaping the new state laws of Virginia in the legislature, picking up where Jefferson had left off before his overseas assignment.[9] Following George Wythe's example to him, Jefferson nurtured Short in France and Madison and Monroe in America in their burgeoning careers while each served as a valuable adviser to their older patron.

---

9. Ellis, *American Sphinx*, 82–83.

Jefferson's fondness for this small cadre of three men was shown upon his return from France in 1789. To this circle that had served him so well while he was away he expressed a desire to form a collaborative community. As he envisioned it, this community would be something akin, in principle, to the "academical village" he later incorporated into his designs for the University of Virginia. In a letter he wrote to Madison, Jefferson described the need he saw for a "neighborhood" that he hoped his colleague would join in, describing this living arrangement as an

> agreeable society... the first essential to happiness... of our existence... I view the prospect of this society as inestimable.... Monroe is buying land almost adjoining me. [William] Short will do the same. What would I not give if you could fall into that circle...? Life is of no value but as it brings us gratifications. Among the most valuable of these is rational society.[10]

What he wanted more than anything was these bright, like-minded young Virginians around him, forming something resembling the French salons he had come to love for their intellectual stimulation and agreeable company. The idea likely brought back to him fond memories of the Williamsburg gatherings of his youth, or perhaps he envisioned it as an erstwhile substitute for his lost dreams of family shattered by Martha's untimely death. This collaboration also had a pragmatic side, for he knew it would be a valuable asset to help sow the seeds of a national political role should that become possible. Clearly it seems Jefferson had ambitions beyond those he spoke of openly.

THE INDISPENSABLE MAN

Among his three Virginia protégés—Short, Monroe, and Madison—one man stands out above the others. The man Jefferson trusted most throughout his life was James Madison. Even at the end, he turned to him only four months before his death as Jefferson wrote his farewell which contained an expression of his uncommonly deep feelings of gratitude for their nearly lifelong partnership and common commitments. He hoped and even expected Madison to protect his reputation against those who would sully it after he was gone, the specter of political opposition never far from his mind:

---

10. Kennedy, *Mr. Jefferson's Lost Cause*, 32–33.

> If ever the earth has beheld a system of administration conducted with a single and steadfast eye to the general interest and happiness of those committed to it, one which, protected by truth, can never know reproach, it is that to which our lives have been devoted. To myself you have been a pillar of support through life. Take care of me when dead, and be assured that I shall leave with you my last affections.[11]

For fifty years they had collaborated in a manner never to be duplicated in American political history. Madison's role in supporting Jefferson as his listening post, adviser, collaborator, defender, and friend is a role that is largely unsung by all but a few. Madison's public actions on behalf of Jefferson allowed the naturally more reclusive older man to remain somewhat invisible yet not lacking serious impact in the national public policy debates or finding success in his deferential campaigns for high public office. Their diaries reveal the great depth of this symbiotic relationship. Madison was the one who most shaped his senior's views and smoothed the consequential actions for the public, as Jefferson was often unpredictable though creative, possessed of a mind that did not go down the usual paths to a solution. Sometimes his ideas needed the practical reality that only Madison could invoke for him.

---

11. Koch, *Jefferson and Madison*, 260.

James Madison, Without Him There Would Have Been No Jefferson

How James Madison became the person who could best articulate the public expression of the private Jefferson's ideas is a tribute to both his intellectual brilliance and his deft reading of his mentor. Madison was always careful to be both sensitive and diplomatic in editing Jefferson's writing and seemed to have an intuitive sense for how to communicate this to the thin-skinned writer of such beautiful prose. Great writers do not like to be edited, as seen in Jefferson's ire at the Declaration's emendations by his colleagues.

One example of Madison's critical role on behalf of Jefferson was the passage of the Bill for Religious Freedom that Jefferson had authored in the Virginia legislature in 1777. Following an inability to see it through on its first offering, Jefferson gave it up, much like he did with the defeated bill on abolishing slavery in 1769. But Madison, who shared Jefferson's passion to curb the role of the established church in the affairs of government, would persist through subsequent revisions in the ensuing years. His quiet, personal appeal to his fellow legislators ultimately led to its passage in 1786 while Jefferson was in France. Jefferson would come to believe its authorship to be one of his greatest achievements, but he also must have known that if Madison had not taken up the task, the enactment of one of Jefferson's signature initiatives would not have occurred.

THE CONSTITUTIONAL DEBATE FROM AFAR

The next year, 1787, saw Madison traveling to Philadelphia as a Virginia delegate to ostensibly amend the Articles of Confederation for the new nation. As is well known now, the task soon morphed into the secret drafting of an entirely new constitution, an undertaking that Madison had been quietly researching for some time. He was well prepared to be the man on the point for this challenge, and it was his brilliance combined with exceptionally hard work that would result in his later being called the "father of the Constitution." But to read Madison and Jefferson's correspondence, it might seem that he was at times channeling his mentor's ideas, deferring to his wisdom. The reality was somewhat different.

The interaction of these two future presidents concerning the drafting of the Constitution gives possibly the best picture of the complex nature of their collaboration over the many years ahead. Jefferson would typically weigh in from a safe distance (across the Atlantic in this case) and Madison would be the one to labor in the trenches, writing, negotiating, and deftly deflecting. Jefferson would hold forth on his pet theories and visions for the new nation, often a bit unusual or idealistic. Madison would then do the practical work necessary to carry out what was pragmatic or wise, all the while assuring his older colleague that these nuances were insignificant changes that captured Jefferson's intent. It was a delicate dance they performed, and Madison led without letting Jefferson feel he was following his partner. It is clear that Madison never resented this less visible role nor did he disdain the sage for his idealism and even impracticality at times. It was a relationship forged in mutual respect.

One key example from the constitutional dance occurred when Jefferson expressed his overall framework for the new American government as one including a federal leadership role reserved primarily to the arenas of foreign policy and trade. In his thinking, the states would provide leadership in *all* matters domestic, which would include both banking and property (slaves). This was the view he wanted Madison to convey to the Congress and Monroe to reassure the Virginia planters with. But as these exchanges evolved, often in cryptic code to prevent suspected snooping, Jefferson's growing utopian views of limiting the federal government in favor of the states put him at odds with the practical evolution of the conversation engaging the Congress in Philadelphia. It was the officers who had served with Washington at Valley Forge who particularly saw a keen need for a balance of powers, but one that ensured a strong, on-the-ground federal governance role. Madison gradually came around to supporting this view as necessary, but he realized it ran contrary to Jefferson's own. Jefferson believed that the saving grace of any imbalance—state or federal—was the American people. He believed it was the people who would, without the taint of either governmental power over behavior or religious constraints on conscience, internalize a local and national moral compass for right governing. This understanding of Polaris arising from the people would turn on his construct of having an *educated* American people capable of right moral choices. Here the utopian and the pragmatic clashed in the framing—and not for the last time.

The tension between those two beliefs was best expressed in the Madison-Hamilton collaboration that today we call the Federalist Papers. It was in these writings that they made the public case for a stronger federal role to solve the paralysis caused by the limitations experienced under the Articles of Confederation. This partnership role supporting the Federalists' and Hamilton's views was one Madison decided he must necessarily keep secret from Jefferson lest he offend him. Jefferson had already begun to be disquieted by this future nemesis, Hamilton, and by the centralized financial philosophy he was beginning to expound as essential for dealing with the great debts incurred from the war.

As this delicate interplay by letter was being carried on between America and France, Jefferson was experiencing the vortex of the French

Revolution, which shaped his own thinking. The upheaval of the monarchy and the priesthood was a denouement he almost uncritically admired when the people began to exert their bloody will on their former rulers. These shocking events and Jefferson's imbibing of the French wine of Enlightenment philosophy likely served to inform some of his more idealistic thinking about forming the new nation across the Atlantic.

The context for his opponents' case was far different as they drew their conclusions not only from their study of history but also as veterans of the Revolution in America. Jefferson's philosophical and scientific studies, coupled with his absence from the revolutionary battlefields, would shape his core political beliefs far differently than the beliefs of those who had experienced the frustrations of a powerless confederation of states.

Although he viewed the proceedings from afar, Jefferson did not entirely withhold criticism of what he understood was the drift. Here he needed Madison's protection. It came to a head when the anti-Federalists and his fellow Virginians, Patrick Henry and George Mason, cited Jefferson as being opposed to a strong central government. Likely they were echoing Monroe's reassurance from his correspondence that this was indeed the case. It was then up to Madison to contradict that claim and carefully defend Jefferson's political leanings.

As Madison later told Jefferson, "I took the liberty to state some of your opinions on the favorable side"[12] (while withholding those on the anti-Federalist side), thus ensuring that Jefferson would continue to be seen as being in the camp favoring a strong federal government. Although Madison knew that some of Jefferson's more radical ideas were to the right of even Patrick Henry, he had also seen that Jefferson was not *consistently* opposed to a strong central government and thus seized on that as his stratagem. Their personal interaction by overseas letters during the time of the constitutional debates gave him the confidence that Jefferson would approve the ultimate outcome while also being protected from future political fallout. This deft interplay stands as a cogent example of where the protégé helped his mentor to learn and later to become successful. Today we might call this "reverse mentoring."

In the end, Jefferson supported the arguments of Madison and others, endorsing the ratification—but with one important caveat. He called these final suggestions merely: "strokes that need retouching. What these

---

12. Ellis, *American Sphinx*, 123.

are, I think are sufficiently manifested by the general voice from north to south, which calls for a bill of rights."[13]

His almost lifelong concern was to first protect individual citizens from the potential excesses of government that lurked in the hearts of men. Ultimately that philosophy led to a break with what he interpreted as a distortion of the past calling the new nation's course increasingly one of veering back toward monarchy. Here, too, Madison would prove invaluable.

Thus, over the next decades, Madison would continue to emerge as being uniquely influential compared to any of Jefferson's other colleagues in a partnership that lasted over half a century. Their closeness would be more deeply forged in the hardships of the political battles that lay ahead as well as in shared personal losses. Madison kept Jefferson from making the mistake of having some of his excessively idealistic views become policy proposals and in every venture not only supported Jefferson but also helped shape his thinking. Madison was so brilliant at it that one commentator has said, in essence, that without Madison there would have been no Jefferson.[14] But Jefferson had good fortune in a second trusted lifelong friend, another protégé and Virginia neighbor—James Monroe. Second only to Madison, Monroe also became instrumental to the man Jefferson was becoming.

A SECOND PILLAR

Near the end of his presidency in 1808, Jefferson would write to Monroe this poignant note of their evolved friendship: "I have ever viewed Mr. Madison and yourself as two principal pillars of my happiness. Were either to be withdrawn, I should consider it as among the greatest calamities which could assail my future peace of mind."[15]

As with Jefferson's own early legal preparation under Wythe, the twenty-two-year-old Monroe began to read law with Jefferson in 1780. Their friendship only solidified in 1783–1784 when they shared rooms as two of Virginia's members in the Continental Congress before Jefferson was called to France. For the next several years, this trusted relationship grew ever deeper as Monroe provided Jefferson with legislative and political intelligence from Virginia. In fact, during Jefferson's years

---

13. Koch and Peden, *The Life and Selected Writings of Thomas Jefferson*, 450.
14. Koch, *Jefferson and Madison*.
15. Cunningham, *Jefferson and Monroe*, 40.

in France, Monroe received more correspondence than even Madison. The collaboration continued when Jefferson returned and they became nearby neighbors.

As his mentor, Jefferson strongly encouraged Monroe to enter a career in politics, as Wythe had done with him. He also steered him toward Professor Wythe's unique law and governance program at William and Mary.[16] Later Monroe would become President Jefferson's trusted emissary to France, concluding the politically sensitive Louisiana Purchase. By 1816, Monroe would be seen as the likely successor to Madison as president with Jefferson continuing as his mentor, offering written advice that President Monroe requested and personal advice when Monroe returned home to visit. Theirs was a collaboration of forty-six extraordinary years, continuing until Jefferson's death. Yet one issue above all would vex them both to the very end—slavery.

16. Ibid., 18.

James Monroe, Jefferson's "Second Pillar"

This fractious issue would cause President Monroe more anguish than any other. It came in the form of the issue of whether to extend slavery to the western territories as they became states. These were the lands acquired by his mentor in 1803 from Napoleon. During Monroe's tenure, many territories petitioned for statehood seeking equal treatment with the South to choose whether to be slave or free. How Monroe and Jefferson once again were brought together to confront this challenge is a tale best left for the last years of the old sage, years in which he and his two pillars would continue their lifelong work on one last great building project together—"Mr. Jefferson's university."

THE VIRGINIA PLANTERS

Even when in France, Jefferson was not far from the questions of slavery and other issues bearing down upon the new nation. What concerned him most back home, beyond the framing of the Constitution and the new laws in Virginia, was the impact of an unauthorized French republication of his *Notes on the State of Virginia*. Originally written in 1782, this small book was compiled as a personal favor to a French diplomat who had expressed a desire to more fully understand the country where he had been posted and the premier state in the colonies—Jefferson's Virginia. The small book was first issued in a limited edition of 200 copies much like many self-published books today. Jefferson kept the authorship anonymous, intending it solely for private use. He feared that a wider reading of *Notes*, particularly those short passages where he expressed an uncommonly progressive view on slavery, would cause severe consternation among his constituency among the Virginia planters.

We will return to *Notes* when we look more closely at Jefferson's worldview. Suffice to say at this point in the story, his paradoxical and long-standing view of the moral incompatibility of slavery with freedom and his highly optimistic prediction of early emancipation would not sit well with his constituents. Although he did not elaborate in *Notes* as to how emancipation would occur, he clearly believed it was philosophically the right thing to do consistent with rights of all men. Darkly, he also predicted a racial conflagration of apocalyptic proportions should such freedom be extended. He felt freedom would also produce "convulsions which will probably never end but in the extermination of one or the other race."[17]

This was an uncharacteristically gloomy view for Jefferson, particularly given his outspokenness in favor of periodic revolution as an essential societal "cleansing." This pessimistic view on rebellion, however unlikely, can only be explained as something he feared could decimate the nascent American democratic experiment. It was a fear that never left him in the years ahead. Taking all this in, he concluded that the wider spread of his ideas in America would put him in political hot water with his main constituency, the Virginia planters.

Madison was quickly consulted from France about the feared adverse reaction to *Notes*. Jefferson was concerned that his views on emancipation would come back to haunt his later political ambitions. Madison

---

17. Koch and Peden, *The Life and Selected Writings of Thomas Jefferson*, 256.

replied that, to the contrary, Jefferson should not fear that his remarks in *Notes* had raised any problems, its impact was unremarkable.[18] It had gone virtually unnoticed.

Although this gratified Jefferson, his biographer Joseph Ellis observes that from this time forward Jefferson never stated a public position on slavery nor did he ever write another book. Ellis attributes this remarkable political and literary silence to Jefferson's fears of the voters' reaction. From 1786 on, it would be Jefferson's view that there was a "need for public opinion to catch up with the moral imperative of emancipation."[19] Instead of continuing as an advocate for changing the public mind and the new nation's policy (as Wilberforce was about to do), Jefferson became instead the cautious diplomat. He would now begin to look to the next generation, not to his own, for the realization of his beliefs on slavery even as the Unholy Triangle ground on year after bloody year. So, while Madison would encourage him, he could not overcome Jefferson's fears and his desire to please his fellow planter society. It would fall to Madison and then to Monroe to lead the next generation in redressing the slaves' bondage; yet they, too, would do so reluctantly and without progress beyond their mentor's.

THE FURTHER CALL TO SERVE

Shortly after Jefferson expressed angst about what he had written on slavery, he was called to return to an even higher duty than emissary to France. He was summoned home by President George Washington to be the first Secretary of State in the new United States of America. As Jefferson accepted that office in 1790, he now had a much larger stage upon which to play and to bring forth his views of the role of the new government—and of ending slavery, had he determined to do so.

Yet, for the next eighteen years, with two brief interruptions, his life would unfold in stark, often puzzling contrasts: vicious personal battles and great achievements. He would find, as would Wilberforce, that attempting to change the culture of a nation brought unsought opprobrium with limited potential for success. The field on which he would choose to battle and the issues for which he would contend tell the tale of Jefferson's emerging national and international leadership. The issues he

---

18. Ellis, *American Sphinx*, 102.
19. Ibid., 103.

was most exercised about would also influence whether he would persist in pursuing his priorities of establishing a good society and ending *all* forms of tyranny.

For Jefferson, at this auspicious point in his life, it was his fellow Virginians, the tight circle of Madison and Monroe, who would ride forth with him, helping him each step of the way in his rise to the presidency. Each would serve as the public face and give private counsel and defense for Jefferson's ideas and ambitions. His fellow planters and slave owners would give him the political momentum to become the voice of a new party and the opponent of what he would come to call a monarchial conspiracy he believed was being surreptitiously led by Alexander Hamilton. His enduring relationship with his two protégés was of the most central importance in helping to shape and to sustain him in the political wars that lay ahead. Here we can see exemplified the ancient proverb: "Though one may be overpowered, two can defend themselves. A cord of three strands is not quickly broken."[20] It was not to be sundered until he died.

KNOWING AND DOING

1. What qualities and contexts do you think might have allowed such amazingly enduring political and personal friendships as those Jefferson, Madison, and Monroe experienced over five decades?
2. How do deep friendships help us in our vocation and in acting on our core beliefs to continue on our chosen path, be it college, professional life, or family life?
3. Are such friendships rarer today than they were two hundred years ago?
4. What qualities do you look for in your own "cord of three strands"?
5. Do you have such relationships? If not, what first steps might you take?

20. Eccl 4:12.

5

The Saints

William Wilberforce is proof that a man can change his times though he cannot do it alone.

—John Pollock, "A Man Who Changed His Times"

When Washington took office in April 1789 as America's first president, Jefferson was also installed as its first secretary of state, marking a singular occasion that the world could not help but take note of. The formation of a democracy was unprecedented. At the same time in England, William Wilberforce was facing a daunting personal decision, one whose ultimate outcome would rival the rise of America. He had thought his calling was to end the slave trade, but his humiliating failed attempt had shown him the entrenched strength of those opposed to him. He could only wonder whether it was still prudent to continue. Perhaps he had "misheard" his call in a fit of idealism or optimism. Maybe, like Jefferson, he would be led to conclude that such a course should wait for a future generation whose sympathies for those oppressed would exceed the selfishness of his own. It was a terrible dilemma for the young MP.

Wilberforce could see in retrospect that his close friend, William Pitt, now the prime minister, had wisely deduced that it would take some time to convince Parliament to have the political and moral will to see the light on slavery. But Wilberforce, seemingly caught up in the moral rightness of the cause, possessed an idealism that likely blinded him to the reality of what it would be necessary to prevail. Perhaps it was a good thing he did not fully know what lay ahead. While the slave trade interests were at first taken somewhat by surprise at the audacity of such a proposal, they would not make that mistake a second time. Their initial tepid response likely masked the difficulty of the task that lay before Wilberforce and his supporters.

Whatever the case, he now stood at the same crossroads as Jefferson had when his slavery bill failed in Virginia in 1769. If anything was to sustain Wilberforce in the struggle to end the trade after his unanticipated defeat, it was the faithfulness of those around him. Soon they were to be given a sneeringly derisive name in the corridors of Parliament: "The Saints."

Wilberforce had attracted a somewhat wider circle of close followers than the small coterie surrounding Jefferson. That was in part a product of the difference in their personalities. Unlike the more private, interior American, Wilberforce was a very public man—gregarious, demonstrative, joyful to be around—and over the years he would count even his enemies as eventual friends. Oftentimes his opponents were won over by his political graciousness and his persistent resolve not to vilify others either publicly or privately. He had also determined after his "great change" to no longer be a party man—except for the party of humanity. He would take cause with anyone who would support his projects to advance the betterment of people and not simply to better themselves politically. He was one of the first independents in Parliament and among its first devout Christians, paving the way for many others who would follow him in the decades afterward. He was slowly making it "safe" for enthusiasts by his example.

In contrast to Jefferson, Wilberforce was not an adherent of an overarching governing philosophy; he was more a man guided by a moral impetus that allowed him to be flexible in tactics but solid in his central beliefs. And, unlike Jefferson, Wilberforce was a brilliant speaker. His friend, William Pitt, who is extolled even today as among the best orators in English history, believed Wilberforce was unparalleled.

With these natural gifts, Wilberforce was also not nearly as private as Jefferson in the way he worked with others, either as a leader or in his legislative tactics. Where Jefferson worked behind the scenes with a few close confidantes, primarily Madison and Monroe, Wilberforce formed a wider circle of colleagues committed to take on the slave trade interests while he became the man out on the point. He foresaw that success for them all would ultimately turn on working together as a large team, but this mode of public engagement also reflected his natural disposition—

to be surrounded by many colleagues. His alliances to end the slave trade were never hidden from view, and they grew inexorably over time. Were he alive today, Wilberforce would be the first to say that the end of slavery in all of Britain was certainly not his accomplishment alone, and he would likely feel that history has given him excessive credit. His refrain until the end of life was that ultimately it was God's doing, working through him and his colleagues. Yet his role as the leader called to do the work cannot be underrated by history either.

"Wilber" was the human engine for change and the leader whose persistence in what he believed to be right saw them all through the darkest times of failure. Good humor and patience under vicious personal and at times physical attack, plus a creative talent for making a moral cause a popular one, clearly marked the way Wilberforce and the coalition of nonpartisan abolitionists slowly influenced Parliament and helped to change society over several decades. "Wilberforce needed the others to make him what he was,"[1] one biographer concluded, but they had to have him as their leader. His was an irreplaceable role in the cause.

One of Wilberforce's blessings, from which he would benefit more than Jefferson, was the sizable group of people who were already focusing on ending slavery even before he first took up the cause in Parliament. These were like-minded men and women he could draw upon for support from the very beginning and who had sought him out. Wilberforce was not alone (as Jefferson seemingly felt about the defeat of his own slavery proposal) once he concluded that he must continue to fight for the slaves after he was first bloodied in the opening political skirmish of a long war.

THE CLAPHAM COMMUNITY

Many of The Saints ultimately chose to live in a small village, Clapham Common, just outside of London. Clapham as their shared locus arose from an idea of Henry Thornton, a close friend of Wilberforce who believed that some type of community needed to be formed around Wilberforce to encourage his struggle against slavery. Henry was the son of none other than Wilberforce's early mentor, John Thornton. In 1792, two years after Wilberforce's first defeat, Henry Thornton initiated

---

1. Howse, *Saints in Politics*, 25.

the community living arrangement in the small village. He purchased Battersea Rise with its thirty-four bedrooms and threw it open for Wilberforce to live in and for the others to use as a place to meet. Guests would often sleep over after long nights of debate and work. Others would soon join the community, purchasing homes nearby. They were regular visitors to each other's homes on a daily basis, as were many of those considered as members who did not live in Clapham. Most also worshipped together in the same Anglican Church where John Venn was rector. Venn became not only a colleague of the Clapham group but also their spiritual adviser for over twenty years.

Henry Thornton had two main purposes in forming this fellowship in the Clapham community. One was to encourage religious faith in the London culture through mutual support and common worship. The other was to have a central place apart from the fray where the group could plan together and encourage each other where their religion would not be the oddity it was seen to be in and around Parliament.[2] Although not all those residing in Clapham were politicians, all shared the view that the end of slavery could come only through concerted political initiative for change—a quest they shorthanded as "the cause." Later generations would give them their name—the Clapham Sect or the Clapham Circle.

These Claphamites were clearly marked by an unusual trait for politicians and professionals—their willingness to submit their careers and egos to the cause they shared. They operated, as one contemporary described, like "a meeting which never adjourned."[3] This group not only gathered around Wilberforce, as Thornton envisioned, but also helped to encourage each other and sustain their commitment in the darkest times through common prayer as well as great times of near-childish frivolity. In a sense, it was not unlike the small filial community that Jefferson envisioned forming near his Monticello, although for Jefferson it never became quite the source of collaboration and encouragement that Clapham did for Wilberforce. Theirs was a decades-long informal relationship that continued to function until Wilberforce's death in 1833.

If Madison and Monroe formed Jefferson's two indispensable pillars, the network of support Wilberforce enjoyed from The Saints was, as one biographer observed, also "indispensable in enabling him to serve

---

2. Metaxas, *Amazing Grace*, 183.
3. Holladay, "A Life of Significance," 72.

effectively in politics."[4] Among the Clapham Circle were many leaders of British society, leaders who operated as a team with their roles determined by their experience and by what was needed in responding to the needs that arose. They also developed an unprecedented strategy, certainly for that time, that evolved through the lessons of experience in success and failure, which enabled them to move inexorably forward, though through fits and starts, over the years.

Also not unlike Jefferson's collaboration with Madison and Monroe, this coalescence of commitment has seen few if any equal in politics for its breadth and longevity. Given that a key to Wilberforce's strategy was to transform thinking in the culture by influencing its leaders, this group proved critical, for many were respected leaders in their own right in England. In effect, they functioned like what we now call a team—an organizational construct far ahead of its time. The effectiveness of a team such as theirs is something that only within the past few decades has been used effectively in modern organizations,[5] and it accounts, in large measure, for their success together.

THE TEAM

The Clapham Circle was made up of relatively few people, but size was not as important as the fact that they functioned as one for a single purpose, despite some tactical disagreements along the way. Wilberforce, clearly their leader, was nevertheless a leader *among* them, not *over* them—a critical distinction. The key members of the team included Granville Sharp, Thomas Clarkson, Zachary MacAulay, James Stephen, James Ramsay, Hannah More, John Shore, Charles Grant, Thomas Gisborne, and Thomas Babington.

Granville Sharp was a self-taught lawyer already respected in abolition circles as the attorney who brought the landmark 1772 lawsuit (four years before the Declaration of Independence was written) that resulted in a ruling that *any* African slave who set foot on English soil was a *free*

---

4. Belmonte, *Hero for Humanity*, 139.

5. In the seminal book *The Wisdom of Teams*, Katzenbach and Smith, 43–64, present their distilled "wisdom," which they drew from researching the experience of hundreds of effective teams. They boil it down to a few basics: (1) a small group of people, (2) who have or develop complementary skills and roles, (3) committed to a common purpose, (4) with a shared understanding of their approach/strategy, (5) and who hold themselves mutually accountable.

man. (Colonial holdings such as the West Indies, where most of the slaves were confined, did not meet the legal test of being English soil.) This ruling led to the immediate freeing of fourteen thousand slaves in England, and later of thousands of escaped slaves from America who fought on the side of the British during the Revolution. Sharp also gained respect by prosecuting the infamous Zong Case. Going against all societal and class norms, he intervened for justice regarding the deaths of several hundred sick and dying slaves who were thrown overboard by the slave ship's captain in order to collect on the insurance. Although the court ruled that the slaves were chattel—property subject to the captain's unquestioned disposal of them—the case galvanized opposition to slavery and led to the formation in 1787 of the first antislavery society in England, headed by Sharp and young Thomas Clarkson. Although Sharp was not a leader, he was a patient and passionate laborer on the voluminous research it would later take to document the case for Parliament.

Thomas Clarkson, co-founder of the antislavery organization came to embrace the issue as a student at Cambridge where he published an award-winning essay on abolition. His first taste of the political climate came when he read his treatise to Parliament, as was the custom for the annual winner. The cool reception by the members showed him how unmoved they were by what he felt were his dire, well-documented findings—oppressive circumstances in the colonies that called for immediate action. From that time forth, Clarkson was committed to doing something to end slavery, ultimately teaming with Sharp and many in the Quaker sect who were determined to recruit a member of the mostly indifferent Parliament to take up their cause. He would spend the next several years traveling over the world to gather irrefutable evidence of the brutality and loss of life that marked slavery's bloody trail, giving up his health and a potentially brilliant career to do so.

Zachary MacAulay was exposed to slavery firsthand while managing different West Indies plantations; he left there in 1789 after trying unsuccessfully to ameliorate the terrible conditions. Thereafter, he became, as one colleague put it, one who had "no concern for his own advantage and with no thought of any rewarding glory, uncomplainingly, year in and year out, bore the burden and the heat of the day. . . . the anti-slavery tutor of them all."[6] So voluminous was his knowledge and so powerful was his memory that "look it up in MacAulay" became

---

6. Howse, *Saints in Politics*, 21.

a byword for the Clapham Circle when they were stumped by a question. Grant, Clarkson, and MacAulay filled the critical research and documentation roles for the team.

Like MacAulay, James Stephen was from the West Indies and refused to own slaves after seeing the barbarity of a "trial" where a slave was burned alive as punishment. A highly skilled lawyer, for five years Stephen gathered firsthand information on conditions in the West Indies, returning to England in 1794 just in time to take the place of an exhausted and discouraged Clarkson. He was the top legal expert on the team and a brilliant writer who was known as one of the finest pamphleteers of his time—a new tactic the Clapham Circle devised, which they leveraged to great advantage.

A slave ship surgeon and later Anglican pastor, James Ramsay published in 1784 a widely read book, *An Essay on the Treatment and Conversion of African Slaves in the British Sugar Colonies,* giving the British public the first eyewitness account of the conditions experienced by kidnapped Africans during the Middle Passage. He also gave gripping accounts of the slaves' lives once they were sold to the plantations in the West Indies.[7]

Perhaps the most publicly famous of all the Clapham Circle, Hannah More, was a renowned woman of letters and with her sisters (purportedly the inspiration for Woody Allen's film *Hannah and Her Sisters*) became a pioneering educator and agent of dozens of philanthropic causes funded by Wilberforce and Thornton. Although not a resident of Clapham, she was there frequently for their ubiquitous conversations.

As a young man, John Shore (later Lord Teignmouth) joined the East India Company, which governed the India colony, and rose to become the governor general of India. He worked with Wilberforce and the Clapham Circle to bring human values to India by eliminating infanticide of girls and the suttee (burning) of widows. He also worked in Parliament to allow missionaries to enter India to help address the human exploitation and indifferent moral behavior often practiced by the British.

Like Shore, Charles Grant joined the East India Company as a young man where they became lifelong friends devoted to common beliefs. He became the director of the Court of Directors for the East India Council, the most powerful position in England over the East and,

---

7. Lean, *God's Politician*, 6.

with Shore, formed a potent and highly informed leadership team for advancing the cause of humanity in India.

Thomas Gisborne, another widely respected preacher, was Wilberforce's roommate at Cambridge, and they remained friends through life. His magnificent home, Yoxall Lodge, near Cambridge, became a second Clapham.[8] He served as a willing administrative and secretarial worker—doing whatever it took to advance the cause.

Like Gisborne, Thomas Babington was not a resident in Clapham, but he was an organizational genius. He was the primary force behind several of the nationwide petition drives that became so important tactically to the strategy that evolved.

TEAM LEADER

Each of these team members shared not only a common purpose but also a common belief. Although they brought different skills to the table and would play different roles over the years, there was constancy to their work that allowed for almost daily accountability as well as encouragement. What they needed, however, was a leader, a voice that would be taken seriously by the public. And so it was that the early visionaries and change agents, notably Sharp and Clarkson, realized a member of Parliament must be recruited to lead the fight. By 1787 they had their man. As historian Ernest Marshall Howse describes Wilberforce,

> ... with all these gifts of graces and character Wilberforce seemed providentially prepared for the task and the time. It was to Wilberforce that Sharp and Clarkson looked when they needed a leader for their cause; it was to Wilberforce that Stephen turned when he came back from the West Indies; it was to Wilberforce that Grant looked to find a champion for his mission schemes. Without Wilberforce all the other men would have been little rivulets in some section of their times; but without Wilberforce the rivulets would never have been gathered into one mighty stream, and harnessed for so many memorable enterprises.[9]

This dedicated band of believers would sustain Wilberforce and each other when each year the defeats in Parliament mounted into a mountain of discouragement. For it was not only the toll of repeated defeats but also the virulence of the opposition in the early years that

---

8. Howse, *Saints in Politics*, 18.
9. Ibid., 26.

was especially daunting. The crown opposed them. The greatest hero of Britain, Admiral Lord Nelson, not only opposed them but also declared Wilberforce a traitor. At one point, the opposition became so intense that Wilberforce was twice publicly attacked, necessitating an armed guard to be dispatched to travel with him. Yet Wilberforce persisted without ever returning the rancor, in no small measure because of the close circle around him.

Failure, however, is not one-sided. It also has a way of being a tutor if people who fail can get past the emotion of public embarrassment and disappointment. Defeat can also instill humility in a politician, where ego is the coin of the realm (sports and media stardom might also be included in our day). Such suffering also leads to dependence—dependence on others—but, in Wilberforce's case, he would say especially upon God. This was the overriding great lesson he learned from both Newton and John Wesley. Their similar admonitions likely returned to his memory time and again along the difficult road ahead.

Failure can also teach new ways of working together when the old ways fail to bring results. Thus, early on, Wilberforce and the Clapham Circle had to develop a different approach to political and societal change if they were to succeed. It was an approach that emerged from the lessons of their past failures.

THE UNIQUE STRATEGY

To understand how Wilberforce and the Clapham Circle began to turn the opposing tide, it is important to see their unique strategy as it evolved. It was one that they adapted to fit the needs of their cause, refined over time, taking two unprecedented lines of attack. These approaches corresponded to Wilberforce's two great objects: the abolition of slavery and the reformation of the corrupt and immoral English culture into a good society. As their strategy emerged, they recognized early, as had Jefferson, that society must be made ready for such a major change as abolition, and that corresponding changes were needed in the moral climate of the nation. Yet, unlike Jefferson, they would not wait for a more benign future. For them, ending slavery became a backbreaking, lifetime task and a *personal* responsibility, unprecedented in scope, as they sought to transform an entire nation. To this day, their persistent efforts remain a singular accomplishment and a goad for future leaders who encounter daunting odds to change a culture and are tempted to give up.

THE FIRST PLAN OF ATTACK

The initial assumption that Wilberforce and his supporters held was that because the 1772 court decision recognized a slave as free once on English soil, it followed that the existence of slavery in the colonies and the terrible mortality in the Middle Passage were not worthy of a civilized people. They also declared that slavery was a demonstrably hypocritical policy. Their argument was that at the root, it was immoral to forcibly deprive human beings of their freedom for a lifetime with no hope of release either through hard work or productive results. The only cause they could see for such deprivations was for the enrichment of their masters. The Clapham Circle consistently used the legal argument that English ships, English crews, and English colonial plantations were mere extensions of England; hence, slavery was not only immoral it was also illegal.

But the impasse they faced when the case was first placed before Parliament and the people was as much a result of public ignorance of the facts as it was a product of the indifference and self-interest of the powerful economic forces arrayed against them. Amazingly, to us today the immoral nature of slavery was not self-evident to most people in the eighteenth century. The problem of securing the manumission of slaves was that the evidence of brutality was too remote, literally across an ocean from public eyes and ears. The cries of the slaves went unheard by all but a few.

The counterargument that the opponents of the Clapham Circle initially mounted was to purport that rather than misery, there was widespread happiness among the Africans to leave their land for a better place. This argument baldly affirmed that these displaced wretches were actually joyful and satisfied to work and make a crop in the comparatively civilized West Indies. Thus the opponents incongruously held that *theirs* was the moral high ground in bettering the lives of Africans, not Wilberforce's. This myth was abetted by an astonishing lack of evidence to the contrary—no one up until The Saints made their case really wanted to know the truth. The vast distances from England where the Middle Passage and subsequent slavery in the West Indies occurred did not have the advantage of today's photos or films or investigative journalists. It was not unlike the studied ignorance of the death camps by the German and Polish populace during World War II. People simply did not *want* to know the price being paid to bring them their sugar, tobacco, and fine cotton clothing; they could simply plead ignorance. Our own era has sweat shops in the East, which were far from our consciousness of what brings us cheap consumer goods in the West until documentation began to change the situation. Theirs was a far blinder time and required vastly more evidence and public debate.

The established facts of the reality of the situation did not yet exist in the public realm save for Ramsay's book. It was to attack this ignorance in Parliament and reveal to the English people the harsh truth that Wilberforce needed the newly gathered Clapham Circle's efforts. Clarkson's research, MacAulay's eyewitness accounts from the West Indies, and Stephen's personal experience all gave precedent-breaking and firsthand credibility to their argument.

For example, to gather needed evidence, Clarkson interviewed more than twenty thousand English sailors from slave ships in the three slave trading ports of England: London, Bristol, and Liverpool.[10] But voluminous documentation of factual evidence alone could not overcome the vested interests of the plantation owners and their beneficiaries in Parliament. The economic interests of the three port cities were particularly persuasive reasons to ignore what was happening thousands of miles away as individual livelihoods and the prosperity of major cities were at stake. It was a question of jobs and money, as it often is in politics today. This overweening self-interest could not easily be overcome simply through debate points based on hard evidence. Sadly, the economic arguments trumped any nascent humanitarian feelings or facts. Typically for the day, Lord Abingdon was to remark to Wilberforce, "Humanity is a private feeling and not a public principle to act upon."[11] In other words, keep personal beliefs out of public discussion. In Wilberforce's time, moral right was simply not a consideration in national politics. But that was about to change.

TAUGHT BY THEIR CAUSE

After their initial defeat, some of the Clapham Circle members began to press Wilberforce to draw the British people into the cause. Unlike our time or Jefferson's in America, the involvement of the general populace in affairs of Parliament was widely viewed with suspicion both by politi-

---

10. Metaxas, *Amazing Grace*, 116.
11. Howse, *Saints in Politics*, 31.

cians and by the crown. In an age where the fear of revolution hung in the air after the Bastille fell in 1789, any monarchy in Europe was opposed to stirring up the people for *any* reason lest rebellion break out. As a man of his times, Wilberforce initially agreed with this prevailing feeling and thought the proposal to galvanize public opinion was tantamount to agitation and would, in the end, be counterproductive. He favored the traditional politics of ideas, arguments, facts, and interests as the only way forward. Gradually, however, his colleagues won him over, as the circumstances dictated the novel approach he finally concluded they must take:

> He did not then favor the use either of corresponding societies or of public meetings. But he was to be *taught by his cause* [emphasis added]. He found that his hopes lay only in the people; and in a short time he and his friends became the most persistent agitators in all Britain. "It is on the general impression and feeling of the nation we must rely. . . . So let the flame be fanned. . . ."[12]

Thus the fire of public opinion was quickened by the bellows of The Saints, ushering in a new era in British politics where the widespread use of educational propaganda served to stir up public fervor. Over the four decades that the Clapham Circle labored together, hundreds of thousands of pamphlets were printed and distributed; thousands of public meetings were called; and corresponding societies without number were formed for the abolition cause, following in the wake of the Clapham team and their supporters' visits to towns across England. For years, letters to the editor were written to almost every newspaper of local import, not to mention the hundreds and hundreds of personal letters to influential friends. Small breakfasts and dinners were used as times of conversation and persuasion, particularly of the key societal leaders. And hundreds of petitions were organized and gathered up by the Clapham team, most often under Babington's leadership.

Behind all this effort was the compilation of powerful research by Clarkson, Sharp, and MacAulay. These men produced voluminous notes, which were then meticulously organized and summarized, most often by Gisborne and by Wilberforce himself, who would produce the distilled results as written testimony or as the basis for his oft-repeated speeches before Parliament.

12. Ibid., 40.

74 CROSSED LIVES—CROSSED PURPOSES

Key Members of the Clapham Circle

THE ART OF CHANGE

One of the best stories about their "agitation" is that of the actions of designer and fellow Clapham Circle member Josiah Wedgwood. He created a special Wedgwood china pattern, with the distinctive pale blue and white colors, that included a provocative imprint of a slave, kneeling in chains, with the inscription, "Am I not a man and a brother?" Wilberforce would use the specially produced china as what he referred to as a conversation "launcher," an opening for dialogue. After the finished meal, the dinner plates were removed leaving the charger plate uncovered, providing the surprise topic of conversation for the rest of the evening. This imploring image also began to appear on many forms of Wedgwood jewelry and on cameos. Whereas some were persuaded by words, others were reached by the message conveyed by images.

Another method to raise public interest and awareness was the pictorial representation of what a slave ship looked like from a cutaway view as it was fully loaded for greatest efficiency. In the cutaway diagram, the human cargo below deck was revealed with its allotted sixteen inches for each prone, shackled human being. The image of slaves lying side by side in layers, not unlike lumber, shocked and horrified a nation that considered itself civilized. The first response was unfortunate. In a callous and cynical move by Parliament, the Dolben Act was passed in 1788 to regulate the number of slaves a ship could hold per ton, but these small, merely symbolic changes did little to ease the torment of the captives,[13] although they delayed the final day of reckoning.[14]

13. Metaxas, *Amazing Grace*, 126.

14. Library of Congress, Stowage of the British Slave Ship Brookes under the regulated slave trade act of 1788. The "easing" of the conditions for transported slaves resulted in regulations of space for a man being six feet one inch by one foot four inches; five feet ten inches by one foot four inches for a woman; and five feet by one foot two inches for a boy or girl.

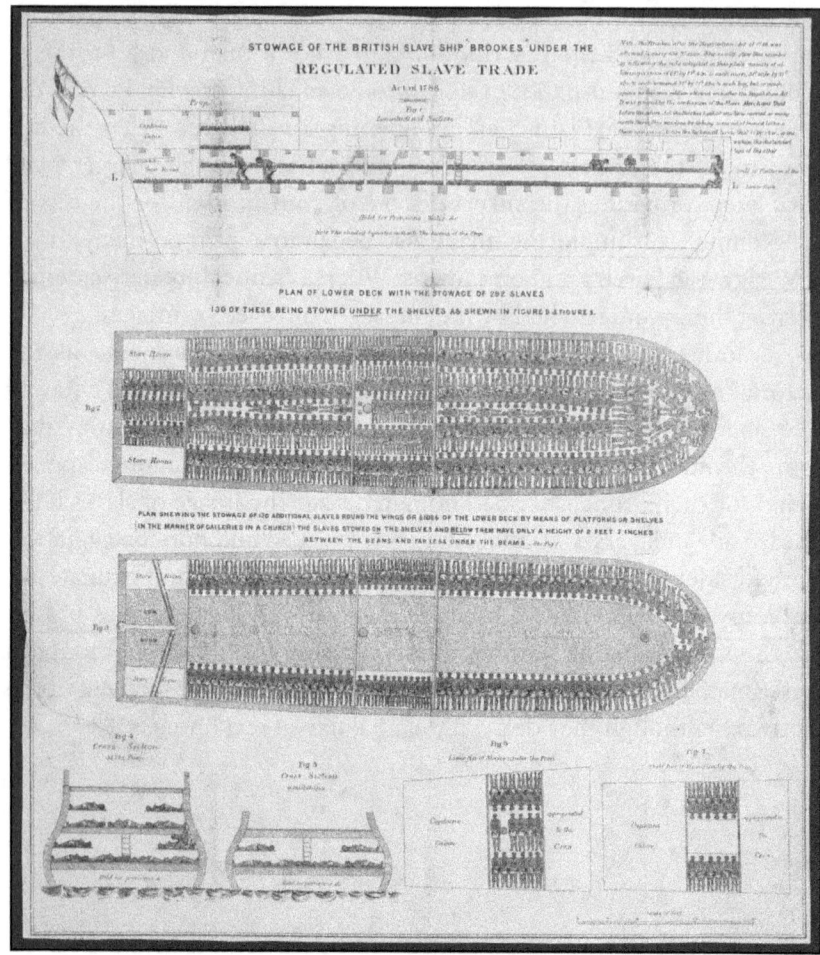

The Brookes Slave Ship Diagram of Slave Stowage

Nevertheless, these vivid displays continued to appear across England as a poignant, true story told at a glance. At least the reality of what sustained England economically could no longer be denied with any credibility by the "happy slave" argument. Many members of Parliament nevertheless implacably continued to affirm the good life that lay ahead in the West Indies while maintaining their fig leaf of compassion in the Dolben Act and downplaying the incidence of any discomfort for the slaves on the voyage.

Even poetry was used in the effort to reach people as the famed William Cowper took up his pen at the urging of his good friend John

Newton. In "The Negro's Complaint," Cowper gave voice to sentiments that struck the hearts of many in England:

> Is there, as ye sometimes tell us,
> Is there one who reigns on high?
> Has he bid you buy and sell us,
> Speaking from his throne, the sky?
> Ask him, if your knotted scourges,
> Fetters, blood-extorting screws,
> Are the means that duty urges
> Agents of his will to use?[15]

The delay by Parliament for further study of the slave trade bill in 1789 may have been the Clapham Circle's first defeat as a team, but it did have two strategic benefits. First, it gave them more time to gather and digest the voluminous research and then to educate the people with their findings, thus bringing in additional petitions from around the country. Second, it gave them an opportunity to assess their approach and to begin to hone the tactics that would become characteristic of their work for the next decades. The penetration of the moral imagination of the British people was only beginning to be felt as the work of conversation, education, art, and poetry slowly spread from city to town. The hideous conditions of the slaves were gradually becoming well known to the beneficiaries of the plantations' exports of sugar, tobacco, and cotton. This meticulous and thorough documentation and the testimony of the first eyewitnesses all began to overwhelm the myths of the manufacturing and port interests despite their heated protests. It also allowed The Saints to fully launch the second part of their strategy in reforming the moral tenor of England.

THE SECOND PLAN OF ATTACK

The Clapham strategy to eradicate slavery ran on two parallel tracks. They had intuited a modern-day understanding of how to change a deeply rooted set of societal assumptions and behaviors, gradually appreciating that this change would take a generation or more. An unreformed society, at least in some measure, would hardly embrace abolition of the slavery of a people thousands of miles away, they reasoned. Thus

---

15. *The Norton Anthology of Literature.*

Wilberforce's "second great object" became an essential part of the strategy to accomplish the first.

The era in which Wilberforce and his Clapham companions labored was a time marked almost throughout by the threat of revolution in Europe that continued to rear its frightening head: a byproduct of the upheaval in France. Even before social networking, the expressions of an oppressed people for liberty from tyrannical regimes had a viral quality. The ideas of freedom spread. More fundamentally, what lay behind the threat of upheaval was a class-based society in England, France, and elsewhere in Europe. Life for most of the common people was vulgar, violent, impoverished, and decadent. The ruling classes and the monarchy in England were not unaware of these forces for change, but they had become indifferent to the needs of the people, comfortable as they were in their own bubbles of prosperity and diversions.

It was a world where alcoholism ran rampant in all classes, child labor was appallingly common, and prostitution was widespread.[16] For example, it is estimated that in the late eighteenth century, 25 percent of unmarried women in London were practitioners of the oldest profession.[17] Punishment for the smallest of crimes was harsh and summary—at least for the poor. Public executions, including dissections, became little more than spectacles for entertainment, not deterrence, and were carried out for such relatively minor infractions as petty theft. The ameliorating impact of religion on this climate of grace was quite small. The years of the religious wars in Europe had not only ushered in the Enlightenment philosophy that science trumped transcendence, but also brought with it a loss of confidence in the efficacy of religion's influence on societal behavior. The upper classes were particularly ill suited to lead a change in the moral culture with their excessive public drunkenness, gross immorality, and appalling indifference to the poverty and suffering of the lower classes. Wilberforce and his Clapham colleagues were among the few of their class who were sickened by the state of affairs in England. Although they were not entirely alone, they were initially at a loss as to how to bring about reform in an entire society.

But then in 1787 the Clapham Circle forged a brilliant strategy that opened the way for decades of reformation that would not only transform the moral landscape, but also undergird the growing sympathy for end-

---

16. Metaxas, *Amazing Grace*, 70.
17. Ibid., 76.

ing the slave trade and its evil entanglements. Without the subsequent changes in the public's sensibilities, ending the slave trade and slavery itself would not have been possible. This is why we see Wilberforce and the Claphamites laboring not only for their most important public objective—ending slavery—but also for the transformation of society—as Wilberforce expressed it, that it might become "fashionable to do good" to those less fortunate.

THE KING JOINS THE TEAM

In retrospect, the method they used was an unlikely one but not all that risky to their cause, couched as it was in historical precedent and royal prerogative. On the surface, the oddity was that it seemingly had nothing to do with the issue of slavery at all. The plan outlined by Wilberforce to Bielby Porteus, the Bishop of London, was one based on the understanding that religion was not a private but a public matter in England. Unlike in Jefferson's America, King George was enshrined as the guardian of the Christian faith as his forebears had been since Henry VIII, and priests were supported by the national treasury. Although for most British subjects, Christianity had become nothing more than a show belied by the hypocritical behavior of its adherents, nevertheless each new sovereign issued a pro forma Proclamation for the Encouragement of Piety and Virtue—which was then widely ignored.[18] However, the historical research by the Clapham team revealed that a similar proclamation by William and Mary in 1692 actually had resulted in a different outcome than the customary indifference. Their initiative in the late seventeenth century was attended by a unique and effective twist—royal encouragement to form Societies for the Reformation of Manners. These societies were subsequently organized by citizens to help the magistrates detect crime and to promote moral and ethical behavior in the people.

Wilberforce shrewdly made the case to Bishop Porteus, a widely respected leader in the Church of England, who shared his view that just such an approach was badly needed for the good of English culture. Since William and Mary's time, moral conduct, especially of society's leaders, had deteriorated alarmingly, and personal responsibility based on mutually held beliefs about the importance of moral virtue was all but extinguished. One consequence was the widespread incidence of unreported

---

18. Pollock, "A Man Who Changed His Times," 59.

and unrestrained crime. The criminal justice system depended upon the victim to bring forward criminal charges and provide the evidence because there was effectively no police force. Not surprisingly, most crimes against the good of the state and its people went unreported, resulting in a climate of general permissiveness and indifference. The bishop was one man who heartily agreed with the Clapham Circle that there was an urgent need for change. He was also wise enough to see Wilberforce's proposal as a once-in-a-generation opportunity.

Thus the campaign to change the moral tone began with Bishop Porteus writing the archbishop of Canterbury that the purpose of the proposed proclamation would be to "check as much as possible the deluge of vice and immorality which was overflowing this country."[19] Wilberforce, with Porteus's backing, then engaged his close friend, Prime Minister Pitt, who arranged a meeting with the archbishop of Canterbury, and finally with Queen Charlotte. King George III himself was then approached by the archbishop, who by now had a very strong hand. The king found the proposal very agreeable, although likely for different reasons than the Clapham instigators. He could see that the security of his throne might be more firmly established if the moral climate improved the lot of the people—and resultant stability came in its wake.

Thus it was that on June 1, 1787, King George issued the Proclamation for the Encouragement of Piety and Virtue. Few knew that behind it all was an inexperienced twenty-seven-year-old William Wilberforce and a few of his friends. This obscure backbencher was the man with the energy, foresight, and persistence to tilt at this windmill, although he is remembered far more for his work on his first great object—slavery—than the second.

SOCIETIES

Borrowing another lesson from history, under the proclamation's imprimatur Wilberforce then organized a national Society for the Suppression of Vice. With the power of the archbishop behind him, he began recruiting the leading members of England. These prominent people would then become his leverage point for changes in society even as he and his colleagues cultivated a mass education campaign for all the classes. The

---

19. Ibid., 60.

head of the See of Canterbury urged his fellow bishops to follow his own example and provide their support for the formation of local societies in their geographic areas of responsibility. Wilberforce also sent letters to like-minded associates throughout the country, encouraging them to organize similar societies for moral reformation in their communities in partnership with the Church of England. His intent was that "men of authority and influence may promote the cause of good morals. . . . Above all things, let them endeavour to instruct and improve the rising generation."[20] As a leader, he wanted the next generation of leaders to exceed his own in piety and moral behavior, these being the foundation, he believed, for continued and positive change in a nation (as he would later write in his book)—not revolution, as was occurring in other parts of Europe.

By 1830, shortly before Wilberforce's death, hundreds of voluntary societies had been formed to ameliorate a myriad of social ills. These ranged widely across a spectrum, including assistance for laborers and the poor, reduction in the number of crimes punishable by hanging, institution of penal reform for women, distribution of Bibles, education for the blind, the first society for preventing cruelty to animals, the end of the brutal spectacles of bear and bull baiting, the cessation of cruel and excessive floggings of navy seamen, the end of the abuse of "climbing boys" (young lads who cleaned chimneys naked), and the promotion of vaccinations.[21] Over his life, Wilberforce was president, vice president, or committee head of sixty-nine charitable societies that grew out of this initial proclamation.[22] Within forty years, English society was transformed, a change unrivaled by any in history save perhaps the conversion of pagan Rome to Christianity under Constantine.

For Wilberforce, his Clapham team, and their allies, this moral transformation was essential in laying the groundwork for abolition of the slave trade and finally for emancipation as well. What Wilberforce recognized as a young man is a principle that is gaining currency today in crime fighting. Recent research has shown that, as Wilberforce wrote to a friend, "The most effectual way to deter serious crime is by punishing the smaller and by endeavoring to repress that general spirit of

---

20. Belmonte, *Hero for Humanity*, 158.
21. Ibid., 159; Metaxas, *Amazing Grace*, 253.
22. Pollock, "A Man Who Change His Times, 224.

licentiousness, which is the parent of every species of vice."[23] We see the success of this principle today in the reduction of murders and armed robberies in New York City, which emerged from the so-called "broken windows" strategy. By prosecuting petty crimes such as graffiti, panhandling, and subway fare jumping, the New York Police Department began to change the message from one of permissiveness to one of intolerance for any type of crime.[24] Wilberforce at age twenty-seven grasped this idea and saw in it the even greater opportunity to create a culture that would eventually support the removal of the grossest of crimes against human beings.

Biographer Eric Metaxas concludes regarding this second strategy, "It's not too much to say that this single observation was the lever by which little Wilberforce replaced an entire world of brutality and misery with another of civility and hope, one that we now refer to as the Victorian era."[25] Wilberforce continued to be engaged in these societies up until his death, although he never took his eye off the prize of the end of the worldwide slave trade and finally, emancipation.

Seizing on the twin strategies, however, was only the beginning of the battle. The final outcome was still obscured in those early days, leading the Clapham Circle to form a philosophy that is known in our day as The Stockdale Paradox: "Confront the brutal facts but never give up hope."[26] In the following decades, The Saints would be tested time and again—a test not only of their persistence but also of their beliefs and of their very friendships and commitments to each other and to their common purposes. Without this Clapham team, Wilberforce would not have prevailed. They helped forge his steel time and again; yet, without his leadership, his fellow Claphamites likely would not have stayed the course. It was a mutual alliance of friends and believers in "the cause"

---

23. Metaxas, *Amazing Grace*, 78.
24. Kelling and Wilson, "Broken Windows,"??.
25. Metaxas, *Amazing Grace*, 79.

26. This maxim has entered the lexicon thanks to Jim Collins's *Good to Great*, 83–87. It comes from his interview with Admiral William Stockdale, highest ranking POW in the Vietnam War, who suffered under the most brutal torture with complete uncertainty of his fate. He explained to Collins that he made it out when others did not because he never lost faith in the end of the story, even when he did not know what it was, nor did he ever fail to confront the fact that he was a prisoner and at the mercy of men who hated him. Collins concludes that it is a good philosophy for a life or for a business.

that did so much to bring about the long, gradual change in England that ultimately spread to most of Europe. His generation offers to subsequent generations a model for cultural transformation.

Like Wilberforce and the Clapham team, our era can also borrow from history. Some key lessons we can draw from their example are relevant for anyone who seeks to bring about significant change in society at any level:

- They did their homework with excellence, not basing their positions on "rights" or on rhetorical passion alone.
- They built a wider support community around them using education, art, images, and personal relationships to galvanize the leaders and the people.
- They had a clear sense of a purpose to accomplish in their lifetime.
- They would not accept setbacks as final defeats, even in the name of pragmatism.
- They stayed the course for the long haul.
- They refused to allow their opponents' virulent personal attacks to be answered in kind—they stuck with the issues and did not retaliate with vitriol.
- They sought to understand their opponents and to engage in civil, meaningful dialogue on common ground.
- They accepted small gains on the road to the larger prize.
- They transcended a single-issue climate by addressing many issues within a need for encouraging a moral climate in all of society: common grace for the common good, not simply "religious" issues.
- As many of them later recorded for posterity, they had a sense of God's providential leading. (It was the same sense of providence that many of the American founding fathers expressed in their against-the-odds separation from Wilberforce's England.)

The irony was that at this moment in time, America stood on the brink of launching a new government under a democratic Constitution with Jefferson as its man for foreign affairs even while England, whose shackles America had just thrown off, stood poised to address the slave trade bill under Wilberforce's leadership. This irony will unfold even further as an even greater paradox as we continue deeper into their stories.

By 1789, despite the brilliance of the Clapham strategy and the excellence of their teamwork, the hard work of turning a promising yet disappointing beginning into results for the slaves and the transformation of society remained embryonic. The repeated contractions of birth lay ahead. Little did they know then how painful, how long was to be their labor—twenty more years of struggle.

And in 1789, little did George Washington, John Adams, and Thomas Jefferson suspect that the heady, early days of this first democracy also held the seeds of an enmity that would burst forth shortly and with great divisive bitterness: a philosophical and political conflict over the next twenty years that would make slavery's ultimate demise much more difficult as the slaves waited in the wings for a savior.

As dawn broke on the next decade, in England and America this all lay ahead.

KNOWING AND DOING

1. We live increasingly in a nation where "sprawl" describes the geography of our closest relationships, contributing to a loss of community. What communal principles of the Clapham Circle might be adapted for a group of people deeply concerned with a great cause in our own time? Would it be a realistic approach?

2. The relationship of William Wilberforce with the "team" that was known as The Saints was a unique one. They needed him; he needed them. What might allow such a team to remain committed through political and cultural failures for decades?

3. The Saints, despite all the heated opposition over the years, were never known to resort to incivility or implacability except on moral principle. What lessons might our increasingly charged political atmosphere draw from this by those who would restore civil discourse?

4. Do you know of other examples where the members of a group and its leader voluntarily suppressed their own personal ambitions

for a moral cause? Would Jefferson have been able to marshal or even join such a team around the cause of abolition?

5. Because the Clapham Circle shared a common faith and openly practiced it, they were initially disregarded by most politicians of their time. It was their persistence and consistency of life that ultimately won the day. Is there a lesson here that applies today? Why or why not?

6. Is there a small or large cause that you might either join or lead that is an issue where selfishness is blotting out compassion?

6

A New Dawn in America: 1789–1808

The storm through which we have passed has been tremendous indeed. The tough sides of our Argosy have been thoroughly tried. . . . We shall put her on her republican tack and she will now show by the beauty of her motion the skill of her builders. . . our fellow citizens have been hoodwinked from their principles, by a most extraordinary combination of circumstances. But the band is removed, and they now see for themselves.

—President Thomas Jefferson to John Dickinson,
March 6, 1801[1]

IN 1789, BOTH JEFFERSON and Wilberforce were widely acknowledged as rising leaders in America and in England. The older man, Jefferson, had the greater world reputation, having been the author of the Declaration of Independence and the American emissary to France. Now, as America's first secretary of state, his star was clearly on the rise. In America and Europe, he was well known for the vast scope of his brilliance and for his sympathy for the French Revolution, an enthusiasm not shared by all of his American contemporaries. Nevertheless, his disquietude toward a strong central government was already not endearing him to his Federalist colleagues.

Wilberforce, still a younger member of the House of Commons and sixteen years Jefferson's junior, was also on the rise, representing the powerful York constituency. He was a close confidante of his good friend Prime Minister William Pitt. With such impressive credentials, he could expect to have realistic ambitions for the prime minister post or an im-

---

1. Koch and Peden, *The Life and Selected Writings of Jefferson*, 561.

portant cabinet position in the not distant future. More importantly to him, however, were his informal responsibilities as the acknowledged leader of a small coalition of those seeking to transform England from its addiction to the economic engine of slave labor and the exploitation of the poor by the ruling classes. As for his work in Parliament to date, he was perhaps best known for two things: precociously voicing his opposition to Lord North for putting down the rebellion in the American colonies in the early 1880s and for quixotically introducing the recently silenced slave trade bill. Neither position made him a man esteemed by most in Parliament. Like Jefferson, he was earning himself admirers, supporters, and enemies.

In short, both men were making their mark as leaders but with against-the-grain personas. What occupied their energies in these next twenty prime years of their lives would tell the tale as to their lasting impact on history.

As he took up his new post in Washington's cabinet, Jefferson began to voice his early misgivings about the imbalance between federal and state powers, which—in keeping with the vision for independence from the crown—seemed incongruous to him. He was also uneasy about the unclear role for the national judiciary. In this he was not alone, for it was the least defined branch of the three. Giving stability to Jefferson's concerns in this time of political uncertainty, he had as both a mentor and a boss the man who would remain until today America's only unanimously elected president, the inestimable Washington.

The former general was well known as a man with an eye for talent, eminently fair and prudent, and a leader not given to passions of impulsiveness or enmity. All agreed here was a man under stern self-control. He was wise, unflappable, the man of personal integrity and respect who kept America together in its darkest hours. Washington also took satisfaction in stilling a raging temper, which he had learned to control under the toughest circumstances imaginable.

While Wilberforce gathered himself to renew the battle in the wake of the deferral of the slave trade bill, Jefferson prepared for his own conflict in pursuit of the "great object" of his life—ending tyranny in all its forms. He would soon find an autocratic seed lurking in the heart of his "brother" and younger cabinet colleague, Alexander Hamilton, ready to sprout at the first opportunity. Not having taken the field against the

British, Jefferson now engaged in a private war that in his first days merely smoldered, largely out of sight—for now.

For both Wilberforce and Jefferson, the period 1789–1808 became the most critical time in both their lives, lived in parallel, as they entered the mature phase of their national and international influence. Together, each faced their steepest challenges as leaders and each was tested in different ways, with divergent results.

For Jefferson it would be a family affair, for in Washington's cabinet the internecine conflicts would become a heartache that only a parent could know. The wounds inflicted would be painfully unlike any Washington had suffered on the bloody and frigid battlefields, and Thomas Jefferson would be at the very center of this trauma.

JACOB AND ESAU

George Washington knew Jefferson in Virginia as a fellow planter, slaveholder, member of the House of Burgesses, and the state's wartime governor. They had served together as delegates to the Congress, and Washington was already quite familiar with Jefferson's writing and organizational abilities. As Washington formed his cabinet, he was meticulously conscious of the impact of everything that he did and said, for all of it was a precedent and each decision weighed heavily upon him. The selection and leadership of his cabinet family was no exception. He set out to manage them much the way he did his officers during the war: first selecting excellent people and then delegating heavily.

Due to Jefferson's noteworthy work in France as ambassador during the time the Constitution was being debated and written, Washington came to respect his diplomatic skills and depth of foreign experience along with his superior mind. Thus Washington decided to place his trust in his fellow Virginian, giving him the honor of becoming the first secretary of state.

Alexander Hamilton, Washington's trusted executive officer throughout most of the war, was similarly brought to the position of secretary of the treasury. Washington also knew Hamilton's strengths extremely well, from his preparations for war to his courage and resourcefulness under fire. Here was a man of keen intelligence and creativity, fearless, with an exceptional capacity to lead in wartime—brave, cool, and decisive. Like Jefferson, he possessed a prolific and penetrating pen, amply demonstrated in the national constitutional debates as primary coauthor with Madison of the Federalist Papers. Colonel Hamilton of New York would prove to be another exemplary choice by Washington as a precedent for the young democracy.

Hamilton was perhaps the one person in America, Madison notwithstanding, who best understood the intricacies and potential for governing within the new federal system, and he hit the ground running. His creative intellectual talents and energy rivaled those of Jefferson; yet, in stark contrast, his political philosophy favored a strong central government rather than Jefferson's natural deference to the states and the people. Furthermore, his distrust of France and favor toward England could hardly be more at odds with Jefferson's own views, who still distrusted Parliament and the king fifteen years after the war's end. Moreover, Hamilton had a reputable war record while Jefferson never served and retained the wounds from the accusation of abandoning his post as Virginia's wartime governor. All this aroused a bitter jealousy and suspicion between the two that caused their "father," Washington, great angst during their years of service together.

An unhappy characteristic of this first American administration was the specter of Hamilton and Jefferson alternatively trading stories about each other in private meetings with Washington. Sometimes these disputes broke out publicly in the cabinet deliberations. One of Hamilton's constant themes in the private conversations he held with the president was that he knew Jefferson was working behind the scenes to undermine Washington's policy of neutrality toward the two major powers, secretly scheming to align the United States with France.[2] More critically, Hamilton counseled, Jefferson was also quietly opposing the nascent federal program to create a national banking system and remove the wartime debts that Hamilton championed.

Hamilton believed that such behavior on Jefferson's part, much of it true as it turned out, was motivated by promoting the interests of the Virginia planters—Jefferson's constituency—who distrusted the Hamiltonian central fiscal policy. The planters' fears were twofold—economic and political. They also suspected that a similar line of reasoning used for justifying the need for a central banking system could be used to lead the federal government to summarily remove the slave system by law. It was well known that Hamilton detested slavery. All this made for a fractious brew from the very outset.

2. Ellis, *His Excellency, George Washington*, 216.

Jefferson was no less paranoid than Hamilton in his own private conversations with Washington. He accused Hamilton of harboring monarchial views, seeking to elevate his own supporters—the New York bankers—as an aristocracy. He accused Hamilton of angling to institutionalize hitherto unforeseen central governmental powers—a clear betrayal of the Revolution's founding purposes. Both younger men agreed on one thing, at least—only Washington could hold the other's dangerous policies in check. Their mutual jealousy served to forge an uneasy allegiance to the president whom they both respected as their leader.

Ironically, both younger men could have learned at least one critical lesson from Washington had they swallowed their bile and paid attention. Washington was a model of how important it was in public life to show restraint in giving vent to personally divisive passions. Washington's common objective for the leadership cadre of the fragile democracy was to hold together the disparate individual state interests with their strong views on exercising the powers granted to them versus those he knew were needed by the federal government if they were to avoid the chaotic errors of the past. His governing philosophy was that personal interests and pride must be put aside in favor of serving a greater end. Both Hamilton and Jefferson erred in nurturing their blind enmity for one another, failing to balance the needs of the new nation against their own personal agendas, and resisting collaboration as a team under their leader. Though Washington sought to show them by example how to properly exercise wisdom in governance and maintain self-control over personal passions, his leadership paradigm and later his personal pleas went unheeded. The honorific title of statesman certainly fit Washington in his persistent efforts to avoid personal and party interests in favor of unity. It was a posture few that followed him ever reached.

Unfortunately, Hamilton would ultimately forfeit his life owing to a lack of emotional restraint when he engaged in the infamous duel with Aaron Burr. In a similar vein, Jefferson's insistence on seeing secret monarchial tyranny in Hamilton and later even in Washington would cause him to lose the trust and support of his two older mentors and colleagues—the president and his ultimate successor, John Adams. Both of these older men might have guided their two younger colleagues toward a wiser course had they been willing to listen.

More to the point, Jefferson's oft-expressed concern to end slavery was now sidelined in favor of acting on his suspicions by quietly suppressing what he saw as the growing accretion of Hamiltonian power over national affairs—and over Washington himself. When Hamilton did propose a solution to slavery at the national level, it was seen as anathema by Jefferson; totally contrary to the decentralized philosophy of governance he held was the true spirit of '76. He held this view until the end of his life: slavery's end was a matter for each state to resolve individually. His rivalry with Hamilton only hardened his views on how to end slavery—and to govern—as he maintained an almost visceral suspicion of any idea with Hamilton's name attached.

BROTHERS AND FATHERS

The test for Jefferson came early in Washington's administration when the House of Representatives took up the questions of slavery and Hamilton's bank reform. The Virginia planters were stunned that the federal government would even consider regulating slavery, for slaves were legally classified as property—the constitutional province of states—and as Southerners they were also highly suspicious of a central banking system that strongly favored the North with its great commercial interests. It was Madison, another protégé of Washington and now Jefferson's alter ego, who took up the fight to oppose Hamilton in the House, representing Virginia. Quietly behind the scenes, Jefferson helped Madison and the opposition forces secretly acting against his own administration.

Despite his earlier written and spoken views on slavery, Jefferson took no *public* role in these very early debates as might have been expected, despite his often-stated opposition to its practice. Instead, he quietly allied with Madison in favor of Virginia's interests in Congress. Historians believe this collaboration likely began during a trip they took together, where they settled on an agreement that they needed to orchestrate a news campaign against Hamiltonian federalism lest it gain the upper hand. As a result, they engaged Philip Freneau as their front man, helping to set him up as owner of the *National Gazette*. Freneau, a muckraker and essayist, also became an employee of Jefferson in the State Department to supplement his income.

As was the practice in the bare-knuckle politics of the time, Madison contributed anonymous essays to the *Gazette* opposing Hamilton's "schemes" while Jefferson quietly assisted him, suggesting lines of thought and contributing some of his own writing as well. Had the president known that both Madison and Jefferson—fellow Virginians and his protégés—were surreptitiously acting not only against Hamilton but also against him, he would have been appalled by their perfidy.

The central issue Madison argued to Congress was the growing consolidation of power in the federal government. In writing and in speeches, he strongly hinted, with Jefferson's approval, that Hamilton's proposed policies were a steady retreat to the monarchial British style of governance with its rigid class system—the type of government America had fought to overthrow little more than a decade earlier.

On the face of it, the accusation was ludicrous. Amazingly, Washington took it with some grim humor, seeing the charge of restoring the monarchy as a wholly foolish notion given that America had *elected* a government, one that was not nor ever could become hereditary because he was childless.[3] As further evidence of his true motives, he also cited his own earlier resistance to the offer of summary rule that some would have thrust upon him during the nadir of the war's end when pay for the officers was withheld by Congress.

Yet he did not deign to strike back by sponsoring his own ghostwriters. Washington remained above the fray, confident that if democracy was to survive, the idealism that Madison and Jefferson sought was inadequate to the task, as he and Hamilton had seen at Valley Forge. He needed little persuading from Hamilton's arguments that the new nation needed strength at its center. For America to compete in the world, a national banking system and liquidation of its foreign debts was the road to building international confidence that the young country, unlike the earlier confederation of states, could manage its fiscal affairs. For Washington and others, stability and mature order, not liberty alone, were the reasons for the new federal government. This was what, in Washington's reasoned judgment, would allow America to become great.

Nevertheless, he took a patient view toward both of his wayward "sons" despite being warned that one of them had fostered secret written and verbal initiatives that undermined his presidency. "Be on your guard," wrote one anonymous Washington supporter, "you have cherished in your Bosom a Serpent, and he is now endeavoring to sting you to death.... His vanity makes him believe that he will certainly be your Successor."[4] Unfortunately, Washington would ultimately find that it was true in the main about Jefferson and that his loyalty lay elsewhere: not

---

3. The principle of a limit to two terms had not been a part of the original constitutional agreements. It took Washington stepping down after two terms to demonstrate that the presidency was not for a lifetime.

4. Ellis, *His Excellency, George Washington*, 219.

to a person but to an ideal. Ironically, this was precisely Jefferson's view of Hamilton, and the view shared by those who followed Jefferson. Here the seed was planted for an embryonic party movement. However, until the final break, Washington and Jefferson were never to speak of his quiet betrayals.

It must be said that for Jefferson's part, he did not express a venal view of Washington, publicly or personally, saving his vitriol for Hamilton and the policies that he saw as orchestrated by Hamilton in his "father's" name. For Jefferson and Madison, Washington, a once revered figure, had seemingly grown somewhat senile. Their rationale ran thus: with this impairment he had been manipulated, even duped, by his other "son." In their eyes, Jefferson, Madison, and those of their followers remained the rightful conveyers of the Spirit of '76.

THE FINAL BREAK

Jefferson resigned from the cabinet in 1793 largely over the political infighting with Hamilton; he hated the constant conflict and must have felt a tremendous strain to secretly oppose his president. He certainly believed he could do little more good there. Instead of serving in the second Washington administration, he retired to Monticello, continuing to work behind the scenes campaigning against the Washington administration and the Hamiltonian federalist initiatives. This would set the stage for his run at the presidency three years later when Washington surprisingly stepped down. It would not be the last time Jefferson stepped away from office.

The final break with Washington followed. In a private letter, Jefferson obliquely called into question Washington's feckless capitulation to Hamilton as stemming from a *lack of courage*. This sensational accusation was later made public as being from an anonymous author:

> In place of that noble love of liberty and republican government that carried us triumphantly through the war, an Anglican monarchial aristocratical party has sprung up, whose avowed object is to draw over us the substance, as they have in other forms, of the British government. . . . It would give you a fever were I to name to you the apostates who have gone over to these heresies, men who were Samsons in the field and Solomons in the council, but who have had their heads shorn by the harlot England.[5]

---

5. Koch and Peden, Letter from Thomas Jefferson to Phillip Mazzei, April 24, 1796, 537.

This public accusation of a betrayal of the Revolution by Washington (though unnamed), accompanied by the incredulous accusation of timidity and foolishness, was a cruel wound to such a proud man. It was a wound that could only be compounded by Jefferson's facile denial of authorship when the president asked its source directly. Washington replied to this evasion, politely but firmly, that he knew Jefferson was the anonymous author. The bond of trust was irretrievably severed and the two never spoke again.

Beyond Jefferson's deeply held beliefs in championing the rights of states over the central government, Roger Kennedy believes it was ultimately Jefferson's loyalty to his planter class's beliefs and his need for their support that overrode any of his earlier beliefs on slavery and the loyalty he owed to Washington. It was his desire, Kennedy believes, to please those who were his supporters and neighbors, even at the expense of his "father":

> Jefferson was driven by an insatiable hunger for the approval of his fellow planters. Such a need for the affirmation of peers is common among political persons. In Jefferson's case it was so intense as to overwhelm his commitment to concepts distasteful either to his contemporaries (abolition) among the planter class or thereafter to their sons. *He sought brothers while attacking the authority of fathers* (emphasis added).[6]

One final note must be added to respond to the question that naturally arises: how could two such insightful, brilliant men as Jefferson and Madison possibly believe that George Washington and Alexander Hamilton had so soon turned traitors? How could one possibly see acts of treachery in a president and his former executive officer who had fought in the fields for eight terrible years of privation and hardship, watching thousands of their countrymen die of hunger, disease, and wounds, all to rid America of British tyranny? How could they possibly turn 180 degrees on their commitments? Was it cowardice? Foolishness perhaps? Jefferson's and Madison's arguments for the monarchial aspirations of Hamilton and for Washington's role in these conspiracies are taken from the same page as the arguments against George III just over two decades earlier. One is left to ponder whether this was simply self-serving hypocrisy—a cynical view by Jefferson that led him to form an opposing political party, giving birth to the system that exists today. Yet,

---

6. Kennedy, *Mr. Jefferson's Lost Cause*, 30.

as amazing as it seems, respected colonial historian Joseph Ellis has concluded that from everything he has reviewed in letters, private journals, and documented conversations, these were indeed sincere views that Jefferson and Madison held; not paranoia but genuine concern based on admittedly wildly distorted perceptions.[7] The disease of suspicion would also unfortunately spread to Jefferson's relationship with his other patron, John Adams.

THE ADAMS FAMILY CIRCLE

John Adams had served as a mentor to Jefferson in Philadelphia and later in France. The bonds of friendship between Adams and Jefferson, first forged during the debates on the Declaration, were made even stronger when both were tasked with negotiating international commercial treaties with England and France beginning in 1784.

Adams and his wife Abigail were well aware of the crushing tragedies that had transpired in Jefferson's life during the eight years since the Declaration had been written: the loss of his two young children and, most painfully, of Martha, his beloved wife. Adams was glad to be reunited with his protégé in France, having extolled his virtues to influential men back in America. And Jefferson was buoyed personally and professionally from his association with John Adams, amplified by Abigail's tender concern, intelligent conversation, and warm hospitality. In Paris, they took him under their wing and helped his heart to heal as he became a regular in their home and at their table. With his reentry into the world of politics and foreign policy after his family tragedies, Jefferson would learn from Adams the skills and insights he would later need as the new minister to France.

But for all the felicity of Jefferson's friendship with John Adams both in Philadelphia and Paris, and despite the personal gratitude and affection he undoubtedly had toward Abigail, deepening philosophical differences began to enter their professional relationship toward the end of their time together in France as Adams was about to be posted to England. It only got worse when both men came to serve with Washington in 1789. It was as if a moving cloud cast a widening shadow over both men. The closeness of the ties with Adams as friend and mentor began to fray before Jefferson's rekindled political ambitions and his

---

7. Ellis, *American Creation*, 171–75.

antipathy toward what he saw as Adams's participation in a growing governmental tyranny engineered by Hamilton.

The eventual break with John Adams tragically included Abigail—an even more painful and searing outcome for Jefferson. The final barrier began to be erected during the time Jefferson unsuccessfully sought the presidency in 1796, opposing Adams. Finishing second in electoral votes, Jefferson became vice president as provided for under the new Constitution. Jefferson had characteristically distanced himself from the premeditated smear campaign he and his supporters waged against Adams. Instead, he once again employed a surrogate—the infamous publisher James Callender—to wage the public battle in print. Jefferson and his protégés, Madison and Monroe, quietly encouraged Callender's actions by providing the written ammunition. Jefferson clearly understood the nature of this clandestine attack as he wrote Monroe, "Don't let my name be connected with the business."[8]

Nevertheless, Jefferson finished a close second making him the Vice President. In his concession speech, Jefferson perhaps exaggerated his true feelings in his initial praise, acknowledging his place as Adams's protégé: "He has always been my senior, from the commencement of my public life."[9] Furthermore, he said he did not ever wish it otherwise. Jefferson even penned a gracious letter to Adams, extolling his virtues to govern and expressing his own lack of ambition for the highest office, recalling their good years together. But as David McCullough relates, unfortunately the letter was never sent. Madison reviewed it and advised against sending it on the rationale that if Adams were to fail, Jefferson would then be bound up in the downfall by such an expression of support. Friendship might dictate it, but politics recommended otherwise.[10]

Yet Jefferson's eye was ever on Hamilton. The incoming vice president privately warned Adams against Hamilton's perfidy, which he saw lurking behind the scenes in the form of his supporters, particularly those key Federalists in the cabinet the new president retained from Washington. There was simply no precedent for turning over the cabinet. But almost immediately as his administration began, Adams rightly saw that Jefferson and Madison were quietly colluding again, this time to

8. McCullough, *John Adams*, 536.
9. Ibid., 465.
10. Ibid., 466.

put their republican, French-leaning approach to foreign policy in place of his own more cautious and more neutral Federalist course—one that favored stronger ties with England in the delicate diplomatic dance with both great powers. Adams sought to avert a war by not favoring one over the other as Washington had advised in his departing speech. The bonds of trust were thus again being stretched to the breaking point between Jefferson and a mentor, one with superior foreign policy credentials even to his own. More ominously for their relationship, the Adams temper was such that it would not allow him simply to look the other way as Washington had done with Jefferson's silent opposition.

From a very early point, the vice president was rarely consulted and quickly became a nonentity. Adams reluctantly concluded that the character quality most lacking in Jefferson was a "want of sincerity"[11] (integrity). When it came to issues close to Jefferson's heart, Adams saw he was not above deceit and a compromise of loyalty, even toward those to whom he owed a deep debt of gratitude. For a second time, Jefferson's response to conflict was to withdraw from office, retreating to Monticello by 1797. He went home to sow seeds—the beginning of a quiet campaign for the next presidential election, which would become a historical watershed for the new republic.

THE SECOND AMERICAN REVOLUTION

The election of 1800 was the nadir of the now distant, distrustful relationship between President Adams and his erstwhile vice president. Although the separation began as an outgrowth of their differing political philosophies and gained momentum amid suspicion of the remaining Hamiltonians, the cutting edge was employed by Jefferson with finality in the consequent campaign vitriol. That these deep divides between them and their supporters would soon become a party system now seemed inevitable. Once again, the very thing the prescient Washington warned against in his farewell address. Now it was all but too late. The amount of vilification from both sides—Federalists and Democratic Republicans—through newspapers, pamphlets, and behind-the-scenes backstabbing was of the most base, distorted, and personal nature. Because voters at that time were concerned more with character than with platform as we are today, defacing an opponent's character by surrogates was the prime

---

11. Ibid., 475.

campaign strategy both sides used while the beneficiary stood above it all. Our time did not invent the politics of personal destruction.

In the campaign of 1800, Adams was caught in a crossfire of criticism: not only did the Jeffersonian Republicans distrust his philosophy, but the Hamiltonian Federalists distrusted his independence from their agenda. The brutal campaign took a painful and personal toll on Adams, culminating in the ignominy of coming in a humiliating third place in the electoral vote, as both the Virginian, Jefferson, and the New Yorker, Aaron Burr, finished ahead of him—in a dead heat. After multiple rounds of voting in the House to break the stalemate, it was ironically Hamilton, Jefferson's nemesis, who persuaded a New York member to change his vote. He explained that he felt Burr was an even greater threat to the nation than Jefferson was.[12] For Hamilton, this was a remarkable turnaround and one that also unwittingly sowed the seeds of his death from Burr's controversial gunshot in a duel on the misty shores of Weehawken, New Jersey.

On the day of Jefferson's inauguration, the defeated Adams left the capital at 4:00 a.m., declining to take part in the ceremony. Perhaps he was uninvited because no sitting president had ever been defeated for office and there was as yet no protocol for passing power. His famous pride may not have allowed him to be publicly displayed at a Republican triumph, which he saw as the product of Hamilton's savage attacks and Jefferson's highly personal vilification. After all Adams had done at the founding he must have felt deeply hurt to be unceremoniously discharged by the people. Although relations between him and Jefferson had been at least publicly polite until then, graciousness on either side that might have allowed his attendance did not seem to have been sought nor was it offered. The wounds between them remained tender and unhealed for many silent years, deepened by the clear-eyed condemnation of Jefferson's perfidy by Abigail, his one-time benefactor and friend. Until they were retired and well along in years, the two founders would not speak until they tentatively began a remarkable correspondence that lasted until shortly before their deaths. As Adams rode out, he perhaps knew he would never return to Washington.

---

12. In this strange turn of providence, Burr became a fatal threat to Hamilton. The shocking duel between two prominent national leaders, although forbidden in their native New York and New Jersey, culminated years of ferocious personal opposition and marked the nadir of Federalist–Republican relations.

Jefferson, for his part, considered his narrow triumph nothing less than a mandate, a "second American revolution" he called it, as the Democratic Republicans turned the so-called monarchial Federalists out of office. The rights of the people were to be restored to what had been intended by the founders. Moreover, not without cause, there were many who were optimistic about the chances for the abolition of slavery now that Thomas Jefferson was president. It was not to be.

In Jefferson's presidency, two key accomplishments stand out that merit our attention, primarily because they shed light on slavery's hold and the president's commitment to end slavery: (1) the seminal event of his presidency, the Louisiana Purchase in 1803, and (2) the abolition of the slave trade in 1808. As great actions often do, these two events triggered unintended consequences that ultimately led to the bloody war to end slavery.

PRESIDENT JEFFERSON

Thomas Jefferson assumed the highest office in the land in 1801, having secured what seemed to him the golden opportunity to see his core purpose of overthrowing the Federalists' tyranny fulfilled. Indeed, in a letter to his daughter Maria in 1800, he came as close as he ever would to succinctly expressing an overarching calling similar to the "two objects" that energized Wilberforce all of his life. As he wrote to her, "I feel a sincere wish, indeed, to see our Government brought back to its republican principles, to see that kind of government firmly fixed to which my whole life has been devoted."[13]

---

13. Ellis, *American Sphinx*, 202.

Thomas Jefferson as President

Whether those principles included slavery's demise remained to be seen as republicanism now reigned triumphant. With a clear opportunity to see him as a leader in full, not as a short-term governor, a committeeman, or a rising leader in support of Washington or Adams, his colors would come clear. In all these previous subordinate leadership roles, however lofty they had been, he experienced frustration either soon or late, and withdrew three times to the friendlier views from Monticello. This time there would be no retirement to his mountain retreat, although he would long for it before the end.

To emphasize that this was a new day and that he was a new type of leader of all the people, he used symbols along with the words of his inaugural to communicate what he believed was a return to the principles of 1776. In Jefferson's view, these principles had been badly corrupted almost from the beginning.

One widely circulated but inaccurate story said that for his inaugural he dressed in what was called "plain cloth," then rode alone on horseback up Pennsylvania Avenue to the Capitol with neither guard nor servant attending him. As the myth went and is sometimes still retold, he could easily have been mistaken for an ordinary citizen and spectator. The truth is more prosaic. He was actually housed close enough to the Capitol to easily walk there, led by a militia from nearby Alexandria, Virginia. A delegation of marshals from the District of Columbia, accompanied by various dignitaries, including Republican congressmen and two of Adams's cabinet members, walked with him to show the flag of continuity.[14] Nevertheless, though less dramatic than the apocryphal story, his choice of conveyance was intended to be a statement of his preference for a lack of pomp. He clearly wanted a contrast to the first two inaugurals, which included horse-drawn carriages, large corteges, and finery. His unspoken message: this was a return to the roots of austerity and simplicity that were the republican expression of government. It was Jefferson's vision for the nation writ in his example.

And, this being Jefferson, there then followed eloquent words to the assembled Congress and dignitaries, spoken in his soft, reedy voice, so quiet that many could not hear him. His purpose, he said, was to put aside the rancor of the campaign and give voice to what his administration sought to recover from the founding ideals:

> During the contest of opinion through which we have passed the animation of discussions and of exertions has sometimes worn an aspect which might impose on strangers unused to think freely and to speak and to write what they think; but this being now decided by the voice of the nation, announced according to the rules of the Constitution, all will, of course, arrange themselves under the will of the law, and unite in common efforts for the common good. All, too, will bear in mind this sacred principle, that though the will of the majority is in all cases to prevail, that will to be rightful must be reasonable; that the minority possess their equal rights, which equal law must protect, and to violate would be oppression. Let us, then, fellow-citizens, unite with one heart and one mind. Let us restore to social intercourse that har-

---

14. Ibid., 201–2.

mony and affection without which liberty and even life itself are but dreary things. And let us reflect that, having banished from our land that religious intolerance under which mankind so long bled and suffered, we have yet gained little if we countenance a political intolerance as despotic, as wicked, and capable of as bitter and bloody persecutions.[15]

Then he laid out the principles upon which he would govern, including:

- Equal and exact justice to all men, of whatever state or persuasion, religious or political; ...
- The support of state governments in all their rights, as the most competent administrations for our domestic concerns and the surest bulwarks against anti-republican tendencies.[16]

Jefferson made no mention of slavery directly, but upon close reading it would seem that for one with his gift of language he took intentional care to limit the equality pursued by the central government to include both political and religious egalitarianism, not that of skin color, red or black, or slave status. He also reaffirmed the right of states to be preeminent in *domestic* issues (including property, i.e., slaves) without interference from the federal government. Was he merely being politically cautious in deference to his supporters, or was he expressing where his new priorities lay?

John Chester Miller perhaps comes closest to an answer, understanding Jefferson's motivations in omitting this critical issue of slave or free from his campaign platform or his inaugural by explaining, "From the beginning of his career, it had been impressed upon Jefferson that he must choose between his political 'usefulness' and active opposition to slavery."[17] Now that he had achieved the pinnacle, he was in a position to act upon his beliefs, but only if he could do so "*usefully*." Would slavery be among his ends, or would it be an impediment to his agenda? The answer would become clear in time, but for now pragmatism overruled idealism.

---

15. The Avalon Project at Yale Law School, Thomas Jefferson First Inaugural Address.
16. Ibid.
17. Miller, *The Wolf by the Ears*, 279.

Jefferson's actions would speak clearest during the next eight years in the highest office. Meanwhile, it was the *inactions* of America and its leaders in the years after 1776 that allowed tens of thousands of additional slaves to live in submission, while tens of thousands of other Africans perished on the Middle Passage. Jefferson would only have had to look upon Monticello's fields or read the news accounts and pamphlets of Wilberforce's widely distributed documentation, easily available in England and America by 1800, to affirm this truth. A man of his broad reading tastes undoubtedly was aware of what his contemporary was doing to act against the tyranny *he* saw as the most egregious. But Jefferson does not speak to this growing cancer as his administration begins, and guessing at his thinking does no good.

THE HIGH WATER MARK

Jefferson's most notable accomplishment, which set the direction for the new nation, was by any measure the Louisiana Purchase. Fortuitously, a cash-strapped Napoleon sought to sell the Louisiana Territory, 828,000 square miles of almost uncharted land, in order to finance his martial aspirations. Jefferson had only set out to send a modest proposal to France to purchase New Orleans, thus preserving the port outlet to the sea from the South. But Napoleon's offer far exceeded the administration's wildest imagination. He needed to fund the ongoing war with Britain after the British suffered unexpected defeat at Yorktown pinned between the French navy guns and Washington's army and French soldiers. Jefferson understandably leaped at the chance as a good Virginian, one who held the acquisition of land in an agricultural nation as of first importance. This view was shared equally by his predecessor, Washington. After some consideration of a constitutional amendment authorizing purchase of land from a foreign power, Jefferson brushed aside the nicety that he had no legal authority to do what he was about to do. Taking charge of the negotiations himself, he dispatched Monroe as his personal emissary to France, not Secretary of State James Madison. Jefferson sought to avoid the congressional prerogative that might complicate the need to act decisively. Yet, as prescient as it was, it was also an act contravening his oft-stated governing philosophy of an executive deferential to the legislature and to the sovereign states. That he appeared "monarchial" he knew all too well, but the immediacy of the opportunity and the necessity to be decisive combined to make him more the pragmatic politician and leader than a political philosopher. Fortunately for him, the people agreed, and it was a wildly popular decision damping any potential legal opposition from Congress.

Not content to simply acquire land, as a forward-looking scientist, Jefferson commissioned his personal secretary and Virginia neighbor, Meriwether Lewis, along with fellow Virginian William Clark, to explore this vast new area to see how to use this new territory. Before beginning the exploration, however, he had them undergo intensive scientific training in Philadelphia with the best scholars and scientists in America. Jefferson's far-reaching vision was to enable the Corps of Discovery, as it was called, to find the fabled Northwest Passage by water. They were charged to bring back accurate sketches of what they had seen; and to properly preserve samples of vegetation, animals, soil conditions, and topography. All this was with an eye toward expanding the nation and employing a precision of discovery that would befit an enlightened people. Lewis and Clark were also authorized to make treaties with the Indians they encountered. Jefferson had a keen leader's vision that a vast population would move west in the wake of their discoveries, and he wanted to reduce the possibility of conflict. In this approach to the Indians he was uncannily prescient, as he realized that success in westward expansion could turn on a peaceful outcome in relationships with the native population. Tragically, it was not to be.

When Lewis and Clark and the Corps of Discovery returned three years later in 1806, it was an enormous triumph, particularly for Jefferson's foresight. His perspective was recognized then and now as that of a visionary genius. His wisdom that the future of America lay in the West with its vast resources and open spaces for agriculture underscored his belief in the primacy of his mythic "hero," the yeoman farmer. And it did not hurt that those settling the West would be predominantly staunch Republicans, people of the land, not of the manufacturing cities.[18]

UNINTENDED CONSEQUENCES

Yet the law of unintended consequences came into play as it so often does, sowing the seeds for an expansion of slavery, a deepened controversy over states rights, and further national divisions. In later years, these factors would draw a retired Thomas Jefferson reluctantly into the

---

18. Ellis, *American Sphinx*, 252–3.

fray far more than he desired or planned for in his old age. The issue of the constitutionality of Jefferson's actions on this geographical expansion would pale in the light of his decision as to whether the newly acquired Louisiana Territory would be slave or free. The need for this decision came about because of the clause Napoleon had written into the agreement that the inhabitants of the Territory would have the same rights as U.S. citizens. Jefferson interpreted this to mean preservation of the right to own slaves, which many in the territory already did to work the sugar and cotton plantations of the new southern lands. Thus he backed away from making a decision that might have gained these slaves their freedom, but rather he allowed the treaty language to govern the outcome for them and the future of the new states. It was a precedent that seemed innocuous at the time, but that had far-reaching and deleterious effects later.

The irony is that had Jefferson forcefully acted on the language of his earlier proposition twenty years previously to ban slavery in the western lands under the Northwest Ordinance, he would likely have been able to negotiate to keep slavery confined to the sugar producing area of Orleans and to ban slavery in its entirety elsewhere. Thus, he could set a critical precedent for the new states which would be added. John Chester Miller concludes that this ill-fated decision was the single *inaction* that sowed the most potent seeds for the Civil War because the struggle over slavery was refought each time a new territory petitioned for statehood in the decades to follow this non-decision.[19]

Moreover, as the West opened up, a stream and then a torrent of settlers began to move across the continent. The hope of accommodating the Indians, who were overwhelmed by the onrush, was lost as treaties entered into by previous administrations for Indians lands were shattered one by one. The great opening of the West to the freedom of yeoman farmers ironically deprived two classes of people of their own freedom: African slaves and Native Americans. As many a leader has learned all too late, not to decide is often the most important of all decisions. It remains one of America's vastly overlooked historical turning points, setting the stage for a century of enmity.

---

19. Miller, *The Wolf by the Ears*, 143.

THE SLAVE TRADE ENDS

By 1807, Jefferson's presidency was drawing to a close. The second term had not gone well, and he was experiencing great conflict, which he loathed. Two years before his term ended, he was already speaking of his beloved Monticello, his books, and his grandchildren. If he had not been the president, he might well have withdrawn from his responsibilities as he had before in similar times of great personal stress and disagreement.

He had yet to do anything directly about slavery over the course of his presidency. In fact, as we now know, his private affirmation in 1786 not to bring up slavery publicly again likely influenced his years in the highest office in the land. He seemingly had decided that benign neglect on the issue was the best course. That there were nine hundred thousand slaves, roughly 17 percent of the American population, living within the tenuous balance of eight slave states with eight states now free must have added to his dilemma about moral rightness, political philosophy, and pragmatic politics. He was clearly uncomfortable with this precarious situation. In fact, he would rather the whole subject be the "great unmentionable," even as it had been at the founding.

Jefferson was not simply courting popularity among his constituents now; instead, he likely did not want to make himself ineffective in finishing his primary purpose as he saw it: reestablishing the republican principles of 1776 and preventing the resurrection of Federalism. Any action on abolition would likely have hamstrung a republican candidate in 1808. The feared national schism over slavery or, even worse, a slave uprising would surely bring about pressure for strong central control, at least in his mind, with great pressure for the forced assertion of federal rule over the states' choice: slave or free. This is likely why in 1806 he failed to support a bill banning slavery in the District of Columbia—though it was not a state per se. In his mind, it was to be treated as one for this purpose lest a precedent be set. Furthermore, during his presidency, despite having what historians believe was the greatest sway over Congress of any president before Franklin Roosevelt, he was to witness "the spectacle of a slave market in the shadow of the Capitol and gangs of manacled slaves being driven through the streets."[20] As at Monticello, he did not have eyes to see what was paraded before him almost every day.

---

20. Ibid., 132.

To complicate the matter even more, he and the political leaders of the day were confronted by the necessity of dealing with a clause in the Constitution, written twenty years before, that allowed the end of the slave *trade*. The antislavery forces were not reluctant to act on this opportunity. In Article I, Section 9, the North–South compromise made by the framers in 1787 prevented an end to the slave trade prior to 1807. Before that time, individual states could end the trade on their own or they could abolish slavery itself, and many did so. No national initiative was allowed until twenty years had passed.

By 1807, although eight states allowed slavery, only one, South Carolina, carried on a trade in slaves at the Charleston port. Over the years, support for the trade had waned not because of human rights but because internal commerce in flesh between the states was sufficient due to the tremendous growth of the slave population. The traffic in slaves was not unlike that in livestock, and it enabled many owners to turn a profit. Even, the incumbent president, Thomas Jefferson, did so.[21]

Jefferson's sole initiative on the expiration of the twenty-year moratorium was to recommend to Congress that it act upon its constitutional authority and pass a bill abolishing the slave trade that some members had been petitioning for since 1805 without his support. He did not even submit an administration bill, though he did express pleasure when it was passed by a 63–49 margin. At last, legally, the *formal* end of the slave trade in America came to pass, following by only a few months the end of the trade in England, engineered by Wilberforce and his colleagues who had labored assiduously for twenty years.

Consistent with Jefferson's optimistic thinking, he felt this was a huge step toward the inevitable abolition of slavery, equating in his mind support for ending the slave trade as a sentiment generally shared by the American people toward ending slavery itself. If this was his political antenna picking up future signals, he was badly deceived. Had he considered the evidence in this matter, he would have found that in no state where the slave trade had been abolished, including his own Virginia, did ending importation from outside the United States have any impact on the "peculiar institution" itself. To the contrary, had he followed the debate over the bill and the wording thereof, he would have seen that

---

21. George Washington was one slaveholder who would not sell off slaves or separate families from each other as a matter of personal ethics. His view of this practice was that it was morally wrong to do so even when he had an excess of slaves he supported after he left office. With him they were guaranteed a sinecure for life.

it was filled with half-heartedness inserted by southern economic and personal interests. Though few were aware of it at the time, his general silence was in keeping with his private, personal vow not to publicly engage the cause.

One measure of the new law's limits was that it allowed forfeiture of confiscated human "property" from illegal transport to be placed under the jurisdiction of the federal district court where a slaving ship was seized. In practice jurisdiction was intended to be carried out under the laws of a specific state. Hence, the confiscated "property" would remain enslaved to be auctioned off, and then transported to other states as trading goods. Obviously this was a complete contradiction of the supposed intent of the bill. Additionally, penalties for violations were light, limited to small fines making the new law a watered-down deterrent at best.[22] Because of these compromises, and because of the vast new territory now open to slavery, the tensions Jefferson hoped to see gradually quelled between North and South were instead exacerbated over time—a denouement that he would live to regret.

LAYING DOWN THE BURDENS

The score of years between 1789 and 1808 was the most formative period of American government and of the emerging American culture. Washington, Adams, and Jefferson are in the pantheon of great leaders by any measure, and they each have had an enormous impact on America. Yet, in Jefferson's case, for all of his seeming success, as he handed over the reins to his republican successor and protégé, Madison, there hung a cloud. He had no sense of triumph as he rode back south to Monticello, only relief and a looking toward home. It probably did not enter his mind that ahead lay perhaps his greatest triumph as a leader as well as *his* last real opportunity to end slavery in America. He relished an end to his public life and a time to attend to financial concerns, his beloved land, and, of course, his books.

Thomas Jefferson's development as a statesman was born from his studies and later his experience as a national leader over a critical twenty-year period. It was also the product of the lessons of personal hardship in both opposition and failure as much as accomplishment. In his wake,

---

22. The Trade and Environment Database.

he left the two older men who had entrusted him with responsibility to become sadly disillusioned by the disconnect between his studied public integrity and his private scheming. That he and Adams reconciled years later says much, but sadly he and Washington never did. The "father" died estranged from his erstwhile "son," although only living a day's ride apart. Further, he and his "brother" Alexander Hamilton were parted by death, never recognizing the brilliance that each could have added to the other's work had they been the family Washington repeatedly pleaded for. Jefferson's ascendancy to the highest office in the land was sullied by the personal rancor of the party system to which he gave birth and which in turn victimized him. The Democratic Republican party and the rights of states and individuals over that of the federal government became, in time, his "true north,"[23] even as slavery's tyranny had once been for him at the beginning of his vocation forty years earlier.

Jefferson's time in national leadership had ushered in a mindset of American individualism and distrust for strong central government that continues to this day—with both blessings and curses. As for the matter at hand, his leadership to heal the "cancer" on our national conscience made little progress during the score of years of the most influential time of his national leadership. Although he oversaw the addition of a legal coda represented in the nearly toothless slave trade bill, it was a hollow triumph. Westward expansion in the wake of the brilliant acquisition of the Louisiana Territory meant slavery's expansion as well in the years that followed. The tacit agreement at the founding of the nation to limit slavery to the old south was undone. When he broke faith with the founders' initial preference for a strong federalism and instead supported the preeminent domestic rights of states favored by his own political backers, it set the stage for the very divisions and bloody rebellion that he said he feared most. What occurred, however, was not the predicted uprising of slaves against masters, but instead of brothers against brothers. Hamilton and Jefferson were merely the play within the play.

In his final retreat to Monticello in his last years, he would have one last opportunity to lend his hand to leadership in ending what, ironically, he both abhorred and abetted. He would pass up this opportunity, however, and instead would take up one last great project he had long thought on, one with which to grow the next generation of political leaders in Virginia. That is the next and last part of his story.

23. This term, meaning "the internal compass that guides you successfully through life," comes from Bill George's excellent book by the same name.

As the new, experimental American government for which Jefferson had labored made the first and now the second voluntary transfer of power in history, it also put the building blocks for its interpretation of human liberty into place, and the cracks were already beginning to show. But what of the oppressive English monarchy America had only recently thrown off? Was it moving toward further tyrannies? William Wilberforce in *his* prime years—the same twenty years as Jefferson—would continue to pursue his own quest for human liberty and for forming a good society. What England was becoming while America made its entrance onto the world stage as the land of the free must have stunned Jefferson and his fellow patriots. That odd turn in history is the next part of our tale.

KNOWING AND DOING

1. How do you think Jefferson made the irrevocable decision not to openly advocate for slavery's end in 1786? To what extent was he being a realist versus serving his own advancement?

2. Looking back, was Jefferson's and Madison's conclusion accurate—that Hamilton was influencing an increasingly debilitated Washington toward a monarchial form of government, and that Adams sympathized with this direction?

3. Was it ethical for Jefferson to surreptitiously oppose his own administration while continuing to serve and then later to anonymously vilify both Washington and Adams, his erstwhile mentors and colleagues, as leaders who betrayed the founding principles? Did they indeed stray from the original reasons for separating from England—tyranny against the people?

4. When Jefferson reached the highest pinnacle possible, why did he not use his position and public favor to find a way forward to end slavery?

5. Do you agree that Jefferson's decision to allow slavery in the Louisiana Territory may have been the key turning point that set the stage for civil war six decades later?

6. What "nondecisions" do you see today that lead to "solutions" that over time only make things worse? Why do today's political leaders seemingly lack the moral courage to speak up and act?

7

The Long Obedience in England: 1789–1808

The essential thing "in heaven and earth" is . . . that there should be long obedience in the same direction; there thereby results, and has always resulted in the long run, something which has made life worth living.

—Friedrich Nietzsche, *Beyond Good and Evil*

AT HIS POST

During Jefferson's twenty-year rise to the presidency ending with his final retirement from public life, William Wilberforce continued on as a member of Parliament from York. He was never to rise to a higher office. For some men, thought at one time to be leaders of promise, this would be a great disappointment, even a tragedy. To have seen their most energetic years go by one after the other with little change in status might unhinge some men in either bitterness or even debauchery. But leadership, at least leadership that serves others, is not necessarily synonymous with office—in fact, they may not be the same thing at all.

Wilberforce was hardly idle in those twenty years, and his accomplishments even absent high official station would by 1808 place him on a par with Jefferson in international recognition. In the minds of some, his only rival for greatness by the end of this era was the first American president. One day he would be compared with him, eulogized as "the Washington for humanity." But we're getting ahead of ourselves. How he came to this place in history is the complement of Jefferson's most productive era and offers a clear contrast between their approaches to leadership and to the nature of their sustained commitments toward slavery's end. From this time on they took two distinctly different paths echoing from choices they made even earlier in life.

As we have seen, this chapter of Wilberforce's story began like many of the stories of great leaders—in failure—but, as with Jefferson, it would end as a time of great accomplishment. Wilberforce's initial hopeful foray on the slave bill with his Clapham team ended in a bureaucratic stalemate—returned to committee for further study. That outcome and its hiatus, however, enabled the Clapham Circle to regroup and forge their new strategies. So while Jefferson took up the mantle of the first American secretary of state, Wilberforce stood more ready than ever to end the odious slave trade.

IF AT FIRST YOU DO NOT SUCCEED . . .

Before his first stunning setback, Wilberforce almost did not make it to the starting line. After his charge from Pitt under the great oak in May 1787 (attended also by Lord Grenville, who reenters the story later—and surprisingly), Wilberforce had given formal notice to Parliament that he would take up the slave trade bill by the end of that year. His strenuous preparations for the debate, the launching of the Societies for the Suppression of Vice, and the press of his other responsibilities as an MP from York all took their toll—not for the last time. An attack of ulcerative colitis brought him near death in early 1788, threatening to cut short his life and end his great aspirations. On his sickbed he returned to Pitt the mantle of champion of the slavery cause, which his old friend reluctantly accepted. Pitt, however, was not willing to believe that his dear friend, Wilberforce, could die so young with so much ahead of him. In loyalty to Wilberforce and risking his leadership capital as prime minister, however, Pitt personally introduced a resolution binding Parliament to investigate the slave trade—almost one year to the very day he challenged his dying friend to take up this cause for him. Great volumes of evidence had already begun to be gathered by the Clapham team, much of it digested and summarized by Wilberforce in the long hours of labor; now it would be added to, *officially*, by the Privy Council of Parliament instructed by Pitt's resolution. He would not leave the cause owing to his deep friendship with "Wilber."

It was about this time that Wilberforce wrote an entreating letter to John Newton, expressing great affection and imploring his prayers for strength and constancy in the cause they now shared:

I believe I can truly declare, that not a single day has passed in which you have not been in my thoughts, and at those seasons too when the mind abstracts itself from the little cares and little concerns to which it is, alas, too apt to addict itself and fixes its consideration on what it most esteems and loves - I trust I occupy a distinguished place in your regards at the times to which I am alluding: and in truth tis often matter of solid comfort to me, and of gratitude to the Bountiful Giver of all mercies, to reflect that the prayers of many of the well beloved of the Lord are offered up for me: O my Dear Sir, let not your hands cease to be lifted up, lest Amalek prevail - entreat for me that I may be enabled by divine Grace to resist and subdue all the numerous enemies of my salvation: My path is peculiarly steep and difficult and dangerous, but the prize is a crown of glory, and "celestial panoply" is offered me and the God of Hosts for my ally.[1]

Surprisingly, by spring of 1789, Wilberforce unexpectedly recovered and was eager once again to lead the abolition fight now that his energy had returned. Perhaps he was thinking his time on earth was now running out as he engaged his cause with a renewed sense of urgency. Having reviewed the evidence that had been assembled in his absence, he was horrified at the incontrovertible documentation of death, disease, and barbarity on the Middle Passage. In his journal, he expressed his deep belief: "A trade founded on iniquity and carried on as this was, must be abolished, let the policy be what it might—let the consequences be what they would. I from this time determined that I would never rest till I had secured its abolition."[2] A bold and even reckless statement, perhaps (imagine Jefferson vowing this as president), but it was one that bound him for the next two decades—and well beyond.

DISAPPOINTMENT DOUBLED

Having brought before the House the overwhelming evidence of the barbarity of the trade, he and the Clapham team felt their cause was morally compelling and could not be ignored in national policy any longer. In short, their conviction was that this injustice could not remain a private matter of conscience for a few religious outliers—as they were seen by their peers. The earlier revelations of horrendous shipboard crowding

---

1. Rouse, unpublished letter from William Wilberforce to John Newton, September 6, 1788.

2. Belmonte, *A Hero for Humanity*, 111.

and shackling of the slaves was to prove only the tip of the iceberg for needed change. The Dolben Bill façade had merely obfuscated the reality. Dolben, an ardent oppositionist, intentionally offered the cynical solution as a sop to The Saints. This determined foot dragging by their opponents was what Wilberforce must overcome. Despite the setbacks, the Clapham team remained optimistic. That faith would be tested time and again in the years ahead.

Wilberforce himself rose to the occasion in introducing his intentions, belying his near collapse of only a few months before. In one of the greatest speeches in human history, according to no less an expert than the estimable philosopher-statesman Edmund Burke, Wilberforce put forth the case with a passion and eloquence, making the daunting evidence a matter of public record:

> The nature and all the circumstances of this trade are now laid open to us; we can no longer plead ignorance—we cannot evade it—it is now an object placed before us—we cannot pass it; we may spurn it, we may kick it out of the way, but we cannot turn aside so as to avoid seeing it. . . . It is brought now so directly before our eyes that this House must decide, and must justify to all the world, and to their own consciences, the rectitude of the grounds and principles of their decision.[3]

He spoke with an unusual directness and without any softening political nuance. He was clear that when a nation's leaders know that a moral wrong is being committed, they cannot evade their responsibility by pleading ignorance or lack of capacity to act.

---

3. Ibid., 112.

The Long Obedience in England: 1789–1808   115

Wilberforce as a Young Member of Parliament

When Wilberforce had said he would not rest until the trade was abolished, he and his Clapham friends and abolition supporters may not have realized the implications of this decision, but they would soon know what they were up against. They brought the slave trade bill to the floor in April 1791, taking it up even as Washington's first term was coming to an end with Jefferson preoccupied with keeping Hamilton in check.

To the chagrin of the Clapham Circle, their bill, despite overwhelming evidence, lost soundly by almost a 2–1 margin—163–88. It was a double blow after enduring the delay for further study, then fully documenting the case for terminating the practice, even having it corroborated by the Privy Council. Still it emerged as a failure. Neither reason nor simple justice could seem to prevail against the powerful economic interests of the port cities and the merchants.

Nevertheless, just one year later, in April of 1792, Wilberforce was at it again with Pitt playing a key public role in the new bill. The young prime minister offered a dramatic and politically courageous speech of his own just as the long night's final debate was ending and the rising sun shone through the windows of Parliament. This fortuitous timing led him to speak extemporaneously of the great opportunity before them to bring a sunrise of happiness to Africa.[4] This event would be remembered decades later as a harbinger of the final justice to come.

Once again, political maneuvers by the trade interests frustrated the outcome for The Saints. Their opponents, seeing a slight shift of sentiment in The Saints' favor, proposed that the trade could indeed be abolished but, so as not to cause undue dislocation and to allow for preparation for the slaves, that it be instituted gradually over five years—not until January 1, 1796. This stratagem was not unlike the tack taken by the southern interests in America during the constitutional debates that led to the compromise proscribing the end of slave importation until 1808.

Wilberforce was roundly congratulated, but he wisely harbored no illusions of victory. He was no longer the political neophyte. Like many of his more savvy colleagues, he read the proposal of gradual abolition for what it was intended—a delaying tactic to gather further opposition that would later stop the movement in its tracks. He did see one small silver lining, however—it was the first time that an actual vote had ever been taken in Parliament to actually abolish the slave trade. In that he took some comfort, even if the delayed enactment would in fact prove to be a ruse.

By 1793, the long threatened war with France finally broke out full bore, an event that served the slave interests well. Now even Pitt urged Wilberforce to defer for a season in favor of national unity during wartime. Public opinion had been running steadily ahead for abolition but now reversed itself with war worries. There was a widespread fear that any

---

4. Ibid., 114.

instability might undermine England's capacity to prevail. Wilberforce's work was equated by his more "patriotic" opponents with Jacobinism and fostering anarchy. Ill-timed events played into this false narrative.

One source of this unease was the uprising of the slaves in Saint-Domingue against their French masters, which only added to the fears in England that rebellion might spread to their colonies. Then, in an ironic and wholly unforeseen twist, Wilberforce was, against his will, made an honorary citizen of France for his work against the tyranny of slavery. He joined George Washington and Thomas Paine as honorees—a tweak of England's nose. France sought to divide its enemy, England, from America in the guise of supporting those who sought freedom. This French ruse threw additional fuel on the fire opposing Wilberforce's purposes. These unexpected events called for a change in tactics if Wilberforce wanted to continue rather than defer to national security concerns for an unknown period of years.

So despite Pitt's call for his temporary strategic withdrawal along with the admonitions of some friends that he was committing political suicide, Wilberforce's conscience simply would not allow him to reverse his commitments. He believed that his higher calling took precedence over a cynical bowing to national war fever. He would stand alone if necessary, he said. He now took a canny political course and introduced a bill to prevent the transport of slaves destined for *foreign* colonial interests such as France. It was a brilliant legislative stratagem. This proposal split the slave ship owners and their investors from the plantation owners and their backers—all the while supporting the war effort. With no other market for the slave traders than the British colonies, the plantation interests rightly saw that the price they paid for slaves would drop and so they gave their support to the bill as a pocketbook issue. The slave ship owners howled that their livelihood was being threatened, that a drop in price would make transport a losing venture for them. Unfortunately, even this ploy failed in 1793, then again in 1794.[5] Pitt's silent opposition as well as that voiced publicly by the king added to Wilberforce's ineffectiveness in Parliament and only increased his unpopularity with the British people. He was censured for openly taking a stance against the war with France, then for supposedly attempting to destabilize the monarchy by threatening the profitability of the slave trade. Taken together, these factors gave him little chance of success.

---

5. Metaxas, *Amazing Grace*, 159–60.

These seemingly endless defeats finally undid the stalwart Thomas Clarkson, whose indefatigable research and wide travels had fueled so much of the debate with solid facts and moral energy beginning with his years in Cambridge. Disappointed and exhausted, he withdrew to the sidelines for the next twelve years as the slave trade claimed yet another victim of despair.

ELUSIVE VICTORY

When 1796 came, the war with France had abated and the public tide seemed to be turning once again. This time the bill to end the slave trade had more supporters and passed its first reading, then its second despite an opposition ploy to bring it up early to an empty house. The third and final reading seemed assured. Maddeningly, once again, failure rose up to snatch away victory. The blame lay squarely at the feet of a handful of Wilberforce's supporters, who chose on the very night of the conclusive vote to attend the opening of a new Italian comic opera rather than Parliament's seminal deliberations. Free tickets, given out by their opponents, lured some of them away. When the count was taken, defeat by a vote of 74–70 was the verdict.

If Clarkson had been crushed earlier, now Wilberforce, the leader, fell into a dark depression. He was heartbroken for the slaves and their never-ending woes and bitterly disappointed by his erstwhile friends and supporters who could have ended the travail of suffering but chose, instead, immediate self-gratification. All this lay hard upon him, and he began to wonder whether to continue. As he wrote in his diary that night, "I am permanently hurt about the slave trade."[6] And he was. Shortly thereafter, he fell very ill and would not recover for several months.

Nevertheless, in the midst of this most egregious setback of his career, Wilberforce somehow kept going, coming out on the other side an even stronger man.[7] Hardly did this occur because of his strength alone. Had he not been surrounded by the team of Clapham and sustained by a sense of purpose and faith, he would likely have folded his cards.

6. Ibid., 165.
7. McCall et al., *The Lessons of Experience*. The research by these authors shows that a little over 20 percent of what it takes to make a leader—the places of the most critical learning—comes out of times of hardship. Particularly is character formed in such circumstances as the testing field that builds capacity to adapt to ever-changing conditions of life and work. Such hardening of purpose in suffering is critical to the will to persist.

WILBERFORCE'S CRUCIBLE TIME

Just a year before Wilberforce's crushing defeat, the seeds of another physical collapse were beginning to sprout. His good friend Pitt remained estranged, and pressure was being brought to bear by many for a revolution in England like that in France to overthrow the government and the king. Parliament was constrained to do something to staunch the growing crisis. Wilberforce reluctantly concluded that his conscience dictated he must support measures against possible sedition during wartime by giving emergency powers to the government as spelled out in the Treason and Sedition bills. Perhaps he thought to counter the accusations of being a traitor. Although he lobbied to keep the measures as benign as possible, seeking to maintain the right of individuals to petition the government, he still came in for harsh public and private criticism for the hypocrisy of supporting the freedom of black slaves while at the same time oppressing the rights of Englishmen. It was not unlike the situation President John Adams would face a handful of years later. In America, Adams would support the Alien and Sedition Act for reasons similar to those of Wilberforce. Darkly, its passage led to the final break with Jefferson, who could not stomach such an egregious suppression of individual rights by the government. This decision likely was the cause that brought Adams's presidency to a premature end in the historic election of 1800. The tensions over government crackdown on opposition had a similar impact in Britain on both Pitt and his colleague Wilberforce.

If Pitt was vilified and threatened due to this egregious bill, his friend Wilberforce was painted with the same brush. Had Jefferson been in Parliament, he most certainly would have been among the first to rise in passionate objection to this act and cast verbal stones at the deprivation of liberty for the common man. Wilberforce's own state of mind was such that he said, "I greatly fear some civil war or embroilment and with my weak health and bodily infirmities my heart shrinks from its difficulties and dangers."[8] Nevertheless, his defense of the monarchy against the individual rights of the people was not one of his finest hours. Wilberforce never did see the threat that a monarchy might hold in maintaining individual liberties the way Jefferson did by instinct. Instead, Wilberforce found the king a source of stability and continuity just as he viewed the class system. Although this blind spot in Wilberforce did not deter his

---

8. Belmonte, *A Hero for Humanity*, 126.

actions in favor of the poor and oppressed, it did place limits on the extent to which he would act in Parliament on matters concerning the king or restructuring class privileges. These views opened the door to accusations of hypocrisy—not without some merit.

The string of defeats, his political stumbles, and the unremitting opposition, combined with physical threats, left Wilberforce in 1796 a sick, heartbroken, and physically exhausted man, one filled with trepidation. He began to seriously doubt whether he was the right man to continue leading the fight for the cause. He had seen Clarkson fall. Was it his turn now? Just as when he had considered leaving Parliament early in his career to enter the ministry, he once again turned to his old mentor, John Newton. He was all but set to end his time in Parliament and his labors for the slaves in favor of the next generation, even as Jefferson had. He told Newton he was convinced that his time of useful public service was likely over. Fortunately, Newton remained the crucial voice that put the issue clearly before the discouraged Wilberforce. Newton wrote Wilberforce that he needed to see this choice in its proper perspective, and he urged him to persist in his vocation as he had ten years before:

> You meet with many things which weary and disgust you . . . they are inseparably connected with your path of duty; and though you cannot do all the good you wish for, some good is done. . . . Nor is it possible at present to calculate all the advantages that may result from your having a seat in the House at such a time as this. The example, and even the presence of a consistent character, may have a powerful, though unobserved effect upon others. . . . You are a representative for the Lord, in a place where many know Him not. . . . Though you have not, as yet, fully succeeded in your persevering endeavors to abolish the slave trade, the business is still in process. . . . Indeed *the great point of comfort in life is to have a well-grounded persuasion that we are, where, all things considered, we ought to be* (emphasis added). Then it is no great matter whether we are in public or private life, in a city or a village, in a place or a cottage. . . . Happy the man who has a deep impression of our Lord's words, "Without Me you can do nothing."[9]

And so Newton reminded him not only of his duty but also of his certain calling and purpose in life—he was right where he was supposed to be—which Newton said can be, paradoxically, a place of rest as well as

---

9. Ibid., 136–38.

one of trial. Once again he reminded Wilberforce that he needed to see that he was never intended by God to carry the load all alone. Newton does not trivialize the woes Wilberforce has undergone in persevering thus far, but neither will he let him think in his depression and discouragement that this whole enterprise has been a failure. Consider, he says, how the conditions of the slaves are likely far better than they would have been otherwise, even though the ultimate goal remains. This is what Steve Garber calls "proximate justice"—not all one would want to accomplish in public life on behalf of others, but an improvement for the good of many while continuing to work for full redress.[10] Newton would have Wilberforce turn to his real "boss," not only for gaining a sense of his responsibility but also for tapping into the strength to endure and to gain the wisdom to see the picture whole, not fragmented by either fatigue or disgust with others.

Five years earlier, Wilberforce had received similar encouragement to remain in his calling from the aged John Wesley in one of the last letters the old man ever penned. Wesley reminded Wilberforce that the huge task before him honestly *was* impossible—without God's strength. Newton's echo of Wesley put the task in full light for the wavering Wilberforce and stiffened his spine, despite the bleak prospects. It is no exaggeration to say, once again, that without Newton there would have been no Wilberforce. He might not otherwise have been able to sustain the fight. We are also left to wonder in comparison what or who might have caused Jefferson to continue his fight against slavery instead of all but abandoning it in his public calling. If Wythe had been more central in Jefferson's consultations, would things have gone differently? Could Madison or Monroe have helped him hold onto the passion to end slavery? The quiet role of an encourager, of a mentor, of a team is one of great, if unseen, import in the lives of leaders.

In the end, Wilberforce did not abandon his commitment to stay at his post until the slave trade was ended. He persisted despite discouragement and failure. He felt not only God's call on his life but also his protection as long as it was his will that he continue. And continue he did, though he could not have done so without some growing frustration, and even trepidation.

In annual motions for abolition, Wilberforce saw his bills defeated in 1797, 1798, and 1799. In 1800, 1802, and 1803, he would have in-

---

10. Steve Garber, "Making Peace with Proximate Justice," 51–56.

troduced the bill, but once again the renewed war with France caused the slave trade proposal to be deferred over fears of a French advantage against Britain. In this light, the near miss in 1796 must have been a growing heartbreak in Wilberforce's memory—so near but yet so far. The ongoing conditions of the slaves could not be forgotten, either by him or by his Clapham brothers and sisters.

By 1804, Pitt, who had left office for two years, now returned once again as prime minister. With Fox, he helped Wilberforce rack up a large majority who would back the bill. By this point, public opinion had been gradually moving forward again due to the widespread and constant educational and propaganda campaign that had been waged for more than fifteen years by The Saints. There was also the parallel rise in the moral tenor of the British culture that began with the measures throughout England in the many societies. The MPs were no fools as far as their political support was concerned, and it appeared the tide of the electorate's support was slowly turning. Even Newton was encouraged enough to write Wilberforce and give thanks to God and congratulate Wilberforce for what was now looking like a real possibility. In a touching close to one letter, Newton wrote of his nearly eighty years on earth and the hope of seeing the vile trade ended before his own end:

> Whether I, who am within two months of entering my eightieth year, shall live to see the accomplishment of that work, is known only to Him in whose hands are all our times and ways, but the hopeful prospect of its accomplishment will, I trust, give me daily satisfaction so long as my declining faculties are preserved.[11]

Wilberforce replied immediately to his old mentor, who had seen him through so much:

> I steal one moment from business and bustle to thank you most cordially for your kind congratulations. . . . Pray for us, my dear sir, that we also may be enabled to hold on our way, and at last to join you in the shout of victory. . . . I shall ever reckon it the greatest of all my temporal favors, that I have been providentially led to take on the conduct of this business.[12]

---

11. Belmonte, *A Hero for Humanity*, 144.
12. Ibid.

THE END GAME

So often, finishing a long and arduous task turns on unanticipated events for which no comprehensive plans exist. Great changes are as much "lived into" as planned, persisted in more than executed. If William Wilberforce were looking for an example of such persistence in an against-the-odds challenge, he would find it in George Washington's leadership of the outmanned American militias.

In 1776, Washington took the field with an untrained, lightly equipped volunteer force. They faced not only the daunting odds of a far superior British army and navy but also a lack of support from a fractious Continental Congress and a deeply divided American people, many of whom actively opposed and undermined their neighbors. International military experts agreed that, on paper, there was no real chance of success. But by sheer persistence, courage, and inventiveness, Washington and his haggard army stayed in the field for eight years despite horrible hardships. The constant loss of experienced soldiers whose enlistments expired was added to by hordes of deserters and periodic pandemics in camp as the army barely survived. Yet there were sufficient victories to retain hope until the French navy entered the fray in force at Yorktown and the stalemated and exhausting war was given a *coup de grâce* as Britain petitioned for peace.

Wilberforce and his colleagues now had more than eighteen years of effort behind them with no victory yet, although they too stayed in the field. Providentially, two unexpected events came together and finally brought about success. One was the impeachment of the First Lord of the Admiralty, Lord Melville, who was replaced by Lord Middleton, an avid abolitionist and devout Christian who had early on counseled Wilberforce to take up the cause after hearing Ramsay's harrowing testimony on slave ship conditions. Thus a strategically key position heading British maritime interests was now filled by a man allied with The Saints' cause. The second important event was Pitt's death in 1806: a personal tragedy for Wilberforce and the loss of the one man who had all these years except for two headed the government and backed the cause. Pitt was the man who had called Wilberforce to the task and who had supported him in so many battles over the years. The irony in Pitt's demise was that Lord Grenville (the third man at the great oak conversation) now became prime minister. He now supported Wilberforce, bringing with him great energy and others who, like him, had long been oppositionists to now join The Saints' side.

The end finally came when one of The Saints, James Stephen, suggested a brilliant strategy for Wilberforce to employ in the House of Commons, the full complexity of which is not useful to discuss here. In summary, it called for sequential passage, first, of the Foreign Slave Bill, which by now had little opposition, and then the bill to abolish the entire British slave trade. The first essentially rendered slave trading unprofitable; hence, the second had far less opposition from those whose motivation was greed. Amazingly, the strategy worked. The final debate on the evening of February 23, 1807, was marked by one member after another speaking in favor of abolition so that by the time the vote rolled around at 4 a.m. on the 24th of February, its passage was certain.

The spirit of the day was such that at the climax, when the outcome had become clear, the House rose to give Wilberforce three hearty cheers. After twenty long and arduous years, the verdict of the British House of Commons was decisive: 283-16. Wilberforce, the leader of The Saints, the once mocked, vilified, and threatened pariah, sat with bowed head and wept. Perhaps he offered a prayer of humble thanks for the strength of "a long obedience" that was brought an end to the Unholy Triangle in England. Doubtless if he prayed, he also gave thanks for John Newton, his friend and mentor at so many critical moments in his life. It was only right that the venerable Newton lived to share in the joy of success as he had wished, dying a mere ten months later. His death on December 21, 1807, was only ten days before the American slave trade was officially ended in the last year of Jefferson's presidency. In this, Newton also would have rejoiced.

And so the Clapham team joined in the celebration as Wilberforce arrived at his enclave in Clapham immediately after the conclusive vote. So many of them had labored alongside Wilberforce for two decades, and some had fought against the trade for even more years. Henry Thornton, who began the Clapham community, Granville Sharp, who had preceded them all in the struggle, Zachary MacAulay, the human encyclopedia—all were there to celebrate with him. Wilberforce is reported to have said in a jovial mood to Thornton, "Well Henry, what shall we abolish next?"[13] Of course he knew the answer. The slaves in the West Indies remained in chains, and this great objective had only

---

13. Ibid., 211.

reached the first strategic point of success—the abolition of the Middle Passage of the Unholy Triangle. In fact, many battles lay ahead, and the first of those would be to ensure that the bill would become more than a paper expression of Parliament by enforcing its adherence. But for a time they could pause and savor what few men ever know—a victory against all earthly expectations.

THE LOST OPPORTUNITY

Perhaps the most intriguing question that these parallel stories of Jefferson and Wilberforce raises at this juncture is whether the two men who are most known for favoring slavery's end ever met or made personal contact. Did they openly or even surreptitiously join forces, encourage one another, share strategy, complain about the difficulties? It would have seemed in some ways a natural occurrence. Although the courses of their lives and their ultimate commitments differed in magnitude, nevertheless their known affections would have made such affiliation seem quite likely. The answer is both fascinating for its possibilities and disappointing in its results.

During the entire twenty years of Jefferson's rise to the presidency, Wilberforce had labored day in and day out to end the trade. Yet, during these two decades, there is no record of contact on either part; although such well-read and prominent men could hardly have escaped the notice of the other. It was not until 1808, when both nations had committed to ending the slave trade, that there was but a single attempt at collaboration.

By then, the most critical question facing both America and England regarding the recently outlawed slave trade was that of intent versus reality: would the slave trade actually be stopped or not? President Harry S. Truman was famous for loudly complaining that although he was president, he could get more done when he was an army captain. Laws and decrees by governments do not necessarily translate into action. In some ways, Jefferson tied his own hands.

Having an aversion to foreign confrontations, Jefferson had promised to draw down the navy before taking office. Thus Jefferson was not able to place any U.S. navy forces off the coast of Africa to intercept American slave traders. In keeping with his philosophy regarding the separate powers of states and the central government, and as the new law's compromised language prescribed, the detection and prosecution of violations of the slave trade act were left to the port cities and their state governments. The only naval force on the seas with the capacity to stop American slave ships in international waters was England's. In this matter of enforcement there existed the one place where Wilberforce's life and efforts might have intersected with those of Jefferson's.

With both countries ending the trade, enterprising slave traders not wishing to lose their lucrative business had already devised a ruse. British ships disguised themselves as American and American slave ships flew the British colors, thus seeking to prevent enforcement by either country. Wilberforce moved quickly to end this deception lest it thwart all of the work that had been done. He wrote to James Monroe and enclosed a letter to President Jefferson appealing for a way to end the British ships' ploy of flying the American ensign to avoid being caught. Despite being internationally known by now, Wilberforce had such humility that he felt it appropriate to go through Monroe rather than writing Jefferson directly. He asked Jefferson to intercede on behalf of "the unknown multitudes whose fate you may form on this particular case."[14] He suggested an Anglo–American agreement that would allow for boarding the ships and freeing the slaves by either country's navy no matter what colors the slave ship would fly:

> A compact formed between our two countries for the benevolent purpose of stopping, perhaps, the most destructive scourge that ever afflicted the human race, may lead to similar agreements with other countries, until at length all the civilized nations of the earth shall have come into this *concert of benevolence*. . . . Surely there can never exist an occasion more proper for resorting to such a measure; and we may hope that the adoption of it would now be followed in Africa by the same happy consequences.[15]

But Jefferson never sent a reply. Wilberforce's moral argument as well as the opportunity he proposed that they combine to lead other nations to do what was right took a back seat, for the American president, to the freedom of the seas. He would not allow a British boarding party to inspect any American ship or one flying under American colors, whether or not it held slaves. This freedom was a higher principle for this founding father of the Revolution, whose memory of British incursions

---

14. Pollock, *Wilberforce*, 228.

15. Isaac and Wilberforce, *The Life of William Wilberforce*, cited in Belmonte, *A Hero for Humanity*, 198.

remained strong. He was also knee deep in one of his most serious and perplexing foreign policy issues—the Barbary pirates, who were operating in the western Mediterranean and playing havoc with U.S. shipping, demanding ransoms in exchange for peace. Jefferson had no further capacity for the use of scarce maritime resources.

Typically, Wilberforce would not give up. Instead, he wrote a year later to John Jay, a fellow evangelical, to intervene with the American government, now under the leadership of Jefferson's protégé, James Madison. Again, it was to no avail. The result was that for a much longer time, the American flag and the Portuguese flag "became a cover for slave runners of all nationalities, and thousands of slaves were transported to the western hemisphere after 1808."[16] It might have been otherwise.

As Frederick Douglass famously said years later, the U.S. simply "winked at the accursed slave trade,"[17] allowing slave smuggling to continue in this country while abetting its continuance by rogue English slave ships. More than fifty years passed before an American president took office and finally ended the last of the U.S. trade in smuggled slaves.[18]

The ending of the slave trade in America and England by 1808, despite all the flaws, went a long way toward saving tens of thousands of slaves from a life of incarceration and death. The rise of King Cotton in the Deep South produced an insatiable demand for slaves in the United States as new states were added from the recently acquired western territories. The internal trade of slaves between the states remained the primary recourse in America, a process that unhappily caused the dislocation of families far more than would have occurred otherwise. Their destination was primarily the dreaded Deep South plantations of Alabama, Louisiana, and Mississippi. Slavery was now more firmly entrenched than when Jefferson took office, despite his optimism that the tide had turned with the trade's legal end. The rest of the story—and of Jefferson's story as well—is what he would do in his last years as an icon of the Revolution and a lightning rod for the growing abolitionist movement in America. Where and how he would focus his energies

---

16. Miller, *The Wolf by the Ears*, 146.
17. Oakes, *The Radical and the Republican*, 157.
18. Ibid., 158.

for the remainder of his days reflected his deepest beliefs. He was still concerned for his legacy.

For Wilberforce, the battle to end slavery itself also lay ahead, as did the enforcement of the new law on the high seas. How he would spend his remaining years is also a tale told best in comparison to Jefferson's. The manner in which both men completed their lives and spent their waning years calls for an examination in bolder relief of the third and last factor that influenced the nature of their youthful commitment to ending slavery—their worldviews. As we look back over their lifetimes, we will see where their foundational beliefs stand out, shaping the last chapter of their life stories. It is an ending that will do much to explain not only *how much* they differed in their worldviews by the time they had finished their courses as old men, but also *why* their endings differed so starkly from their beginnings.

KNOWING AND DOING

1. How does getting your calling and your purpose in life in clear focus help in continuing along a difficult road of frustration, disappointment, and lack of success? Or does it?

2. Do you think Wilberforce was able to focus more effectively on his two great objects because he discarded the ambition to aspire a higher office? Could he have been even more effective in ending the trade in a shorter time if he had become the prime minister?

3. Would Wilberforce have been considered a failure if Parliament had never passed the slave trade bill during his lifetime?

4. Was John Newton the one man who kept Wilberforce in his vocation, or do you think the Clapham Circle was just as instrumental, if not more so? How might this be instructive for your own life?

5. Why do you think Jefferson never responded to Wilberforce's letter proposing a common cause in stopping the circumvention of the slave trade laws in each country?

6. What does success (or failure) look like for you in your vocation?

8

A Fitting Epitaph

> *Here was buried Thomas Jefferson*
> *Author of the Declaration of American Independence*
> *Of The Statute for Religious Freedom, &*
> *Father of the University of Virginia*[1]

IN 1809 NEITHER THOMAS Jefferson nor William Wilberforce knew how many years they had remaining on earth. For Jefferson it would be seventeen, while for Wilberforce it would be twenty-four. By their last years they had become esteemed "elders at the gate"—men sought out by others for their opinions, for their support, and for their wisdom. Although they were not yet free from personal and political opposition, even in their latter years, many of their earlier enemies had melted away, having been converted to their points of view, becoming simply tolerant, or dying. Both men remained respected, mature leaders, but a new generation was emerging, and others began to take their place in the sun; some of these were men they had mentored, helping them advance in their public careers. Both men now found themselves freer in their last years to tighten their focus on what continued to matter to them. Each man expressed his own sense of urgency—that was brought on by the recognition of dwindling years. But they still had significant family responsibilities, growing financial pressures, and aging bodies, causing them to alter their habits of action. Their energies were waning. Nevertheless, each man held ever more firmly to his now strongly held beliefs. These worldviews had great implications for writing their final chapter, when additional accomplishments would mark their last years,

---

1. Koch and Peden, *The Life and Writings of Thomas Jefferson*, ii, taken from the image of Jefferson's original design and instructions.

further establishing their legacies. In what measure they sustained their early commitments and how they continued to influence their countries and the world is a large part of their last act. As the stories of their lives conclude, these legacies to the next generations, ours included, become ever clearer. Monuments would be built to honor them by their admirers, commemorating them for posterity. More importantly they left an impact on the lives of others—perhaps the most enduring outcome of leadership in any era.

A VIRGINIAN AGAIN

If Jefferson had a yearning that eclipsed all others, often voiced amid his many political trials, it was to be home with his books, his gardens, and his beloved family at Monticello. When he spoke of "family," he paradoxically included all those who were his slaves on the plantation—that is how he liked to think of them—and those favored few closest to him in the house returned the favor. By 1809, he seemed to have become genuinely tired of public life once again. Unlike his previous temporary strategic retreats to his mountain home, this time it seemed sincere. Yet ahead lay family difficulties, more death, increasing debts, another huge building project, and the resumption of an old but fractured friendship. Two choices he made in these latter years were particularly reflective of his remaining priorities. The first is what he gave himself to until shortly before his death, considering it worthy to be included in his epitaph. This was the project he had in mind for many years dating to before the presidency—to design, fund, and construct a great university in nearby Charlottesville. In this endeavor, he would once again be joined and supported by his two closest Virginian protégés and colleagues—Madison and Monroe. The second choice is what he did *not* give himself to, despite repeated requests, as the younger generation drew upon his often repeated statements of sympathy and commitment to the abolition of slavery. Why his energies were sufficient for the one task and not the other opens the window even wider on our understanding of Jefferson vis-à-vis Wilberforce.

AN ENLIGHTENED VISION

In May 1817 there occurred an auspicious gathering of the Board of Visitors for tiny Albemarle Academy in Charlottesville, Virginia. It was the board's first meeting, and found among the members were two former presidents and one sitting president: Thomas Jefferson joined by James Madison and President James Monroe. The old collaboration held firm, and this day the board voted to take the first steps toward a purpose that Jefferson had held onto since his early days in the House of Burgesses and had been quietly at work on in his retirement. These three men came to lend their leadership and visibility, thus giving credibility to the enterprise, with Monroe and Madison present not only out of loyalty to Jefferson, but also with an eye toward establishing a top-tier academic institution in the first state of the South.[2]

The beginning was modest. The Albemarle Academy was essentially defunct, having no students and nothing remaining but its founding purpose—to educate the sons of Virginia planters in the classics and to prepare them for leadership among their peers. That day the board voted to change the name to Central College, to establish it as a new institution, and to seek the resources necessary to buy land and to begin fund raising in earnest for a far more compelling educational vision. Jefferson, in keeping with his personal dream, already had detailed sketches of what he called an "academical village" that would rival Harvard College or the College of New Jersey (later Princeton) in prestige. He described it to his colleagues with brimming enthusiasm, seeing it as a place that would not only develop the intellects of the students, but also refine their moral sense based on the Aristotelian virtues. It was also to become the second American institution of higher learning not founded under religious assumptions,[3] thus leaving its students free to believe as their consciences led.

Over the next several years, as Monroe remained occupied by the affairs of state, Madison and Jefferson continued their remarkable collaboration, working together on many critical aspects of founding a university: securing repeated appropriations of funds from the state legislature, procuring a suitable site, recruiting the faculty, and even designing the curriculum.[4] Here was an enterprise for which they were particularly well suited. Being arguably among the most educated men

---

2. Crawford, *Twilight at Monticello*, 150–51; Koch, *Jefferson and Madison*, 270.

3. Benjamin Franklin founded the College of Philadelphia (later the University of Pennsylvania) as the first university established without religious origins or curriculum. Jefferson and Franklin shared a common commitment to the Enlightenment and were its two greatest proponents in late eighteenth-century America.

4. Koch, *Jefferson and Madison*, 263–70.

of their time (along with John Adams), they saw their work as preparing the next generations of Virginia scholars with a true Enlightenment curriculum, rooted in the classics and the rapidly emerging sciences. Monroe was kept fully informed and lent his support in every way possible to advance the ideas of his mentor, Jefferson, and his close friend, Madison.

Much earlier, Jefferson had described to many correspondents, including Dr. Joseph Priestley, that his vision was for something brand new in education: "An University on a plan so broad and liberal and modern, as to be worth patronizing with the public support."[5] This letter to Dr. Priestley, a noted European academic, was written in 1801, shortly after Jefferson took office as president. His unique plans for higher education for his native state had been a long time in the making and were likely never far from his mind as he continually refined them over the next years—he even designed a diet for the students! But it was the curriculum and the campus architecture into which he poured most of his vast creative energies.

As the foremost proponent of reason in America, Jefferson was keenly and particularly interested in the sciences. As he expressed it, these would include "botany, chemistry, zoology, anatomy, surgery, medicine, natural philosophy, agriculture, mathematics, astronomy, geography, politics, commerce, history, ethics, law, arts, and fine arts"[6]—all were to be taught. As for languages, his love of his classical education bequeathed by his father would accept none other than Latin and Greek, thus enabling the students to read the ancient authors in their original voice. He foresaw many of the faculty taking on the teaching of more than one subject across disciplines, and he was convinced the professors should be drawn from the finest universities in Europe, believing their Enlightenment understanding and classical preparation superior to most of the religiously trained academics in America. Certainly he must have thought of that revered Scot, William Small, his mentor, as the prototype for his overseas recruiting venture.

What was most notable for the American scene that occurred Jefferson intended this to be a university that specifically would *not* teach theology or religion. In his mind there was no place in a modern university for anything other than a secular education. He drew upon his earlier

---

5. Koch and Peden, "Letter to Dr. Joseph Priestley, January 18, 1800," 552.
6. Ibid., 553.

observations in Europe that church-affiliated institutions were inimical to science. He believed that most Americans were destined to fall behind as they continued to mimic church-founded European institutions as Harvard, Yale, and Princeton had done. He concluded that the only remedy for this growing dilemma was to "replace what he considered the obscurantism of the church with the precision of the Enlightenment."[7] This new university would be its outpost in America. Jefferson was not opposed to religious teaching per se; however, he thought each religious branch should teach its own adherents privately, not under the imprimatur of state- or school-supported clergy who would bias the purpose of higher education.

For his "academical village," Jefferson created a unique design in universities, eschewing the usual grand buildings in favor of one-story dormitory rooms, apartments, and pavilions with walkways where students and professors could intermingle. The rotunda that housed the library was to be the centerpiece, dominating the scene much like the place that the chapel held in other institutions of higher education. And finally, one end of the campus would be entirely open to the forests, the skies, and the surrounding hills as a means to draw the eye to the wide possibilities that lay ahead, signifying that students and their teachers were to have free and open minds that looked toward the future.

On October 16, 1817, President Monroe laid the cornerstone. The first construction supervisor was none other than the school's architect, the aged ex-president, who had assumed oversight of one of the single largest construction projects in America up to that time.

Four years later, on November 5, 1821, Jefferson and Madison journeyed to the university grounds, still under construction, to honor the visiting Lafayette for his singular contributions during the Revolution almost fifty years before. In the preceding four years, Jefferson had begun to fail badly, becoming so weak that he required a substitute to read his speech. The words he penned were a passionate appeal for the final funding for the project he held dear, embodying his hopes for the future of America and its next generation. As he expressed it,

> In this feeble state if I can still contribute anything to advance the Institution within whose walls we are now mingling . . . it will be, as it ever has been, cheerfully and zealously bestowed. And could I live to see it once enjoy the patronage and cherishment of our

---

7. Crawford, *Twilight at Monticello*, 153.

public authorities with undivided voice, I should die without a doubt of the future fortunes of my native State.[8]

Although additional funding was granted by the state legislature, it was another four years, on March 7, 1825, before the university was formally opened to its first students. True to his wish, Jefferson had lived to see his dream completed—a bare year before he died. The venerable old scholar served as the greeter for the incoming students the first day the doors were opened. What a scene that must have been for the young men!

A SINGULAR ACCOMPLISHMENT

Of all the great things Jefferson accomplished in his life, perhaps no project exemplified the very best of his personal leadership more than the work he did in becoming the "father of the University of Virginia"—a title much to his liking that he included in his concise epitaph. In fact, this may have been his proudest legacy.

To begin with, he had the vision for something unique in America and Europe to help grow the next generation of leaders in Virginia. This long-held image arose from his belief that "education was the greatest of all human causes as it was the indispensable road to liberty."[9] Second, he not only conceived this great plan, he also built it into a purpose shared among the leading people of his day, including his two closest friends and members of the "President's Club." He also needed local political backing and worked diligently and sacrificially to secure funding and to gather support among the leaders in Virginia. With his old friend and colleague Madison, he was able to influence those who had the final decision to endorse his unique curriculum plans and his unusual architectural designs, although many of his concepts were also highly controversial for his day. It was perhaps the one time in his long life when he did not shy away from personal and public conflict on a major issue. He had built a wide circle of supporters by the time the cornerstone was laid; yet, despite the necessity arising from failing health to turn the final tasks over to others, he continued to keep his hand in every aspect of the project, including the final selection of the faculty.

---

8. Ibid., 206.
9. Koch, *Jefferson and Madison*, 268.

That he lived to see its completion and be present at its opening is a fitting tribute not only to his leadership but also to his persistence, as he all but ignored the ravages of time until it was completed. The University of Virginia stands today as the kind of institution that he hoped it would become—and offers even more that he had consciously excluded. It is certainly in the top tier of universities in America. Ironically, despite Jefferson's fervent wishes, the university, though still secular, houses both a lively Department of Religion and a Christian Study Center that have influenced the faith of many graduates over the years.

SLAVERY: ONE MORE TIME

Jefferson's last years were marked by his final, bold project, the founding of "Mr. Jefferson's University" as it was called by the locals. Yet these were also years marked by what he did *not* do in response to the question of providing leadership in the festering cause of abolition. It should have come as no surprise to Jefferson that the growing move toward abolition—one he had predicted after the outlawing of the slave trade—would continue to seek him out.

From his earliest days, he had been a man who spoke and wrote against slavery, seeking whether through legislation or commentary to persuade others of the rights of man. Even though he had ceased taking an active public role after 1785, his admirers did not interpret this silence as reflecting a change in his private views. To those followers, "all men are created equal" was the truest expression of his beliefs, even though four decades had now passed since these ringing words had announced America's founding values. The annual observance of the birth of the nation, celebrated on the fourth of July, was a reminder of the power of language to kindle a vision. Yet arriving at the core of his actual beliefs is not an easy task in the face of his long inaction. No biographer or historian has yet mined his private thoughts and beliefs with great confidence.

Jefferson did leave for posterity one explanation of why he gave his leadership energies in his last years to building the University of Virginia while not acting to support the antislavery cause. Some have branded this failure as hypocrisy, some as latent racism, while others have simply seen him as a man of his times. Speculation has it that he had a classical philosophical bent toward human rights in general unhindered by forceful action, because he simply could not make up his mind what to do. Whether the subject was slaves, Indians, or women, some would say his head and his heart wrestled with each other as he famously described to Maria Cosway concerning the subject of his enchantment with her.[10] Each of these scholarly explanations, it would appear, has some grain of truth. But his own most fulsome explanation of his reasons for demurring came in an exchange with an earnest young leader destined to become a great man like Jefferson himself one day.

AN INQUIRY OF HOPE

In his latter years, Thomas Jefferson became even more paradoxical in his response to slavery. His own internal struggles about national policy seemed to be mirrored in his private life in the latter years. Well established in the Monticello redoubt, his slaves labored to sustain his lifestyle now that the master had returned for good. Yet he seemingly tried to keep himself from being overly aware of their labors by having their quarters physically screened from the view of the great house.

He reluctantly admitted to his close confidantes that, somewhat contrary to his Enlightenment beliefs, that "morals do not necessarily advance hand in hand with the sciences," and that the younger generation growing up under freedom had sadly become even less moral and less idealistic than his own, much to his disappointment. Their preference, he believed, was to make money and to take its pleasures from the fruits of slavery.[11] That his own life and example reflected just such a choice seemed to elude his thoughts. If the young Virginia planters were paying attention to the old sage, his personal choice to continue to hold slaves likely spoke louder to them than his words written a generation ago. Self-deception can occur in the most intelligent of men, and that seems to have been part of Jefferson's malady. At the very least, it was "compartmentalization" as we like to explain today.

But one young man was not disillusioned with the founder and thought him the ideal person to take up his cudgel once again against the long American oppression of Africans. On July 31, 1814, Jefferson received a letter from young Edward Coles seeking both his opinion and his possible support. Coles was no ordinary aspiring Virginia country gentleman or casual correspondent. A man of great promise, he had

---

10. Peterson, "Dialogue Between My Head and My Heart," 866–77.
11. Miller, *The Wolf by the Ears*, 204–205.

been private secretary to James Madison, was a neighbor of Jefferson's, and remained an ardent admirer. He was also an abolitionist. In his letter, he requested that Jefferson take a public leadership role to encourage the gradual emancipation of the slaves in Virginia, even as he had first proposed in 1769. Coles argued that if Jefferson were to put his full imprimatur on the antislavery movement, it would be his crowning achievement; success would be certain to follow. Coles pressed home the idea Jefferson had often expressed—the people must be led by their natural leaders, primarily the planters, "to arouse and enlighten public sentiment which in matters of this kind ought not to be expected to lead *but to be led* (emphasis added)."[12] Coles shared his plans, embryonic as they were, to sell his plantation in Virginia and move to the free Illinois territory, taking his slaves with him and there giving them land as free men. He saw it as an example to the Virginia aristocracy that it was indeed feasible to free their slaves while demonstrating to his fellow planters that no deleterious effects would occur.[13] He must have felt Jefferson would be certain to concur.

But if Coles thought he would get encouragement from the Declaration's author, he was to be sadly disappointed. In Jefferson's elegant response, first he applauded the moral sentiments of Coles. Then Jefferson reiterates his now hard and fast position:

> Mine on the subject of slavery of negroes have long since been in possession of the public, and time has only served to give them stronger root. The love of justice and the love of country plead equally the cause of these people, and it is a moral reproach to us that they should have pleaded it so long in vain, and should have produced not a single effort, nay I fear not much serious willingness to relieve them & ourselves from our present condition of moral & political reprobation.[14]

Jefferson subsequently goes on to express his long-held hopes and expectations that the younger generation, the first to be truly free from their births, would more readily see the evils of slavery than his own

---

12. Ibid., 206.

13. Edward Coles did in fact carry out his plan and moved to Illinois with his free slaves. He later became governor of the State of Illinois and devoted much of the remainder of his life to the cause of abolition.

14. Peterson, "Emancipation and the Younger Generation: Letter to Edward Coles, August 25, 1814, Monticello," 1343–46.

generation and consequently act upon their moral sense. He had given up on his own peers, he said. Incredibly, he then states that Coles is the *first* person to bring the cause of abolition to him, the evidence of which he long ago concluded indicated a continued apathy in the people and in their leaders. His advice to Coles is essentially to follow his own example of keeping a low profile while quietly fanning the flame of hope until a more fortuitous time would arrive in the vague future. As for the idea of moving to Illinois and freeing his slaves, Jefferson derides this notion based apparently on his unchanged views of the benighted state of the Negroes and the need to prepare them for freedom:

> I have seen no proposition so expedient on the whole, as that of emancipation of those born after a given day, and of their education and expatriation after a given age. This would give time for a gradual extinction of that species of labour & substitution of another, and lessen the severity of the shock which an operation so fundamental cannot fail to produce. For men probably of any color, but of this color we know, brought from their infancy without necessity for thought or forecast, are by their habits rendered as incapable as children of taking care of themselves, and are extinguished promptly wherever industry is necessary for raising young. In the meantime they are pests in society by their idleness, and the depredations to which this leads them. Their amalgamation with the other color produces a degradation to which no lover of his country, no lover of excellence in the human character can innocently consent.[15]

This statement reveals Jefferson's perspective that Africans are unlikely to become useful citizens. Even more darkly, he has an underlying fear of the Scylla and Charybdis of abolition. One the one hand, the likelihood of miscegenation would spell doom for the republic. On the other, freedom without immediate deportation might well mean a racial war. He can see no end other than that of a very gradual emancipation coupled with resettlement back to Africa so as to avoid the things he fears the most about a free slave population. He will maintain this apocalyptic view until his death.

As for the request by Coles that Jefferson provide public backing for the abolition cause, Jefferson responded that he did not want his name even associated with abolition of the type championed and urged upon him by young Coles. Because of his advanced years, Jefferson felt this

15. Ibid.

was now a matter for younger men. Yet in this response, he belied once again his other often stated view of leadership—that slavery's end rested upon elite leaders who "would set the example to the American people of devotion to the public good, the practice of self-denial, and disdain of 'mere money-making.'"[16] Still, Jefferson was not inclined to stand either in the company of those leaders or at their head. With the exception of his great university building project, this was to be his time in life for reflection on the past, no longer looking ahead as he had earlier in life. Even though Coles would make one more attempt, the old man would not budge.

MISSOURI LOOMS

Two years after responding to the letter from Coles, Jefferson was presented with the opportunity to help his protégé, now President Monroe, deal with the festering national issue of slavery. Monroe was vexed by the mounting pressures of a decision made each time a new state was added—whether they would be slave or free. As Monroe took office in 1817, Jefferson had one last chance as a wise adviser to help address the blot against the American body politic and its darkening future as a united republic. It was here that the final, fateful lines were drawn that ultimately brought Gettysburg and Appomattox into infamy.

As each new territory in the westward population explosion petitioned for statehood during Monroe's tenure, the Missouri question finally brought matters to a painful head. Monroe sought the advice of the sage of Monticello. As he wrote to his old mentor in 1820, "I have never known a question so menacing to the tranquility and even the continuance of our Union as the present one." Jefferson readily concurred, calling it the "most portentous one I have ever contemplated,"[17] but he had little practical advice to offer his protégé, having avoided these sorts of difficult choices himself for thirty years.

As Jefferson considered the Missouri question, his thoughts must have returned to his earlier role on the very same issue—the extension of slavery to the western territories. This situation arose after the end of the war and before Washington was elected president. Jefferson had just re-entered public life after Martha died and the Virginia legislature

---

16. Miller, *The Wolf by the Ears*, 209.
17. Cunningham, *Jefferson and Monroe: Constant Friendship and Respect*, 56.

named him to the Confederation Congress in 1783–1784 to work out the newly independent nation's common issues, laying the groundwork for self-government. Britain, in recognizing American independence at the Treaty of Paris, had ceded all of the territory west of the Alleghenies as far as the Mississippi River to the victors. It was in the debates in Congress that Jefferson's vision for the West first began to come clear.

He saw that America's future was in the West, not knowing the role he would later play in the breathtaking expansion all the way to the Pacific. "He was convinced that the West would be the key to defining the character of the new nation; he hoped to encourage the spread westward of a republic of individual farmers, each tilling his own land and committed to personal and national independence and liberty."[18] Jefferson would begin to formulate his thoughts for a good society, one that was self-governing, with loose oversight by the central government, and a nation whose centerpiece was the yeoman farmer. He believed each territory could petition to become a state equal with the original thirteen when it reached a critical population mass rather than simply expand the size of the existing states into the new territories.

To carry out this expansion project, Jefferson proposed two significant policies for the Congress to consider. First, he recommended that the land be divided into rectangular grids, individual farm-sized plots that would encourage westward movement by enterprising families. Second, he pushed for the proscription of slavery anywhere in the new western territories, confining it to the original southern states.[19] The Northwest Ordinance of 1785 enacted by the Congress adopted his farm grid plan for the formation of states, and it was later written into the new Constitution, continuing to govern land use in the Midwest and the Far West to this day. Except for one unfortunate incident, the illness of the delegate from New Jersey, the ban on slavery in the new territories would have been adopted as well.[20] Though the Northwest Ordinance of 1787 did ban slavery in the western territories it had no teeth and was ignored in many places. Thus, with no clear national policy on the expansion of slavery when a state from the western territory was to be added, the addition of each new state posed a unique problem, and when Missouri petitioned to enter the Union, Monroe's dilemma became a national crisis.

18. Bernstein, *Thomas Jefferson*, 53.

19. A tacit, unwritten understanding between North and South in the early days of independence agreed that slavery would be confined to the original Southern states.

20. Bernstein, *Thomas Jefferson*, 53–54.

Despite his earlier expressed desire in the deliberations in 1784 that slavery be proscribed from the new territories, Jefferson reluctantly supported the Missouri Compromise, which allowed its entry as a slave state along with Maine's entry as a free state. This agreement also stated that no future slave states would be formed north of 36°30°. Jefferson rightly saw "this momentous question like a fire bell in the night. . . . as the death knell of the Union. . . . This is a reprieve only, not a final sentence."[21] Yet he backed the compromise as a way to keep parity between slave and free states in hopes of preserving the Union by continuing to balance the states numerically.

Sadly for posterity, he saw no other way out than to reverse himself on the western states issue he earlier supported and to support widening slavery's introduction into the West. This must have been a painful admission for Jefferson, whose hopes for the future of America at the end of his life had been placed with the generation to follow. Yet he had nothing of wisdom to offer to his younger colleague, Monroe, as he faced the storms ahead.

Neither Jefferson nor John Adams as elder statesmen recently reconciled could do anything but avoid this great issue facing the nation they had helped to found under the conditions that now threatened its very existence.

THE GREAT SILENCE REDUX

The remarkable reconciliation of the two old colleagues of the Revolution—Adams and Jefferson—occurred through a benevolent ruse by their mutual friend and correspondent, Dr. Benjamin Rush. Rush considered them the north and south poles of that singular Revolutionary period, and although he had sided with Jefferson in the Adams–Jefferson election, he remained a trusted friend of both. And thus began an unsuspected and mutually treasured fourteen years of correspondence that lasted until the end of their lives—a remarkable treasure for posterity that each man knowingly preserved for our edification.

It may seem puzzling at first that in the blizzard of letters between Jefferson and Adams over those final years, there was but one scant conversation about the deep national wound that slavery was becoming. Jefferson seemingly carried out his earlier vow to think no more on the

---

21. Peterson, "Letter from Thomas Jefferson to John Holmes, April 22, 1820, Monticello," 1434.

subject, even with his old comrade. Perhaps this silence can best be explained not so much as an oddity but as being much like what occurred in their early days during the founding of the republic.

The unspoken agreement that existed among the founding generation of leaders was evidenced in the great hush on even discussing slavery's resolution. No one wanted to stir up sentiments that would split the fragile and embryonic union of states that was slowly being born as a single nation. Now almost forty years later, the two surviving founders seemingly could not bring themselves to write to each other concerning their feelings about the expansion of slavery, knowing how the other likely felt. In this, they were more than north–south poles of political party. One was a slave owner, the other decidedly not; one saw it as a federal issue, the other as in the realm of the states' authority alone. Only in a single instance did it come up between them in these years: regarding the Missouri question that Jefferson was trying to get his mind around in order to help advise Monroe.

On January 21, 1821, Jefferson wrote Adams: "The real question, as seen in the states afflicted with this unfortunate population, is, 'Are our slaves to be presented with freedom and a dagger?' For if Congress has a power to regulate the conditions of the inhabitants of the states, within the states, it will be but another exercise of that power to declare that all shall be free."[22]

Jefferson explains this growing, fractious issue in terms of what he has said before—if then freedom was to be granted to the slaves, then it will be war, either between the states or between the races. He reveals his continued philosophical discomfort with the federal governing principle he has opposed since his days of contention with Hamilton on the national banking system, as well as with Adams. If the federal government can regulate whether a *new* state is slave or free, he holds, then it can free the slaves in *all* the states—granting them full emancipation without the consent of any state. For Jefferson, this amounted to his definition of the supreme tyranny—a despotism worse than that of slavery. Ultimately this is the view that would break the Union.

In his return letter on February 3, Adams agrees with the portentous matter of slavery and expresses the fears he shared with Jefferson for their country's future: "Slavery in this Country I have seen hanging over it like a black cloud for over half a Century.... I have been so ter-

---

22. Capon, *The Adams-Jefferson Letters*, 570.

rified with this Phenomenon that I constantly said in former times to the Southern Gentlemen, I cannot comprehend this object; I must leave it to you. I will vote for forceing no measure against your judgements. What we are to see, *God* knows, and I leave it to him, and his agents in posterity."[23]

Adams simply could not accept the Southern argument that deprived anyone living in America of liberty. He knew, however, that forcing his colleagues to his views in prior days would have made it impossible to form a federal government. He himself had help on his farm and in the household, but these were either day laborers or live-in help. Adams apparently does not want to raise in his letters the seeming contradiction inherent in Jefferson's political beliefs and his slave owning, nor does he comment on Jefferson's foolish idea that the "diffusion"[24] of slaves into the new territories would be the ultimate, almost magical solution to the issue now confronting them.

In Adams's opinion, this notion of diffusion's felicitous outcome he knew Jefferson had proposed earlier was a fantastical view, and he had denounced it to others in the most dismissive terms—but never to Jefferson. Yet Adams did agree with Jefferson that he also could see no way forward. Had they been privy to a glimpse across the Atlantic, they would have seen that a bill introduced in Parliament the very year they exchanged these letters would be enacted twelve years later, setting an example of freedom for America and the rest of world to follow. Arguably two of the greatest minds in America could see only disaster in the "wolf" they held by the ears. It would fall to their successor, Lincoln, to take up the gauntlet they had not and would not.

AN AUSPICIOUS FOURTH OF JULY

As they penned their single exchange on slavery, Adams and Jefferson had barely five years of life remaining, and neither had the stomach for tackling this vexing question upon which, in the main, they still disagreed. At the end, they left the issue in the hands of posterity and of posterity's God, who indeed barely forty years hence would be "tram-

23. Ibid., 571.

24. "Diffusion" was the scheme Jefferson grabbed hold of to explain how slavery's expansion westward would be the root of its demise, somehow diluting its evil effects the more widely it was practiced until it disappeared. This issue will be taken up in more detail in chapter 10.

pling out the vintage where the grapes of wrath are stored." The deaths of Adams and Jefferson on July 4, 1826, ended their remarkable generation. The book was closed on the founders and their hopes for an end to the problem that vexed the land of liberty all their years.

LAST WORDS

As he roused himself from a deep unconsciousness in the last hours of his life, Jefferson was heard to whisper the beginning words from the *Nunc Dimittis,* "Lord, now lettest thou thy servant depart in peace."[25] Taken from what is called the Song of Simeon in the Gospel of Luke 2:29, it receives its title from the first two words in Latin. In the English Book of Common Prayer of 1662, which Jefferson would have been very familiar with, these words were part of the traditional Evensong or Compline Prayer at the end of the day. The Song of Simeon finishes with these words:

> For mine eyes have seen thy salvation,
> Which thou hast prepared before the face of all people;
> To be a light to lighten the Gentiles
>   and to be the glory of thy people Israel. [26]

Simeon was an old man who had been promised in a vision that he would not die before he saw the Messiah of Israel. As Joseph and Mary bring the baby Jesus to be consecrated in the Temple, Simeon somehow senses this is the young Messiah and takes the baby in his arms, offering his prayer. That these were among Jefferson's last earthly words is a final puzzle concerning his life, or it certainly would have been to those who knew him best. Was he hedging his bets? Whether Jefferson's Enlightenment beliefs against what did not accord with reason and experience stood the test of his last great battle on earth remains an intriguing mystery whose answer is known only in the realm he entered.

Then, even as Jefferson's first memory of life was his being carried in on a pillow by a slave, his last scene occurred when an old, beloved slave, Joseph, adjusted his pillow after bending down to hear his master's indistinct voice only he could understand. The final irony is that a slave offered Thomas Jefferson his last earthly comfort—and his first memory.

25. Crawford, *Twilight at Monticello,* 241.
26. Wikipedia, http://en.wikipedia.org/wiki/Nunc_dimittis, accessed May 16, 2009.

CARVED IN STONE

As for Jefferson's legacy, it was not only the one he entreated Madison to protect after he died but also the one he sought to shape with his own hand. Not trusting others for this task—not even Madison—he had designed his own spare tombstone with its accompanying epitaph—those three achievements for which he most wanted to be remembered by those who came after him: the Declaration of American Independence, the Statute for Religious Freedom, and the University of Virginia. He would allow no additions either by his heirs or his admirers. Neither was any credit given to those who had been a great part of these accomplishments: not to his colleagues who edited the Declaration into its final form; nor to Madison who had steered the religious freedom bill through the Virginia legislature while Jefferson was in France; nor to those who funded the building of Mr. Jefferson's university. It would lie with his readers and successors to glean the final meaning of this extraordinary, long life. His role in ending slavery would likewise be assessed by time. That evaluation continues.

Thomas Jefferson maintained to the last that his youthful commitment to ending slavery remained his lifelong belief. But in the Enlightenment milieu he occupied, he separated private beliefs from public truths. These early beliefs had gradually given way to a fear of revolution, distrust of a national solution, and ultimately silence. His hope came to be placed in fantasy and in the progress of man—thin reeds to be sure. We can only regret that there was not one more line to add to his legacy: *He Led the African-American Slaves into the Land of Freedom.* That task would pass to another president almost forty years later as he presided over the surrender of the South that Jefferson helped to create—in thought and in culture. The freedom for slaves that Jefferson wrote of with both passion and disquiet was destined to be purchased by the lives of six hundred thousand of his fellow Americans—and the life of one persistent and exhausted president. That, too, was Jefferson's legacy.

Jefferson had left the "wolf" to roam until other youthful, idealistic leaders would emerge to dispatch it with their blood. The epitaph he wrote was apt; his legacy is obviously a great one, and this failure alone does not subtract from all that—not entirely at least. Yet the lessons of his life and leadership remain a perplexing moral blot to this day. Why did he voice such optimism that slavery would see its end in the vague and distant future, yet fail to see that he himself was implicated to lead and to set an example? It is a question we take up next in examining the whole story—after we finish the last chapter of William Wilberforce's days on earth.

KNOWING AND DOING

1. Jefferson chose to give his last years to founding the University of Virginia. Do you believe this was a good choice for his remaining strength, or was he simply seeking one last grand gesture that would enshrine his memory?

2. Edward Coles was convinced that Jefferson held the key to galvanizing the abolition movement: if he as a Virginian, beloved former president, and author of the Declaration were to get behind the movement, the South would come along. In retrospect, was the judgment of Coles or of Jefferson correct?

3. Could Jefferson have been a better mentor to President James Monroe when he sought advice on the slavery issue surrounding Missouri's entry as a state—or even before in preparing him to face this question? If yes, in what way?

4. In their late correspondence, Jefferson and Adams made a seemingly self-conscious effort to spell out for posterity the two different views that the founders held in framing and interpreting the Constitution. How have their differing perspectives affected our own views today as to the original intent?

5. What thoughts do you have as you think about your last years on earth and how you might best use the remaining time you have?

9

One Task Remains

Up clearly is the direction of greatness. From the world's perspective it is the only direction to go. Just as a compass needle points north, the human needle points up; in each heart is a built-in mechanism that craves self-promotion and advancement, the climb of ego. Our role models and heroes reflect the theme: Ascend and flex the muscles of your self-will. Whether you do it blatantly or use the disguise of humanity, make yourself upwardly mobile. Why? Because that is the direction of greatness.[1]

THE EXHAUSTING TWENTY-YEAR BATTLE that ended the slave trade had seemingly not dulled Wilberforce's love for whimsy. His "What next?" comment to Henry Thornton in the aftermath of their great victory revealed both his great sense of humor and his continued commitment to emancipate the slaves. While Jefferson was making plans to begin his retirement at Monticello and to build the University of Virginia, Wilberforce, the younger by sixteen years, soldiered on as a statesman who had gained unexpected worldwide respect. Although Wilberforce would soon find his always fragile health gradually failing him, his passion still burned brightly, not only for the slaves but also for the dozens of other causes to which he gave leadership—both moral and practical. The Saints team members neither rested nor went their separate ways as they might have been reasonably expected to do after two decades of laboring in the mean trenches of politics. They continued on with him even though he would move out of Clapham Common to accommodate his new wife, Barbara, and their growing family. But as the movement widened, Clapham was by now beyond being a geographical boundary:

---

1. Hybels, *Descending into Greatness*, 16.

it was an ever-conversing conclave of like-minded individuals who had been through the cultural change wars together. They had learned not to be daunted by the size of the task before them. No longer young men and women, they would sustain a commitment to each other and to "the cause" that would not end until Wilberforce's death a quarter century later.

His new, larger home in Kensington Gore, across from Hyde Park, was more suited for a growing role as father and husband, and it was only a short mile's walk from Parliament. It soon became "a sort of clearing-house for British philanthropy and moral reformation" with Wilberforce at the center of an often chaotic scene. Ever ready to encourage, revise, or rebuke inappropriate strategies, he made his home an open bazaar for good causes to come calling. His biographer, John Pollock, calls Wilberforce at this time in his life "a conducting rail for the charitable sparks of others," with small groups of committed instigators for various charities arriving daily for advice and to be connected to his network of social initiatives. Although his Clapham colleagues tried their best to help screen these inquiries and bring order to the process, Wilberforce would good-heartedly meet with one after the other of these groups in his home, despite his daily fatigue."[2] This was simply who he was. Robert Thornton, his early mentor in London, would have beamed at his protégé's charitable heart.

Jefferson, thirty-eight hundred miles away, would have sympathized with his counterpart as even in his retirement from public life he was constrained to also entertain a revolving throng of admirers, extending the hospitality expected of a plantation scion. Even though it would only add to his financial woes, he could not escape from his duties of hospitality. Unlike Wilberforce, however, Jefferson was content that Congress had passed the slave trade bill and gave little attention to emancipation. He would likely have advised Wilberforce to let time and progress take the measure of slavery's end. But that was not William Wilberforce's calling or his custom.

2
Pollock, *Wilberforce*, 218.

AN INTERNATIONAL CAUSE

In some ways, Wilberforce's final years were not all that dissimilar to his earlier days, despite his growing fame and the lengthening shadows. He continued to engage Parliament and English society on the reformation of manners while moving methodically toward ensuring that the trade was not surreptitiously resumed and the cause embraced by other nations. His energies now began to be directed to a larger stage. Perplexing to some, ending slavery was not taken up by Wilberforce immediately; in fact, it would be sixteen more years until the final battles for emancipation were seriously begun. In Wilberforce's mind, the timing for the last battle was critical, and he understood, intuitively perhaps, that premature moves could actually doom the final legislative success if false hopes were raised without solid preparatory groundwork. In that cautious assessment, he was not unlike Jefferson. His prudence, however, did not preclude *all* action. Even so, for this cautious but still forward-leaning course, he found that some questioned the strategy as being far too timid.

Simply put, Wilberforce felt that more time was needed primarily to ensure the end of the trade and the terrible suffering it engendered. He knew that the complete demise of the lucrative practice hinged on far more than simply passing a bill. Now the hard work of implementation lay ahead. The full ending was still fragile, and the continued existence of slave trading by other nations weakened the impact of the British and American actions. International agreements would be critical if the trade was to be fully extinguished. And so the Clapham team turned their eyes toward the world and called now for moral leadership on an international scale. As many nations have realized since then, such a role is not welcomed when one nation is seen as imposing its beliefs and values on another—especially when national economic interests are at stake and religious sensibilities are the motivation.

One initiative by the Clapham Circle in the ensuing years ultimately resulted in the formation of a society they named the African Institution. Its founding purpose was to secure European agreement on ending transport slavery and resettling those who had been captured. The end of the wars with France following Napoleon's defeat in 1814 offered a window to take on the slave trade among all the signatories as part of a wide-ranging peace settlement. Through the same vehicle the Clapham group lobbied to better the lot of those freed slaves that were relocating to Sierra Leone in western Africa. Wilberforce, now a recognized name in the embassies of the other European nations, assumed the responsibility for seeking an International Convention to stop all slave trading. His first move was to personally press Tsar Alexander of Russia to be its head. The primary barrier to such an agreement was France's refusal to assent to these terms in the peace treaty with England. Resuming the slave trade after the war was seen by England's vanquished foe as a key to recovering its vastly diminished prosperity.

After the long-awaited end of the war with France, Wilberforce's opposition to the treaty due to such a "minor" issue was viewed by most of the leaders in England as unpatriotic and unnecessarily sanctimonious in light of the urgency of concluding the long-awaited peace agreement. Yet he would not yield in allowing France to resume the slave trade. Once again, his foes in Parliament painted him as disloyal, acting contrary to the good of his country. The terms negotiated by Lord Castelreagh allowing France's request for resumption were greeted by a cheering House of Commons who were ready for approval. But Wilberforce was unswerving in his purpose and seemingly oblivious to the emotional appeal to be reasonable. Even though he was almost in tears as he opposed what others believed to be right, he rose to passionately speak against Castelreagh's proposed agreement with France: "I cannot but conceive that I behold in his hand the death-warrant of a multitude of innocent victims, men, women, and children. . . . When I consider the miseries we are about to renew, is it possible to regard them without the deepest emotions of sorrow? . . . No considerations could have induced me to consent to it."[3] Unheeding of the majority view, he then proceeded once again to stir up the British people by encouraging over a million of his countrymen to sign the Clapham Circle's petitions on behalf of the slaves by opposing the treaty with France.

At the end, implausibly it seemed, the French barrier of national pride (and avarice) coupled with English temerity fell before the persistent, visible specter of the slaves trapped within the unholy triangle. Wilberforce simply would not let Parliament forget the slaves—even at the price of delaying the peace. Soon thereafter, the International Congress of Vienna also reached agreement with Spain, the last nation to yield to the arguments of the British delegates for universal stoppage. Among those representing Britain were none other than a rejuvenated

---

3. Ibid., 242–43.

Thomas Clarkson and the brilliant Zachary MacAulay, who had earned the right to help shape the final outcome as revered elder statesmen. When the agreement with Spain was finally forged, Wilberforce became a man of such widespread international reputation that the princes of Europe clamored to meet the man who embodied concern for humanity.[4] A movement that began in England had now spread to all of Europe. America (surreptitiously) and Brazil, with Portugal's backing, were the lone remaining practitioners of the foul practice.

THE DESCENT OF THE LEADER

One of the enduring questions concerning leadership of any stripe is whether acquiring greater power and status helps the cause for which one labors. The perspective of most of the world in the nineteenth century as well as now is that to be a great leader—even in serving humanity—your focus must be on achieving the highest possible office, which can then be the platform to give added leverage to your purpose. Jefferson seemingly believed in this approach, although the reality of the presidency may in time have attenuated his belief. Wilberforce, however, did not ascribe to this commonly held view. He had earlier abandoned the possibility that he would become prime minister, first when he associated himself with the slave trade controversy, then by openly being a practicing religious "enthusiast." His decision on personal ambition was a conscious one that he recorded in his journal as a reminder of the stake that he had put in the ground: "Whatever dreams of ambition I may have indulged, it now seems clear, that my part is to give the example of an independent Member of Parliament, and a man of religion, discharging with activity and fidelity the duties of his trust, and not seeking to render his parliamentary station a ladder by which to rise to a higher eminence."[5]

He would not put his ladder up against the wrong wall; in fact, he would not climb the ladder at all. In the aftermath of his victory on the slave trade bill, followed by his move to the new house in Kensington Gore, he came to a critical decision point as the elections loomed in 1811. For twenty-eight years, almost his entire tenure in Parliament, he had been the member from Yorkshire—one of the two most prestigious and powerful districts in all of England. It was his Yorkshire district that

---

4. Metaxas, *Amazing Grace*, 245.
5. Hague, *William Wilberforce*, 311.

gave Wilberforce a strong, visible platform from which to conduct his campaigns for reform and to support Prime Minister Pitt on almost every front. But this key district also required of him a great effort in serving his many constituents and in conducting assiduous campaigning to hold the seat. It required him to churn out mountains of correspondence and maintain the serious committee responsibilities attendant to such a powerful position. Once again, he wrestled with a question for which he did not clearly know the answer: should he step down to a safe "pocket borough" and thereby lessen his load? At this time it was a seemingly counterintuitive move given the major policy changes he continued to strive for. Stepping away from power, once done, would be an irreversible and life-changing decision.

What had led Wilberforce to this critical point? One factor, of course, was his health. The ongoing battle he waged with colitis necessitated the commonly prescribed opium treatment. It was a devilish bargain he had struck that plagued him always and made him appear far older than his years, particularly weakening his already poor eyesight. He was now quite frail with a bad pallor, yet implausibly he still projected a winsome and energetic personality to those who did not know the effort it took. In addition, he also experienced severe curvature of the spine, a condition becoming so grave that gradually, over time, his head rested on his chest and he was forced to surreptitiously wear a steel cage underneath his clothes to support his arms and head—a fact discovered only after his death.

These health concerns gave him pause and caused him to think of his family's future. If he was to have a shortened life, he wanted to spend more time with his six children and his wife. Unusually for his time, Wilberforce loved reading and playing with his children in an age when fathers were typically remote models of the "be seen and not heard" school of parenting.[6] He became an example to many men of his generation that a balanced life for a person of prominence was a plausible and even an enjoyable course. Still, for him, the decision to step down was a wrenching dilemma. At this key crossroads, Wilberforce must have yearned for Newton to consult once more on a critical, life-changing decision. His death shortly after the success of the slave trade act left a great hole within the Saints and particularly for his protégé of many years.

---

6. Pollock, *Wilberforce*, 232.

In the end, after much prayer and consultation with his Clapham team, he decided not to stand for re-election to Yorkshire but took a lesser borough, Bramber. The truth was that despite his stepping down so far in the prestige of office, his authority was now a moral one, being "the conscience of Parliament" as some called him, if not of England itself. His capacity to shape events rested now on the earned authority of character and not on the power of position.

In his typically self-effacing manner after this decision, Wilberforce movingly said, "It is like closing my account and I seem to have done so little, and there seem some things which it would be so desirable to try to do before I quit Parliament that I shrink from retiring as from extinction."[7] Although he had not retired from public life, he seemingly felt that lessening his responsibilities in 1812 was tantamount to full retirement. Of course, this was hardly the case. In fact, it likely allowed him to concentrate his energies far better though no less vigorously, beginning with securing the international agreements.

Alongside their wide-ranging international initiative to end the slave trade, bringing moral transformation to British colonial rule in India became an important parallel Clapham effort. In the end, the Claphamites saw the changes wrought in India's rule as satisfying a victory as any—save for slavery's end. At this point, Wilberforce could justifiably have retired to a calmer life as Jefferson did.

Although political and practical delays with abolition still bedeviled him, Wilberforce had learned—in contrast to his first attempts to end the slave trade twenty-five years earlier—that patience must be coupled with perseverance and steady action. So while Jefferson's health began to fail even as he watched his university grow toward completion, Wilberforce took the final steps that would lead to the opening shot to end the war of oppression on the Africans.

ONE MORE BATTLE

In the intervening sixteen years since the end of the slave trade, in addition to ensuring the enforcement of the ban on British traders, Wilberforce and his colleagues felt it imperative to pass the Registry of Slaves Bill as a priority to pave the way for emancipation. This act would ensure that each slave in the West Indies was accounted for, thus

---

7. Metaxas, *Amazing Grace*, 223.

preventing undercover attempts (Cuba and Spain were the primary culprits) to circumvent the law and sell slaves to the English plantation managers. The registration bill had a dual purpose: to prevent smuggling by keeping an accurate, current accounting of the slaves and to compel the plantation overseers to treat slaves more humanely. The reasoning was that if there was registration, the deaths usually produced by overwork and lack of care could not easily be compensated for by the next secret slave boat arrival. This step, Wilberforce believed, was also necessary to help prepare slaves for emancipation by coupling registration with education and apprenticeship. These preliminary steps would allow the slaves to be qualified to join the ranks of British free laborers in time. Such preparation was important if the slaves were to live not only freely but also independently, able to sustain themselves. This delay for preparation was to counter Wilberforce's opponents who often opposed liberation by charging—as Jefferson had—that the slaves could not be assimilated into society but would become parasites.

Although passing the registration bill was Wilberforce's final legislative priority before taking on emancipation, the prime minister pressed him instead to have the government instruct the colonial legislatures to take up this initiative on their own without England's forcing their hand by law. It was not unlike the dilemma being faced at the same time in America where many saw the federal government as unconstitutionally coercive if they intruded on states' rights in regard to slavery. In deference to the prime minister, Wilberforce reluctantly gave up the bill, which soon led to unforeseen, tragic results.

As it turned out, the slaves in the West Indies had already heard false rumors that Wilberforce was working toward their *immediate* emancipation. They were now wrongly told that these efforts had been thwarted by the colonial leaders. In rage and frustration at hope again deferred, they staged a bloody revolt in Barbados that ended in heartbreak and many grisly deaths. It also brought down upon Wilberforce's head direct blame for causing such unrest and led him to feel deep remorse and guilt. Insurrection was precisely what he had sought to prevent by his efforts to establish the registry and to provide adequate preparation. In some ways it showed that even Wilberforce did not fully understand how precious freedom was to those he would one day liberate.

To add to these trials and difficulties, the insurrection in the Indies was soon followed by unrest at home as crop failures in 1816 and 1817 led to terrible hardship in England. The plight of the slaves in the far-off colonies was no competition compared to the possibility of revolt by the poor in England. Wilberforce was heartsick at these delays and characteristically believed he should have been wiser in his earlier decisions. He second-guessed himself wondering if perhaps he should have taken the planters at their word in 1796 when the trade bill almost passed and the planters had accepted a compromise, agreeing to emancipate the slaves if Wilberforce would only delay the slave trade bill for four years.

By 1823, he could wait no longer. The plight of the poor in England had improved with a return of better weather, and open revolt due to hunger was no longer an issue. The Saints sounded the trumpet, calling a massive meeting to form what they named as the Anti-Slavery Society for the Mitigation and Gradual Abolition of Slavery Throughout the British Dominions. For his part, Thomas Clarkson began to draw upon the new moral tone in Britain by distributing numerous pamphlets that described in frank detail the plight of those held in slavery, thus echoing the earlier strategy of explicitly exposing conditions on board the slave ships. Wilberforce's first public action was to publish in March of that year of his "manifesto" on slavery—*An Appeal on Behalf of the Slaves in the West Indies*. This treatise of almost one hundred pages had a huge impact in Britain and Europe. Reading it moved one plantation owner to repentance. He wrote Wilberforce to tell him of this remarkable change in his life: "[It] so affected me, that should it cost me my whole property, I would surrender it willingly, that my poor negroes may be brought not only to the liberty of Europeans, but especially to the liberty of Christians."[8]

Yet Wilberforce's argument was less against the plantation owners themselves than with the evils of the system for slave and owner alike.[9] In this extended essay, Wilberforce laid out his strategy of emancipation, using the example of how free blacks in Sierra Leone had been successful in governing themselves. He further contended that adequate preparation and kindness would give the slaves in the Indies hope while allowing them time to be ready, once emancipation came, to become British free laborers.

8. Belmonte, *Hero for Humanity*, 272.
9. Martin Luther King, Jr., echoed this theme one hundred forty years later in his great speeches on the mutual evils and ill consequences of segregation for both blacks and whites.

PASSING THE MANTLE

Before the final emancipation battle, William Wilberforce chose to take one additional step—downward once again. He had come to this decision somewhat reluctantly but also realistically. With the insights of age, he realized that in this culminating challenge his calling was no longer to be at the head, even though others were not seeking to displace him. It became clear to him that his task was to prepare and aid the generation of leaders who would follow him. This meant giving up his visible role in the front ranks and letting the legacy pass to another whom he would mentor. Although Wilberforce still longed as ever to see his first great object fully completed and he believed the time was now at hand to take on emancipation, he knew one other thing. In his bones he saw that his own powers of health and energy were waning rapidly despite his greatly reduced parliamentary responsibilities. Thus, in 1821, two years before formally launching the last crusade, he turned over the Parliament's leadership on the emancipation bill to a younger man, Thomas Buxton, a Quaker MP and staunch advocate of prison reform.

The argument Wilberforce made to convince himself first and then others in the Clapham Circle was that to forego overall leadership of this great cause was to recognize he could be doing God's will as much by retiring as by leading. He had come to believe that there is such a thing as a season to a calling, and he knew his time of fruitfulness was heading toward winter. He came to this conclusion using the principle that John the Baptist had sounded eighteen hundred years before when the Messiah he prophesied began to draw the crowds that had once followed him into the wilderness: "He must become greater; I must become less,"[10] the Baptizer said. Wilberforce saw that it was time for him to bring the next generation to the fore replacing him and his own. He said he hoped he had already begun acting in this way, opening opportunity "to other and younger men."[11] His decision he believed would make the transition to those coming behind him that much easier. He would not cling to power.

In much the same way that Newton had mentored him during his early parliamentary career, Wilberforce now looked toward Buxton, much as a father to a son. He seemed quite comfortable to step aside and

---

10. John 3:30, New International Version.
11. Belmonte, *Hero for Humanity*, 274.

turn over to Buxton the mantle of leadership. In many ways this decision was easier, unlike the torment of his earlier dilemma when he stepped down from the Yorkshire representation. In a moving letter, he set forth his charge to Buxton—and to the next generation:

> Now for many, many years I have been longing to bring forward that great subject, the condition of the negro slaves in our Trans-Atlantic colonies, and their advancement to the rank of a free peasantry; a cause . . . recommended to me, or rather enforced on me, by every consideration of religion, justice and humanity. I have been waiting for a proper time and circumstances for . . . introducing this great business, and . . . for some Members of Parliament, who, if I were to retire or to be laid by, would be an eligible leader in this holy enterprise. I have for some time been viewing you in this connection. . . . Let me entreat you . . . should [I] be unable to finish [this work] you would continue to prosecute it. . . . May it please God to bless you. . . . But above all, may He give the disposition to say at all times, "Lord, what wouldst thou have me to do or suffer?" Looking to Him, through Christ, for wisdom and strength.[12]

His were the paradoxical themes of persistence married with dependence on God that Newton and Wesley pressed on a younger Wilberforce when he was discouraged and facing great odds.

And so it was on May 15, 1823, three years before Jefferson died, that Thomas Buxton stood up in the House of Commons and introduced the antislavery motion for gradual abolition. Wilberforce himself rose to speak on its behalf, giving an impassioned speech complementing Buxton's more legal depiction and, in the bargain, giving him a lesson in how to approach a divided House with a matter of great moral urgency. Wilberforce's main theme was that he wanted the slaves not only to have their conditions made better to prepare them for emancipation, but also to give them hope in the hopeless world in which they had lived for so very long.

Unfortunately, even as in the slave trade debates of many years before, the legislators did not make an immediate decision. Instead, Parliament passed a delaying tactic that simply ameliorated the slaves' condition on paper, making their betterment a matter to be decided by the colonial governments, not Parliament. The final bill contained

---

12. Buxton, *Memoirs of Sir Thomas Foxwell Buxton*, cited in Belmonte, *Hero for Humanity*, 275–76.

no promise of ultimate emancipation. It was such a subtle tactic that even Wilberforce and the Clapham team thought at first it was a good start before the true implications sank in. And although Buxton was the point man, Wilberforce still took the slings and arrows of the opposition, being seen as the power behind it all. One consequence was that Wilberforce was blamed for a second unfortunate misunderstanding that led to another tragic slave insurrection in the wake of the stymied vote. This outbreak of rage was triggered again by a rumor, this time that Parliament had decided to lessen the slaves' plight but that the colonial governments had suppressed any redress. This revolt was also thwarted and led to an immediate counterattack by the slave interests directed at Wilberforce as the "agitator."

The opponents' rejoinder to emancipation this time went directly to Wilberforce's character. In the *Weekly Register,* William Cobbett, its editor, printed an open letter denouncing Wilberforce's *Appeal on Behalf of the Slaves* as full of lies and distortions of fact. Cobbett accused him of rank hypocrisy by saying the old man wanted the Negro slaves to have all the freedoms of English laborers, who themselves were equally poor and downtrodden. In essence, he accused Wilberforce of cruelly ignoring his own countrymen in favor of the Africans:

> Never have you done *one single act* (emphasis added) in favour of labourers in this country.... What an insult it is, and what an unfeeling, what a cold-blooded hypocrite must he be that can send it forth; what an insult to call upon people under the name of free British labourers; to appeal to them in behalf of black slaves, when these free British labourers; these poor, mocked, degraded wretches, would be happy to lick the dishes and bowls, out of which the Black slaves have breakfasted, dined or supped.[13]

Much like the surrogate attack ads in the political battles waged by Jefferson against the federalists Washington and Adams, this false charge stuck to Wilberforce for many years, even after his death. Those who disagreed with him believed it entirely, while its monstrous deception infuriated those to whom he had become both a hero and the man they most respected in Parliament. His followers in the Clapham Circle well knew how long and indefatigably he had worked for the poor in England, and that he had the legislative and personal record to show for it. Characteristically, Wilberforce himself was not moved by these at-

---

13. Pollock, *Wilberforce,* 287.

tacks, knowing that he had assiduously helped those in need in hundreds of ways. Nevertheless, he was concerned that the politics of personal destruction would become a deterrent to those who had sensibilities for social justice and might aspire to public office. "All too often," he worried, "people are not willing to risk their reputation or aspirations in a great cause, especially if they have to endure venom and vitriol on the way to victory. One has to be willing to take up his cross."[14] He could easily have had in mind Jefferson's withdrawal twice from public life when he was under attack by Hamilton and his Federalist followers. Wilberforce felt he needed to encourage his younger colleagues to stand firm and endure the nature of political life—persisting in their responsibilities as leaders despite vilification.

As it turned out, the response in Parliament to these scurrilous attacks on Wilberforce was not the one the oppositionists had imagined. Instead, this bit of political nastiness led to a backlash, followed by an intense investigation into the colonial slave system. The result was an independent, official, and detailed documentation of the abuses that were a common occurrence for these shackled people. Indeed, it corroborated the findings documented earlier by the Clapham team, some of whom testified to this firsthand as former plantation managers.

However, Wilberforce would still not rest entirely, and once again he oversaw the further gathering of evidence, even though he could no longer be a key participant in its presentation. As the campaign pressed forward in the next two years, he knew the time had now come for him to step down. The pace was simply too much for his failing health. Finally he announced his intention to leave public life on February 22, 1825, one year before Jefferson's death.

Although many urged Wilberforce to accept a lifetime peerage, as was the custom for prominent men at the end of their active political careers, after consultation with his Clapham brothers and sisters, he declined. He wanted to remain plain William Wilberforce, not to end his life as a lord. He did not want people to conclude that becoming a peer of the realm had been his ultimate motive all along. His only regret upon retirement was that he had done so *little*. He would amazingly say, "I am filled with the deepest compunction from the consciousness of my having made so poor use of the talents committed to my stewardship."[15]

14. Belmonte, *Hero for Humanity*, 278.
15. Metaxas, *Amazing Grace*, 266.

Given his character, this does not seem false humility in search of affirmation but rather a genuine, heartfelt expression. The finish line for the slaves was still far off.

His retirement left a hole in Parliament that neither Buxton nor others could fill, not entirely. Nevertheless, as to the significance of the changes seen from his decades of public service, few would quarrel that he had made a mark unlike almost any before or after. One colleague, perhaps typical of most, put it to him this way:

> It must be a satisfaction to you to have observed that the moral tone of the House of Commons, as well as of the nation at large, is much higher than when you first entered upon public life. . . . There can be no doubt that God has made you the honoured instrument of contributing much to this great improvement. There are, I hope, some young men of promise coming forward, but . . . would that there were many Elishas on whom your mantle might fall.[16]

What a few began to realize in retrospect was that quietly, year by year, a movement had been conceived, given energy, and was now moving forward apace that changed the moral underpinnings of England. It became "fashionable to do good." A new generation had arisen whose culture reflected years of small, persistent improvements in every corner of society. They had broken with their forebears on that score—not by education but by the example of a few, faithful leaders who would serve others, not themselves. The Victorian era was being born.

FINISHING WELL

By 1831, as the move toward emancipation continued to build steam, Wilberforce judged himself so weakened in body and mind that he determined he would not speak again in public. Even his eyes had failed him, and he could no longer read a newspaper owing to the accumulated effects from years of opium treatments. But still there came a final request that called him back for the last battle: the old war horse responded to the trumpet one final time.

The repeated delaying tactics by the slave owners and their allies had begun to wear thin on an impatient public. The Clapham team and their abolitionist colleagues had learned their lessons well by now,

---

16. Belmonte, *Hero for Humanity*, 293.

and they knew the impasse must be engaged head-on. Employing their time-tested strategy of thorough research, extensive documentation, widespread public meetings, voluminous correspondence, and canny use of the media of the day—newspapers, pamphlets, and word of mouth—they put forth their final and overwhelming case. They argued, quite correctly, that the ostensible easing of conditions that had been introduced by the colonies to prepare for eventual emancipation was, in truth, not even a fig leaf any longer. The severe floggings and inhuman working conditions not fit for beasts had only gotten worse in the past ten years—by now well documented and verified as evidence sent to every corner of England confirmed.

The ensuing national campaign of the abolitionists gathered hundreds of petitions from the length and breadth of the country and secured over one-half million signatures, bringing the full weight of public opinion to bear on slavery's end. Ultimately these signatures were laid literally at the feet of Parliament. Ironically, it was during this petition drive—by now a common undertaking by the Claphamites—that the reluctant wisp of an old man would roar one last time.

Wilberforce and his wife Barbara had by this time come to live with their son, Robert, in Maidstone, having suffered the ignominy in the past two years of seeing their oldest son, the ne'er-do-well William, become bankrupt. William's purchase of a dairy farm, for which his father had unwisely cosigned the note, had failed due to his poor management. To cover the debts his son incurred, Wilberforce was forced to give up his own home on Highwood Hill and take lodging with his two other sons for the last years of life. Like Jefferson, he would die deeply in debt, without even his beloved home to comfort him and his wife in their last years. Characteristically, he saw it as an unforeseen blessing to be in the bosom of his extended family at the end.

It was at that time that Robert persuaded him to put forth an antislavery petition for the region of Maidstone at a large gathering to be held on April 12, 1833. The old man agreed; he could not resist his son or the opportunity. It was classic Wilberforce, risen one last time from the shadows of age. If he was dimmed in voice and shrunken in body, the words he spoke to the assembled populace from Maidstone were nevertheless electric: "I say and say honestly and fearlessly, that the same Being who commands us to love mercy, says also, "Do justice." . . . I trust I now approach the end of my career. The object of emancipation is bright before us, the light of heaven beams on it, and is an earnest of its success."[17]

As he began to conclude, as if on cue, a bright ray of sunshine burst into the hall and inspired his closing comments. This was reminiscent of William Pitt's memorable speech at the day's dawning in Parliament so many long years ago. Thus, with shaking hand, Wilberforce joined his name to the petitions that came in from every corner of England as, once again, the question of slavery was to be brought to a vote by the voice of the people.

The truly remarkable part of the proposal before Parliament, in addition to the sustained, indefatigable moral courage of its purpose, was that it contained a provision to compensate the planters and slave owners £20 million—*one quarter of the entire national budget*—to purchase freedom for more than eight hundred thousand slaves. That decision alone by England was a breathtaking precedent in a dangerous international time.

As the bill progressed, Wilberforce continued to advise and encourage Buxton as he led the cause in Parliament, writing to him frequently not to allow the delaying tactics of the slave interests to prolong the call for further documentation and to bring closure to the matter. The time to act was at hand.

To the Anti-Slavery Society he had helped to found, his advice to his colleagues in 1831 could well have been written on his coat of arms: "Our Motto must continue to be *perseverance*. And ultimately I trust the Almighty will crown our efforts with success."[18] By the spring of 1833, a wave of popular opinion drove the issue to a certain and immediate consideration. Wilberforce wrote to his protégé, Buxton, to go forward with purpose, much like Henry at Agincourt encouraged the small English "band of brothers" drawn up before the massed French army.

Lord Stanley, the Colonial Secretary, put forth the Government's proposal, which included, in addition to the generous compensation for the planters, an apprenticeship provision for the freed slaves. The bill before the legislators would result in freedom in the colonies, but with one last pernicious hitch: it would also require that the slaves continue to work without compensation for their former masters for twelve years in order to "learn" their newfound freedom and their technical duties.

17. Ibid., 318.
18. Pollock, *Wilberforce*, 304.

Wilberforce was aghast at this last ploy and urged Buxton to obdurately resist its inclusion. Simultaneously he wrote to an old friend in Parliament to encourage Buxton, who was now coming under the kind of opprobrium that Wilberforce himself had been subjected to in the past and was growing understandably daunted.

Perhaps this last burst of energy he expended and the disappointment of the dozen year delay being proposed was the proverbial straw, for now Wilberforce's strength was waning rapidly. In May he went to Bath for some last possible palliative remedy coincident with the very time the resolution was introduced in London. By July it was clear his life was ebbing away; yet he had reserved for him one last joy, the one he had so long awaited. The bill to abolish slavery was looking certain to pass with the promised £20 million redemption fund intact and the egregious twelve-year apprentice provision stripped.[19] After so many disappointments, it was now a near certainty.

Wilberforce could only say, as the word of final assurance was brought to him, "Thank God that I have lived to witness a day in which England is willing to give twenty millions sterling for the Abolition of Slavery."[20] Tom MacAulay, son of Zachary MacAulay, now an MP, who had grown up with the Clapham team, reported after his visit with this news that Wilberforce "exulted in the success . . . as much as the youngest and most ardent partisan."[21]

On July 29, 1833, William Wilberforce left his earthly responsibilities behind, his two great objects having been achieved. Two days after his death, the third reading made final what was unprecedented in the history of mankind. In one year from the date of the bill, all of the slaves would be free.

---

19. Hague, *William Wilberforce*, 502–3. Hague, an MP himself, points out that the widely held understanding that Wilberforce received news of the bill's passage on the third reading on July 26 was erroneous because Parliament did not meet on that date to discuss slavery. The bill passed a week later. This myth began with his son Robert's biography and is reported by most of his biographers. Nevertheless, before his death, he was fully assured that the end had at long last come and he did die content in that hope.

20. Ibid., 308.

21. Metaxas, *Amazing Grace*, 275.

William Wilberforce, Shortly Before He Died

THE RISING OF THE DAWN

So it was on July 31, 1834, one year after William Wilberforce's burial, that eight hundred thousand slaves were freed from their captivity. Over three hundred years of suffering sanctioned by England's worldwide sea power and energized by their greed had ended. Unlike Jefferson, Wilberforce had not written his own epitaph or selected his burial place. Others would do that for him, specifying that it be with kings and heroes in Westminster Abbey—an honor he would likely have declined. Later England erected a memorial statue in his honor—much akin to Jefferson's perpetual recognition on the banks of the Tidal Basin in Washington. Yet the one glorious sight that his eyes could perhaps see from his heavenly vista that day was the only earthly epitaph he would ever have wanted. It was certainly one of the most important and dramatic events in the history of the world, yet it occurred far from the eyes of the powerful and the great. The historian G. M. Trevelyan tells of that auspicious morning: "On the last night of slavery, the negroes in our West Indian islands went up on to the hill-tops to watch the sun rise, bringing them freedom as its first rays struck the waters."[22]

Those to be freed wanted to watch their own emancipation as it rose upon the earth. Once again, the dawning rays of light, which had been but a portent in the past, now welcomed the end for which so many had labored for so long, pouring their energies out on behalf of men and women they never even met. In many ways this coda of the rising sun was the earnest for the "well done, good and faithful servant" that William Wilberforce received as he entered his well-deserved rest. The epitaph on his statue said the rest:

> To the memory of
> William Wilberforce
> (born in Hull, August 24th 1759,
> died in London July 29th 1833);
>
> For nearly half a century a member of the House of Commons,
> and, for six parliaments during that period,
> one of the two representatives for Yorkshire.
> In an age and country fertile in great and good men,
> he was among the foremost of those who fixed the character
> of their times because to the high and various talents to warm
> benevolence, and to universal candour,
> he added the abiding eloquence of a Christian life.
>
> Eminent as he was in every department of public labour,
> and a leader in every work of charity,

---

22. Ibid., 277.

whether to relieve the temporal of the spiritual wants
   of his fellow men
his name will ever be specially identified
with those exertions
which, by the blessing of GOD,
removed from England the guilt of the African slave trade,
and prepared the way for the abolition of slavery
in every colony of the empire:
In the prosecution of these objects,
he relied, not in vain, on God;
but in the progress he was called to endure
great obloquy and great opposition:
he outlived, however all enmity:
And, in the evening of his days,
withdrew from public life and public observation
to the bosom of his family.
Yet he died not unnoticed or forgotten by his country:
The Peers and Commons of England,
with the Lord Chancellor, and the Speaker at their head,
carried him to his fitting place,
among the mighty dead around,
here to repose:
Till, through the merits of Jesus Christ,
his only redeemer and saviour,
(whom, in his life and in his writings he had desired to glorify,)
he shall rise in the resurrection of the just.

KNOWING AND DOING

1. Do you think Wilberforce was being too cautious when he did not take up the abolition bill for fifteen years after the trade was abolished?

2. Was his time well spent focusing on the relief of exploitation of people in the India colony, or was it a strategic diversion from his purpose?

3. What allowed Wilberforce to step back from holding one of the two most prestigious seats in Parliament? Was that perhaps a good *personal* decision but not a wise move for advancing the *cause* of abolition? What kind of man steps down from an opportunity for greatness?

4. From what you know of William Wilberforce, what can you imagine as his approach to mentoring Buxton as his replacement to lead the last battles on slavery? What lessons might he have passed on? Do you think it unusual that he did not select someone from the Clapham Circle who had been closer to him in the trenches of the slave trade work?

5. "Finishing well" is a phrase taken from the Apostle Paul as he assessed his last days for his protégé, Timothy, hoping for freedom from a Roman jail but knowing he likely faced execution. Was Wilberforce correct in his dissatisfaction with what he had done, or do you think he finished well? Did Jefferson? Why or why not?

Interregnum

Quiet resolution. The hardihood to take risks. The will to take full responsibility for decision. The readiness to share its rewards with subordinates. An equal readiness to take the blame when things go adversely. The nerve to survive the storm and disappointment and to face toward each day with the scoresheet wiped clean, neither dwelling on one's successes nor accepting discouragement from one's failures. In these things lie a great part of the essence of leadership, for they are the constituents of that kind of moral courage which has enabled one man to draw others to him in any age.[1]

—S. L. A. MARSHALL

THE END OF THE earthly stories of William Wilberforce and Thomas Jefferson does not complete the larger story: the one in which their impact on history continued to play out into our own time. Neither the good nor the bad was interred with their bones. It all began with the common idealistic purposes of two young, privileged men whose countries would war with each other, make peace, go to war yet again, and then finally conclude with an unspoiled era of peace. They each died with their own separate and great legacies, yet they also ended at odds with each other. They finished their stories with the commitments of youth still intact in their minds; yet, as we have seen, so divergent in their actions in their last decades that the next generation continued on the strikingly different trajectories each man launched. Thus, their differing legacies on slavery—the Victorian Age and the Civil War—remained behind them to live on in shaping even more perplexing stories. Their times continued as conundrums for following generations to unravel in

---

1. *Armed Forces Officer.* The text of the book is found at the Air University website (the corporate university for developing Air Force leaders), Montgomery, AL, and was compiled by the U.S. Marine Corps Association for a 1975 edition.

social progress, the loss of empire, spilled blood, iron, and lasting racial and religious enmity. Despite these paradoxes, the lessons of their lives remain important to us, perhaps even more relevant to our own perplexing times as we see the need for wise, unselfish leaders who can put aside differences to bring about critically needed changes. We have a moral leadership gap ourselves that grows wider with the passing of these dangerous years.

Today both men are still cited to support one cause or another: sometimes wrongly, sometimes aptly. We have only to look at the number of recent biographies on the Founding Fathers or Jefferson's prominence in Supreme Court decisions, for example, to see the old sage's impact still. His writing is frequently drawn upon for expressions supporting freedom and denouncing government tyranny and his ringing words in the Declaration are still the most foundational expression of human liberty echoed across the globe.

As for Wilberforce, several books have recently been published about this once obscure man. There are "societies of benevolence" in America and England bearing his name that continue his focus to assist the poor and the oppressed. The release of the 2007 movie *Amazing Grace* also helped to reintroduce him to our era. The legacies of Jefferson and Wilberforce regarding human dignity and liberty are still powerful examples used to confront the problem of slavery, which has reappeared in a different guise in our own time.

These new yet ancient forms of slavery still have as their objective to derive a profit from human flesh. Traffic in human beings generates an estimated $32 billion annually, enslaving and exploiting an estimated twenty-seven million men, women, and children. Often this occurs in a type of bondage that pushes the limits of the human moral imagination even as the Middle Passage did centuries ago. For example, it is estimated that two million children are imprisoned in the international sex trade while another million are jailed, primarily with adults, awaiting sentencing for minor offenses simply to take them off the mean streets.[2] As trust in political leadership across the globe plummets to unprecedented low levels, the theme of an inability to resolve these and other seemingly intractable modern human problems grows ever larger.[3] In

---

2. These data are taken from the International Justice Mission website, http://www.ijm.org/ourwork/injusticetoday.

3. The dearth of effective leadership is a constant drumbeat. In "the paper of record,"

part, the events in 2007 surrounding the bicentennial observance of the end of the slave trade in England and the United States helped people remember the nature of these extraordinary events of long ago, linking them to our own challenges and offering a possible way forward. The examples of singular leadership by Jefferson and Wilberforce in transforming their cultures—although in strikingly differing ways—remain both legacies and lessons for our generation's concerns, whether global or local. We have a sliver of hope that the impossible may not be so; we may yet learn from these two men and their times.

The relevant question for today from their stories thus remains not so much "what?"—what is it that they actually did?—or even "how?"—how did they accomplish what they did?—but "why?" Why did their paths begin so promisingly yet end so differently on the towering moral issue of the eighteenth and nineteenth centuries with which both were so identified? In even tighter focus, why did one man succeed beyond all possible expectations, and why did the other man, a great man by any measure, still fail to lead or even lend a strong hand toward the end of slavery?

Beyond these two stories we also must ask how slavery could have been ended peacefully in a nation governed by an unbending monarchy committed to colonial rule. Equally perplexingly, why at the very same moment in history could slavery thrive in the nation founded on liberty, the colony that broke from England over the individual rights and liberty of men arising from created equality? Why was England prepared to pay an enormous portion of its national budget to free its slaves while so many in America held slavery to be an inescapable economic necessity though ultimately paid for in the currency of the blood and treasure of five savage years of war?

These are not easy questions in any sense. Perhaps we can only make a beginning response in these pages; nevertheless, they deserve serious reflection for our times to learn from and for we, ourselves, to

---

The New York Times, the search for effective leadership was a theme voiced repeatedly in a single month by national Op-Ed commentators Thomas Friedman and David Brooks and also in Senator Evan Bayh's valedictory. See, for example, Brooks' "What Next Mr. President?" February 12, 2010, and "The Power Elite," February 19, 2010; Friedman's "Adults Only Please," January 27, 2010, and "The Fat Lady Has Sung," February 21, 2010; and Bayh's "Why I'm Leaving the Senate," February 21, 2010. Also see "A Study in Paralysis," *The Economist*, February 18, 2010, for a more in-depth discussion of the need for leadership in American democracy.

learn from. We will then be in a better position not only to answer the three broader questions with which we began this quest but also to gain instruction for a time in a desperate search for effective moral leadership. Every era has its conundrums and hypocrisies, as do the individuals living in those times, so perhaps we can profit from theirs. At least we ought to begin to learn from these stories and their era.

To do so, we need perspective, some way to step back and reflect upon these two stories as if there were a balcony above the dance floor of life allowing us to see the entire, swirling scene whole.[4] Reflecting upon the stories of the comparative decisions and outcomes of the lives of Jefferson and Wilberforce, we can perhaps better take stock, by way of contrast, so that we can draw our own conclusions.

THE ROOT OF THE ANSWER

In any age, says eminent British historian S. L. A. Marshall, the essence of leadership is moral courage. At the root, the answers to our questions are to be found in timeless lessons emerging from fundamental beliefs that reside at the center of every person and guide every leader. The term we give to this core set of values is "worldview." Ultimately a worldview—what we deeply believe and how we interpret the reality of the world around us—is what transforms the vagaries of life into meaningful knowledge and action for an individual or for a nation. One's fundamental beliefs shape character, that tempered central place in a person that people sense and hence are willing to follow far more than title, charisma, or even power—at least for the long haul. If history is to be our teacher, the type of leadership that transforms cultures, institutions, and nations springs from timeless personal qualities we can observe if only in retrospect.

We have already seen that the life stories of Jefferson and Wilberforce demonstrate the powerful influence of *mentors* in shaping a course for their lives from the time they were young. These mentors did not simply help these young men in their professions; they also *embodied certain beliefs* and a clear sense of *purpose* and *vision* of their own—a worldview—that influenced their young protégés. It was the lives of these older men as much as their conversations and ideas that encouraged, instructed,

---

4. This metaphor is most effectively explored in the seminal leadership text by Heifitz and Lipinski, *Leadership on the Line*, 51–74.

and, most importantly, shaped each man, particularly in their early days, along the trajectories of life ahead.

It was also the network of followers, supporters, and colleagues—their historically unique *communities*—within which each man was able to execute and sustain exceptional efforts and accomplishments that neither man could ever have achieved alone: Madison and Monroe; Newton and Clarkson, et al. Here, too, Jefferson and Wilberforce were shaped as leaders by those around them in the experiences and ideas that they shared together and in the battles of life—even against all odds. As we have seen, it is not always possible to discern where our two protagonists ended and where their circles began, so intertwined were their ideas and applied energies. The community surrounding each man in America and in Britain held complementary worldviews within which they responded, often as one, and mutually helped to form each other into mature leaders that had a seminal impact. Indeed, these communities helped shape national movements toward change, whether it was the removal of poverty and oppression in England or the removal of the tyranny of the monarchy and the birth of republican liberty in America.

Finally, then, there is this third factor—worldview—that has quietly, almost unobtrusively, been on the stage during the telling of these stories. In many ways we will see in these next pages that it was their worldviews, above all, that forged their persistence and their critical decisions in sustaining their ultimately divergent life purposes. Here may lie the single most important clue for understanding the ultimate differences between these two men and their final accomplishments as leaders as they grew into maturity. It is at this juncture the missing piece by which we may best be able to answer, imperfectly to be sure, the "why" questions that remain before we draw our final conclusions. No better source exists than their pens. These next two chapters examine first Jefferson's and then Wilberforce's key writings to give us our final clues as to their stories, different courses, and eventual crossed purposes.

10

The Conundrum of Optimism

In every government on earth is some trace of human weakness, some germ of corruption and degeneracy, which cunning will discover, and wickedness insensibly open, cultivate and improve. Every government degenerates when trusted to the rulers of the people alone. The people themselves therefore are its only safe depositories. And to render even them safe their minds must be improved to a certain degree. This indeed is not all that is necessary, though it be essentially necessary. An amendment of our constitution must here come in aid of the public education. The influence over government must be shared among all the people. If every individual which composes their mass participates of the ultimate authority, the government will be safe . . .[1]

—Thomas Jefferson

Jefferson had long championed two key themes in the pursuit of the ideal form of liberty. One was an educated people progressively growing in knowledge and reason thus consequently in goodness. This advance would increase their capacity for self governance. The second, depended on the first: a nation ruled by the will of people not by the tyranny of national government or religious imposition. Well before he came to the presidency, these ideas were clearly set forth in his only published book. For a man whose writing was voluminous—it has yet to be fully catalogued—and whose scholarship, especially in the sciences and the classics, was at the forefront of any academic circle in that age, Jefferson surprisingly wrote only one full-length volume.

---

1. Peterson, *Thomas Jefferson*, 274.

As briefly discussed earlier, his *Notes on Virginia*[2] was originally intended to be a private project for a French colleague and a few friends. When its far wider publication occurred in France, it was a denouement he came to rue and perhaps his fear of its reception was the reason he never sat down to publish anything else of great note.

THE BOOK OF THE CENTURY?

This work is little known today except among Jefferson scholars and aficionados, but his eminent biographer, R. B. Bernstein, agrees with the assessment of many that it was likely "the most important American book published before 1800."[3] The depth of Jefferson's scholarship in a wide range of scientific, political, and sociological fields speaks of his being among the best and the brightest in America. It helped to solidify the recognition in France that Jefferson was one of the important Enlightenment thinkers of the day.

Characteristically, Jefferson also used the occasion to write at great length on the benefits of freedom and liberty enshrined in Virginia's state constitution, which he helped to draft. But governance was hardly his entire focus. There is no single source that expresses so much of Jefferson's thoughts on a range of subjects from science to geography, from farming to the nature of Virginia's people and the ideal form of economy—which rested on the noble yeoman farmer as its foundation. In *Notes* he also included important observations on slavery and the indentured African peoples. It was, of course, this section of *Notes* which had caused him the greatest reason to wonder whether he had gone too far beyond his peers in Virginia. It is also the place where we get Jefferson's most candid thoughts on the issue that troubled him all his days.

While a close reading might possibly have upset some plantation owners, for those seeking to understand his worldview, *Notes* may be the fullest expression, in one place, of the beliefs he held regarding the "peculiar institution" that characterized the American, postcolonial form of slavery. Here he expresses the thoughts on Negro inferiority and the nascent resentments he believed they must hold. These expressions he would later integrate into his more mature beliefs to explain his ambiguity about slavery's end and his lack of any desire to spearhead an aboli-

---

2. Ibid.
3. Bernstein, *Thomas Jefferson*, 60.

CHANGING AMERICAN MANNERS

Wilberforce was not the only one with a concern for the manners and morals of his native land. Jefferson's concern, however, was not necessarily to *reform* manners, but rather to describe them in *Notes* with more than a hint of disquiet. Query XVIII from his French friend asked about the manners and customs of the people inhabiting Virginia. Jefferson, while responding that it is a difficult question to answer—manners really being habits of which an individual is largely unaware (today we might use the term "culture" to describe this)—turns to slavery's impact on the owners as his response:

> There must doubtless be an unhappy influence on the manners of our people produced by the existence of slavery among us. The whole commerce between master and slave is a perpetual exercise of the most boisterous passions, the most unremitting despotism on the one part and degrading submissions on the other. Our children see this and learn to imitate it. . . . The man must be a prodigy who can retain his manners and morals undepraved by such circumstances.[4]

Jefferson keenly observes that one generation nurtures the habits of another. Not only is behavior affected but also the hearts of the children are marred. He had seen that slavery corrupted masters and slaves alike by the forced oppression that characterized this unusual way of daily life based upon the tacit assumption of superiority and inferiority that it engendered. So what roles *should* Virginia's or the nation's leaders play in this question if such moral corruption is evident?

Although it was not asked of him, Jefferson goes on to share his beliefs about what so-called statesmen have wrought in allowing slavery to continue, beginning with British rule and now carried forward on the ship of American independence. He could only anticipate ultimate and even grave consequences from such oppression:

> And with what execration should the statesman be loaded, who permitting one half of the citizens[5] thus to trample on the rights

---

4. Peterson, *Thomas Jefferson*, 288.
5. Ibid., 213–14. Earlier in *Notes* Jefferson responds to Inquiry VII on Virginia's

of the other, transforms those into despots and these into enemies, destroys the morals of the one part and the *amor patriae* of the other.... This is so true, that of the proprietors of slaves a very small proportion indeed are ever seen to labour. And can the liberties of a nation be thought secure when we have removed their only firm basis, a conviction in the mind of the people that these liberties are of the gift of God? That they are not to be violated but with his wrath? Indeed I tremble for my country when I reflect that God is just: that his justice cannot sleep for ever: that considering numbers, nature and natural means only a revolution of the wheel of fortune, an exchange of situation, is among the possible events: that it may become probably by supernatural interference! The Almighty has no attribute that can take sides with us in this contest.[6]

At once, Jefferson reiterates his belief that human liberty comes from God, the creator of men as he said in the Declaration, and that the nation that violates this truth courts God's wrath: his supernatural intervention will likely one day turn the tables on slave and master—if there is any justice in the universe. This is a paradox he somehow cannot resolve in his own mind over the course of his life. The problem for him was this: slavery is morally wrong; yet ending it unwisely might unleash the wrath of the oppressed slaves, with justice rightly on their side. That result would be worse in Jefferson's mind than the status quo. What, then, is the solution for a nation facing this dilemma? He responds in *Notes* with a hope, a careful optimism he is later to elaborate on as an agenda for the *future* generation raised in liberty and educated as none were before them:

> We must be contented to hope they will force their way into every one's mind. I think a change already perceptible, since the origin of the present revolution. The spirit of the master is abating, that of the slave rising from the dust, his condition mollifying the way I hope preparing, under the auspices of heaven, for a total emancipation, and that this is disposed, in order of events, to be with the consent of the masters, rather than by their extirpation.[7]

population that it is between half a million and six hundred thousand, with the ratio of free to slave being 11 to 10 with the gap narrowing. This led to the end of importing slaves in the first Virginia legislative gathering after 1776 and likely was part of the reason for Jefferson's long-held fear of revolt.

6. Ibid., 288–89.
7. Ibid., 289.

Twice citing his "hope," he would later repent of using these optimistic words as he declined to make future public comments on the course of slavery after 1786. Even though he saw the justice of the Almighty as being firmly on the side of the Africans, he chose from this point on to remain a neutral actor. He placed his trust not in any form of legal intervention by the state but rather in the gradual awareness of the masters that theirs was an immoral course needing correction. Self-awareness of his own culpability did not make it onto the pages of *Notes on Virginia*. His compartmentalization, as we would say today, seemed to allow for this manner of moral thought.

ON BEING HUMAN

In *Notes* Jefferson also responds to a question from his interlocutor concerning the laws of Virginia and their administration. Again, he moves from the descriptive narrative to his own philosophical and sociological reflections, this time on human differences. In his recounting, he dryly discusses courts, local governments, the origin of laws under British rule from 1607 up to his day, and the laws framed after independence which he had a large hand in drafting. He then discusses the intent to end slavery he drafted under these new laws, one which had originated with his first bill as a young man in the House of Burgesses.

The original bill authored in 1769 for emancipation in Virginia and a later amendment to it were to begin the process of liberty for the slaves by freeing the children born after the act was passed. The children were to be trained and equipped in order to foster their emigration back to the land of their parents' and grandparents' origin while simultaneous provision was to be made to import whites to take their place in the plantation labor market. Jefferson then asks the question, a natural one given the seemingly complete impracticality of his ideas: "Why not simply free the slaves and allow them to become free laborers?" (As we have seen, this is precisely what England did in her colonies in 1834.) Then he answers his own question:

> Why not retain and incorporate the blacks into the state, and thus save the expence of supplying, by importation of white settlers, the vacancies they will leave? Deep rooted prejudices entertained by the whites; ten thousand recollections, by the blacks, of the injuries they have sustained; new provocations; the real distinctions which nature has made; and many other circumstances,

will divide us into parties, and produce convulsions which will probably never end but in the extermination of one or the other race.—To these objections, which are political, may be added others, which are physical and moral.[8]

Here Jefferson begins to voice what he intends as his scientific views of their human differences, pointing primarily to his conclusions about the inferiority of African Negroes. His observations sound intensely racist and offensive to modern ears, not remotely expressing the sensibilities of the equality of birth he voices elsewhere. Although he responds as an eighteenth-century scientist, confining himself to what he believes are objective contemporary observations of a particular people's physical and behavioral characteristics, he also completely ignores, even as a scientist, their unique situation as a people. In this he sounds more the Virginia planter than the dispassionate scientist. It was a way of thinking and seeing he would never fully find his way around—even when the evidence contradicted it.

Jefferson is unable or unwilling to incisively address or even speculate upon the consequences for the slaves of their African forebears being forcefully uprooted, having their families and tribal affiliations destroyed, and then having their culture all but extirpated in a foreign land. Added to this complete dislocation was that they were purposely prevented by most masters and by some state laws from learning to read or write in this new culture where reading was essential. The hopelessness of this situation and its impact on people Jefferson cannot seem to bring himself to think upon. He confines his analysis to observation rather than speculation. He has no hypothesis to test, as a scientist might. He begins with the difference color makes:

> The first difference that strikes us is that of colour. . . . And is this difference of no importance? Is it not the foundation of a greater or less share of beauty in the two races? Are not the fine mixtures of red and white . . . preferable to that eternal monotony, which reigns in the countenances, that immoveable veil of black which covers all the emotions of the other race? . . . The circumstances of superior beauty, is thought worthy of attention in the propagation of our horses, dogs and other domestic animals; why not in that of man?[9]

8. Ibid., 264.
9. Ibid., 264–65.

One is left a bit slack-jawed at the seemingly dulled sensibilities he has of beauty, using the simile of farm animals. This is no less than a reflection of being a man of his times. The irony is that he clearly possessed the unexamined "habits" of thought he had earlier described as being obtuse. He seemingly has no recognition of how beauty is seen by the beholder; rather, his view of beauty is confined to the province of one race. This is an example of how emerging scientific discoveries such as those in sociology and anthropology concerning different people groups get caught up in false paradigms, as Thomas Kuhn has shown is common in science, a paradigm that cannot accept any anomalies.[10] The consequence of Jefferson's fixed paradigm only serves to distort the objectivity of his inquiry.

Similarly, Jefferson, through observation alone, addresses those differences in behavior that further his argument for his quixotic racial export-import scheme:

> In general, their existence appears to participate more of sensation than reflection. To this must be ascribed their disposition to sleep when abstracted from their diversions and unemployed in labor. . . . Comparing them by their faculties of memory, reason and imagination, it appears to me that in memory they are equal to whites; in reason much inferior . . . and that in imagination they are dull, tasteless, and anomalous. . . . But never yet could I find that a black had uttered a thought above the level of plain narration; never saw even an elementary trait of painting or sculpture.[11]

That conclusion of racial inferiority was later challenged by Benjamin Banneker, a freed Negro slave who had become a scientist and mathematician. He had devised a complicated astronomical almanac and wrote Jefferson as secretary of state in 1791 to convince him that the American societal conclusion of racial inferiority was unfounded. He also took Jefferson to task for ignoring his own stated principles in 1776.[12] Ignoring the slur, Jefferson wrote back:

> No body wishes more than I do to see such proofs as you exhibit, that nature has given our black brethren, talents equal to those of the other colors of men, and that the appearance of a want of

---

10. Kuhn, *Structure of Scientific Revolutions*.
11. Ibid., 265–66.
12. Miller, *Wolf by the Ears*, 76.

them is owning merely to the degraded condition of their existence, both in Africa & America. I can add with truth, that no body wishes more ardently to see a good system commenced for raising the condition of their body & mind to what it ought to be, as fast as the imbecility of their present existence and other circumstances which cannot be neglected, will admit.[13]

Jefferson wrote Banneker that his almanac would be conveyed to the Marquis de Condorcet, a French *philosophe* he knew from his days in Paris, as verification of Banneker's thesis. This response held two problems. One was that Banneker was seeking to encourage Jefferson to take up the cause of black equality he had written of almost twenty years before. Banneker was deeply disappointed. The second was that Jefferson made it clear to Condorcet that he considered one man no proof of an equal race. Later Jefferson would say it was likely Banneker had received help from his white neighbor and that in subsequent communications he had found him to be of a common mind and even "childish."[14]

Nevertheless, the Banneker correspondence would boomerang on Jefferson as his political opponents in 1796 would cite his calling blacks "brethren" and his writing to Banneker proof of Jefferson's unwise fraternizations.[15] It only sealed for him the conclusion he had earlier reached to remain silent on slavery.

Jefferson's doctrine of racial inferiority remained for his lifetime cloaked in scientific detachment, awaiting observed truth in a population of slaves. For these two reasons—the danger of revolt and the incompatibility with white society owing to stark human differences—Jefferson held that emancipation, when it finally came to the Africans in their midst, must be paired with return to their native Africa. Subsequently, this loss of hand labor must be overcome by the immigration of a similar number of white laborers who will work as free men.

These paradoxical and even fantastical views became more and more the beliefs that Jefferson would hold to as he came to higher office and finally to the end of his years. His thoughts here and later were an odd admixture of hope, detachment, and fantasy. He would continue to support slavery's demise based on the philosophical equality of man combined with an awareness of its immorality before God. But his re-

---

13. Peterson, *Thomas Jefferson*, 982.
14. Miller, 76–77.
15. Miller, *Wolf by the Ears*, 78.

sponse to moves to abolish slavery as seen, for example, in his interaction with Edward Coles, was to call for measures that could only be seen as unworkable or wildly idealistic, as in the diffusion "strategy" after the Missouri Compromise. His lifelong belief in the Negroes' inferiority and differences as expressed here, along with what he assumed would be their demonic rage for revenge when freed, prevented him from considering other solutions, such as England's approach in using reparations for owners and government fiat to bring its end. The near paralysis in his mind expressed itself in his steadfast inaction. It was a worldview that placed hopeful trust in future progress—morality and science going hand in hand—but no sense of personal responsibility. This was the heartbeat of his Enlightenment thinking, a perspective that framed his beliefs into his final days.

Biographer R. B. Bernstein observes that Jefferson's worldview was essentially complete shortly after the publication of *Notes* in 1787 as he returned from France for the last time: "He brought with him a strong commitment to a coherent ideology that ever afterward shaped his vision of the world and his place in it. . . . The fears and suspicions he developed by his forty fourth year will haunt him for the rest of his life."[16]

SELF-DEFENSE

A second written source for gaining a grasp of Jefferson's worldview lies in his reflections at the end of his life in 1821. As discussed earlier, Jefferson felt it imperative to write his own version of his life, or at least those few parts he considered important to him and to his legacy—the key events in which he participated, such as the writing of the Declaration. He did not trust posterity to get the story right as he never quite forgot his many opponents, even in old age. His own framing of events of his time and his thoughts thereon offer us further clues as to how his worldview had been formed regarding slavery particularly. Curiously devoid of personal detail it seems intended to put the author in a good light for posterity.

In this short *Autobiography*, Jefferson reiterates, if anyone doubts, that political and religious tyrannies are the gravest threats to man. No longer is it slavery as when he first began his vocation. He wants to make clear his principled opposition to the way the Constitution has been reinterpreted by the "monarchists," which he avers was an unpleasant sur-

16. Bernstein, *Thomas Jefferson*, 80.

prise to him when he returned from France. He claims that Washington secretly agreed with him in his opposition to both Hamilton and Adams in their misinterpretation of federal powers. Jefferson viewed these two men as misrepresenting the republican democracy of the spirit of '76. To the end, he saw Hamilton as the main instigator and archenemy.

Furthermore, Jefferson wanted to clarify, contrary to what others said, that he was a Christian, not an atheist as proclaimed in political attacks during his time in office. As proof, he offered his writings on Jesus, who for him was the prime ethical example for his life and whose moral teachings he sought to follow.

Finally, Jefferson attempted to clarify his role in ending slavery and his antipathy against its depredations to slave and owner as well as to the nation. His views against slavery, he said, expressed a belief he had held all of his life, using those words that Lincoln would later quote to support emancipation: "Yet the day is not distant when it must bear and adopt it [emancipation] or worse will follow. Nothing is more certainly written in the book of fate than that these people are to be free."[17] But Jefferson continues, as Lincoln would not, voicing the same concerns and solution he had written about forty years earlier: emancipation could not occur without deportation. Any other solution courted disaster:

> Nor is it less certain that the two races, equally free, cannot live in the same government. Nature, habit, opinion has drawn indelible lines of distinction between them. It is still in our power to direct the process of emancipation and deportation peaceable and in such slow degree as that the evil will wear off insensibly, and their place be *pari passu* filled up by free white laborers. If on the contrary it is left to force itself on, human nature must shudder at the prospect held up.[18]

Jefferson's mature views remained essentially unchanged despite forty years of life's experiences as America transformed from a British colony to a global power. Not for the first time have these questions been posed about why Jefferson's tortured internal conflicts led to inaction rather than to working toward emancipation. Two of the most common answers for this disconnect between his beliefs and his actions will help set the stage for a third answer that emerges primarily from telling these two stories together. The first theory that has been offered is

17. Peterson, *Thomas Jefferson*, 44.
18. Ibid.

that Jefferson and others of his age thought the task of abolition simply impossible. The second theory has been that Jefferson made a calculated choice that his career, or perhaps his aspirations to unseat the federalists and his posterity, precluded taking on the slavery issue.

AN IMPOSSIBILITY

One response to the question of Jefferson's retreat on slavery is represented in Joseph Ellis's excellent biographical study[19] in which he focuses primarily on understanding Jefferson's character. Ellis posits that the main reason Jefferson did not play a more active leadership role in the abolition of slavery is that he saw the problem as impossible to overcome. Ellis believes that the most important issue in Jefferson's mind was also expressed in his writings—emancipation had to be coupled with expatriation to avoid the racial conflagration he envisioned and to obviate the possibility of racial mixture that would dilute the white race.

Given such dire possibilities existing in his mind, to solve the decades-long issues which were ultimately raised during the Missouri question, 1.5 million slaves would necessarily have to be moved back to Africa. In addition, their owners would have to be compensated at a cost upwards of $900 million. This Jefferson calculated would take at least twenty-five years to accomplish, at which time the Negro birth rate would overtake events. He calculated that by then there would be three million former slaves, with many refusing to go back "home" now that they were free.[20] In Jefferson's thinking, emancipation was grossly impractical and could end only in a bloodbath with slaves killing their former masters. Of course, he did not foresee the consequences that inaction would foment forty years later on the plain of Gettysburg and in the dark forests of The Wilderness.

Jefferson's diffusion answer to the dilemma of either revolt or misogyny was even more fantastical than his deportation and immigration scheme. In Jefferson's own words, the spread of slavery was paradoxically to be its demise: "Diffusion over a greater surface would make them [slaves] individually happier, and proportionately facilitate the accom-

---

19. Ellis, *American Sphinx*.
20. Ibid., 320.

plishment of their emancipation, by dividing the burden on a greater number of coadjutors."[21]

When John Adams heard of this proposal, he called it "madness" and said this supposed "remedy" to the westward expansion of slavery was a distinct contradiction to the original agreement of the founders in the constitutional compromises which tacitly decided to confine slavery to the South. Their original understanding, Adams said, was to look toward a future when gradual abolition would occur in the few states that might still practice it (also an optimistic view, but not approaching Jefferson's fictions). Adams rightly held that diffusion would only guarantee a worsening of the problem and heighten the possibility of a civil war. In this, Adams was clearly prophetic even while Jefferson held to his theoretical fantasy, an inexplicable optimism for defining his vision for future public policy led by the next generation.

Ellis argues that Jefferson's procrastination on the vexing issue of slavery only exacerbated the problem for later generations, and the so-called diffusion solution obviously did not help resolve it as Jefferson seemingly believed it would in time. Instead, slavery's move westward into the Louisiana Territory only heightened the tensions and raised the stakes that change would bring about. A collective public rigor mortis set in as one generation gave way to another and tensions grew apace. The ever temporizing political response continued through a series of feckless administrations until war was the only option remaining.

Ellis's main thesis is that Jefferson's views evolved as he came to see the issue not as a slavery question per se. Rather, in his mind the proposed slavery solutions were merely a stalking horse for legislative tyranny; the real intent in abolition was consolidation of power by the "monarchist" successors to Hamilton. These were the shibboleths Jefferson maintained he had fought against all his adult life. Bringing about slavery's end at the hands of federal law he saw as being a mere pretext to assert federal power over the South in other domestic matters. Ellis calls this Jefferson's time-tested response to many perplexities: to see in every issue the opposing forces of good and evil, with evil always being defined as the consolidation of power in the hands of the few. Hence, Jefferson's response to many issues, this one being the most

---

21. Ibid., 321.

illustrative, often became oversimplification and exaggeration practiced in tandem.[22]

According to Ellis's perspective, what can be seen of Jefferson's leadership on the issue of slavery was a simple principle most leaders know very well: not to decide is to have decided already. In deferring action because of the seeming implacability of slavery's hold, Jefferson sowed the seeds of a far worse tragedy than the mythical black-on-white war he darkly envisioned at the onset of emancipation. Later, his argument became a pretext for the South to remain obdurate. In short, the principle Ellis sees operating in Jefferson is that states' rights prevail over federal governance (tyranny in his mind) of domestic issues. This principle then trumps the moral question about the rights of any one particular class of human beings. That group included not only Negro slaves but also American Indians and likely women as well.

One of Jefferson's successors, Harry Truman, made famous the saying "the buck stops here" as shorthand for his philosophy of governing. He had learned as a young captain in war and as a politician at local, state, and national levels that responsibility lay with the man at the top. There was no dodging it. Unfortunately, Thomas Jefferson walked away from any effort to end slavery and passed the buck to the next generation, although not without a great agony of soul it would seem.

PROTECTING POSTERITY

Jefferson's inaction on slavery was not solely a matter of a reasoned and reflective response to a political Everest. It also seems he thought long and hard about how history would come to see him, and his actions and beliefs on slavery concerned him. His careful, systematic saving of his papers and correspondence to the point of famously copying each letter he sent with a unique personal invention makes clear he knew that those who came after would judge him. Thus, a second perspective on Jefferson's reluctant leadership on slavery takes just this point, arising from perhaps the most comprehensive look at him and his decisions on the issue of emancipation. In John Chester Miller's classic work, *The Wolf by the Ears: Thomas Jefferson and Slavery*, we find a thorough mining of what lay behind the paradoxical combination of optimism and inaction in Jefferson.

---

22. Ibid., 324.

Miller agrees with Ellis's analysis that Jefferson saw in diffusion a possible answer to his dilemma over how it all would end, conveniently removing the specter of federal intervention and compulsion. Thus, consolidation (federal control of the resolution of slavery) was the greater enemy to oppose—one far worse than slavery itself. That is why Jefferson could reluctantly support the Missouri Compromise as a measure that supported states' rights while hoping the widening of slavery's practice to the west would somehow peacefully end slavery in time. For someone who did not believe in supernatural miracles, his diffusion hypothesis seems an odd departure for Jefferson as the man of reason. But Miller goes beyond this argument to posit an even broader explanation for Jefferson's reluctance to act on abolition:

> Jefferson read in the book of Fate that slavery was doomed, but the sequel of that event was not revealed to him. On the other hand, it was also legibly written in the Book of Fate that had Jefferson made himself conspicuous as a fervent, militant, and uncompromising abolitionist on the model of William Lloyd Garrison, or had he even gone so far as to suggest that whites and blacks ought to enjoy equal rights as citizens of the United States, he would not have succeeded in doing the things in which he took the greatest pride and by which he wished to be remembered by posterity. Nor would he have had the slightest chance of becoming President of the United States. . . . From the beginning of his career it was impressed upon Jefferson that he must choose between the preservation of his political "usefulness" and active opposition to slavery. In spite of his real and abiding abhorrence of the "peculiar institution," he was too much the political pragmatist, too intent upon achieving the lofty but realizable goals, and too much the product of his background as a Virginia slaveholder to grapple with this particular example of man's tyranny over man with the same fervor he had displayed contending against British tyranny.[23]

In Miller's judgment, Jefferson *did* make a choice: he chose his career over keeping hard on the trail of emancipation. Unlike Wilberforce, Jefferson achieved the highest office in the land, in part by silencing his voice on slavery in favor of raising it against the Federalists' tyranny. To have proposed to end slavery as a policy of his administration, Jefferson

---

23. Miller, *Wolf by the Ears*, 278–79.

would have had to embrace both federal intervention legislatively and the Federalists' philosophy generally. It was a bridge too far.

Thus, Thomas Jefferson chose instead to focus his waning energies on one last enduring cause—education for young Virginians in a great university that was free of religious tyranny. Had he instead chosen the course that Wilberforce had, he would not have been president nor would he likely have built the University of Virginia. But, as Miller also says, if he could only have seen the sequel, he might have chosen differently.

WHAT MIGHT HAVE BEEN

Fervent American abolitionist William Lloyd Garrison was one man in Jefferson's own time who regretted the absence of his leadership in never following up the beliefs on emancipation he expressed in *Notes* and in his drafting of the Declaration. Garrison felt that if Jefferson had acted decisively, "what an all conjuring influence must have attended his illustrious example."[24] He saw Jefferson as uniquely positioned to have led in putting an end to slavery in a way that would have had a powerful effect on his fellow countrymen. But Jefferson could only plead in his latter days—as he did to anyone like young Coles who came to him for support—that old age and exhaustion in public service left him with nothing to give to their cause at the end. It was the next generation's turn to solve the challenges of their day as moral consciousness grew. He believed he had done his part. But had he?

Was Garrison right about Jefferson? Would the most prominent remaining founding father have been the one voice that could have turned the tide toward abolition in the hearts of the people of the South? In C. S. Lewis's *Prince Caspian*, little Lucy similarly asks the great lion Aslan how something might have turned out had she only acted differently, to which Aslan replies: "To know what would have happened, child? No. No one is ever told that."[25]

Both Ellis and Miller have given us good answers on the Jefferson paradox: fanciful optimism for the future in the face of impossibility; career pragmatism in the face of failure. But there may be an even deeper answer to why Jefferson did not sustain his commitment to end slavery that emerges more clearly from the stories of his and Wilberforce's paral-

---

24. Ibid., 278.
25. Lewis, *Prince Caspian*, 380.

lel lives. Whether he was a revered leader in the highest offices in the land or afterward as an elder at the gate, the early fire of his youth for ending slavery had cooled. It seems his very beliefs had shifted markedly over these many years, even though in writing his commitment seemingly remained intact. Hence, the perspective that can allow us to bring together these other explanations for his inaction and add one more may be that of how his worldview evolved as he gained years and experience. Here may lie the seed that grew into the Jeffersonian tree that bore the fruit of temporizing for decades afterward, even as his political and philosophical progeny took their places at the helm after him.

EMBODYING BELIEFS

One of the most fascinating revelations that emerges from comparing the worldviews of Jefferson and Wilberforce is that each man was considered *in his time* to be almost the perfect embodiment of his core beliefs. Their worldviews—Enlightenment rationalism and Christian theism—then as now, lie at cross purposes in many ways. Not surprisingly, then, each man spoke forcefully against the ideas held by the other, even though they never met or debated their ideas with each other in writing. The disparity in their foundational beliefs existed simply as theirs uniquely; these were the two most important and contradictory philosophies of their day and they remain so in our time. This is a major reason why their stories remain so compellingly relevant for this millennium.

Jefferson's worldview sprang from a philosophy often referred to today as modernism. Modern philosophy is generally thought to have originated in the musings of René Descartes in the seventeenth century and is a manner of thinking that eschews all that has gone before. Hence, this was initially termed skepticism, a way of thinking about the world that did not rely either on past tradition or on the revelation contained in the Jewish Torah or the Christian Bible. It was also called rationalism in their day for its focus on reason alone as the source of knowledge. Indeed, this era would be called the "Age of Reason"[26] as science replaced theology as "the queen" of academia.

Descartes' purpose in starting from scratch so to speak was not to debunk religion but arose out of his desire to discover a different basis for arriving at the truth about God and life, one that was separate from

---

26. Will and Ariel Durant, *Age of Reason Begins*.

the disputes over truth that had been waged in the wake of the breakup of the Church into its Catholic and Reformed camps and the bloody wars that followed. He believed that by pure reason one could arrive at commonly shared truth by all who would seek to follow God, which, in turn, would not give rise to armed conflict over doctrine or authority. However, once he opened the floodgates to the separation of theology from revelation and tradition through use of reason, subsequent thinkers like Locke, Kant, and Rousseau carried the argument further. They sought in different ways to justify supplanting religion with science as the source of all truth and debunking revelation, miracles, and anything in the Bible that did not accord with modern thinking. This was the rising worldview of the eighteenth and then the nineteenth century into which both Jefferson and Wilberforce entered as boys and then men—the Enlightenment era. This shift in thought among intellectuals also explains the backdrop for many of the revolutionary tensions both men lived through in this time of transition for both their nations. Although each began life as a baptized member of the Church of England, ultimately they went their separate ways in the choices they made between religion and reason. This dichotomy remains today as a prominent source for public square debate even as a postmodern worldview is also on the rise, seeking to debunk any overarching truth whether it is from religion or from reason.

We have already seen that the young Jefferson was first nurtured in this new Enlightenment belief system in Williamsburg and then the lessons were extended by his law tutor, mentor, and colleague, George Wythe. It was a guiding perspective also shared by his two "pillars" and successors, Madison and Monroe, as well as by many of his colleagues in the founding and subsequent generations of the new nation. In his most important writings, speeches, and letters, Enlightenment thoughts stand out as they do in the major decisions he made in life. They are likewise carved in his epitaph. All three milestones for which he wanted to be known reflected the new underlying beliefs of his era: self-evident truth, private religious expression, and the central role of education in moral progress.

The worldview the Enlightenment began to supplant in the eighteenth century was that of the transcendent, whether it was the Catholic tradition or the outworking of the Reformation in Protestantism. In France, the revolution spawned by the Enlightenment was directed against the monarchy and the Catholic priests who were seen as in league with each other. In England and Scotland, the Church of England and the Church of Scotland (Presbyterian) replaced the Catholic Church and lasted as primary influences on the culture long after Wilberforce's death, engendering the Victorian era. In America, freedom of religion and the eventual removal of state support for a single church created an ethos of personal piety and community but, with exceptions, not a strong influence on national policy.

For Wilberforce, his Christian worldview was the one nurtured by John Newton and the "enthusiasts," who were among his most ardent supporters. It was not a set of beliefs that were inimical to reason but, as the Reformers and Wesley among others had affirmed, Scripture was the *prime* source for truth along with tradition, reason, and experience. However, for Christians this was hardly an "Age of Unreason."

The Christian worldview reflected a belief in the existence of God and in the universal reality of the four-chapter metanarrative of the Bible that provided meaning to history and embraced the life stories of individuals as part of the great story.[27] Knowledge was seen as not restricted to observation and reason alone. Transcendence encompassed certain verities that lay outside the realm of science and rested on God's self disclosure—revelation. Beauty, moral truth, the ultimate origin of life, the nature of love, and the life of virtue—these remained resistant to the probings of the scientist.

The Enlightenment fully expected moral progress in mankind as knowledge grew. This would allow man to control his own destiny more effectively than had superstitious and fractious religion. The objective of the Enlightenment was the same as that of Plato and Aristotle—to form a good society founded on what was true and real.

In contrast, the Christianity of Wilberforce and his Clapham colleagues held that Christ's resurrected presence in his Spirit affected all of life and indeed transformed a person's heart, resulting in an imperative for action—a clear *responsibility* to help "the least of these" even as Jesus

---

27. The four-chapter story of the Bible is I. the creation of the world; II. the fall of man and woman and nature itself to evil; III. the redemption of humanity and the world from the consequences of the fall by God's self-giving and substitutionary death in his son, Jesus; and IV. the restoration of all creation beginning quietly with the coming of Jesus and his kingdom on earth and ending in a new heaven and a new earth with the return of Jesus where bodily resurrected people would inhabit it eternally as originally intended.

did. This was where progress originated for the Christian—in extending the kingdom Jesus had proclaimed when on earth. Hence, knowledge led to action, but in *dependence* on God, whose Spirit provided guidance and strength. Transformation, moral transformation of a culture, was not based upon political power alone even as Wesley and Newton had admonished Wilberforce. Thus, education, while important, was not seen as the prime engine of social change.

In the Christian worldview, total self-reliance on man's reason that the Enlightenment posited made individuals little more than idol worshippers, placing hope in man, not God. However, the Christian perspective did agree in some measure with Jefferson's early view that the dignity of men as equals arose from creation. Human equality was not seen as simply a free-floating "right" secured by government alone, but rather as one to be protected by government. For Jefferson, this truth of equality emerging from creation is not necessarily a revelation gained from the Bible but rather a "self-evident" truth deriving from human reason—a common Enlightenment construct.

The interpretation and consequences of that meaning were to play out differently for Jefferson than they would for Wilberforce. Each man responded to the implications of his own worldview. Their lives reflect the truth that "ideas have consequences";[28] even more so, *beliefs* have consequences. Hence, contradictory beliefs ultimately led in their lives to contradictory actions and consequently divergent results as reflected in their parallel life stories.

DECODING JEFFERSON

One of Jefferson's most exhaustive biographers, Dumas Malone, makes the case that Jefferson's passion, his core purpose in life, was the eradication of "every form of tyranny over the *mind* (emphasis added) of man," and in this pursuit Jefferson gained a deep conviction that the course laid out by the Enlightenment philosophers was the right one—the one by which to live his life and to choose what most needed to be done during his time on earth. Malone perceived that Jefferson's belief, indeed his faith, was that:

> . . . human intelligence can unlock not only the treasure house of the past but also the secrets of the universe, thus leading man-

---

28. Weaver, *Ideas Have Consequences*; see also Lewis, *Abolition of Man*.

kind onward to a richer and better life, and that he personally was proceeding on that assumption.... This faith was so essential a part of his spiritual nature and of the framework of ideas within which he operated that he generally took it for granted. It was in the air that his spirit breathed; it was a major element in the intellectual climate in which he chose to dwell."[29]

In this Jefferson was hardly alone among his fellow revolutionaries, with Franklin serving as his spiritual predecessor and then colleague among the founders. But Jefferson would prove to be their leader in the new age, succeeding Franklin after his death in 1790. This was particularly true in the length to which Jefferson extended Franklin's system of thought and belief, which would exclude the transcendent and supernatural while embracing ethical teachings, particularly those of Jesus. For Jefferson, Jewish and Christian revelation was excluded as a valid source of *public* knowledge. For him, it was to be confined to the private sphere alone.

Bernard Bailyn, writing of the colonial era's philosophical influences, cites Rome as being the most prominent exemplar in informing the Revolutionary generation of what a great nation could be—more so than even Greece's democratic attempts. The founders also took note of how a nation could decay as its moral and political underpinnings eroded. Bailyn concludes:

> The classics of the ancient world . . . are everywhere illustrative and not *determinative* (emphasis added) of thought. They contributed a vivid vocabulary but not the logic or grammar of thought. . . . More directly influential in shaping the thought of the Revolutionary generation were the ideas and attitudes associated with the writings of Enlightenment rationalism. . . . It is not simply that the great *virtuosi* of the American Enlightenment—Franklin, Adams, Jefferson—cited the classic Enlightenment texts and fought for the legal recognition of natural rights and for the elimination of institutions and practices associated with the *ancien regime*. . . . In pamphlet after pamphlet the American writers cited Locke on natural rights and on the social and governmental contract, Montesquieu . . . on the character of British liberty and on the institutional requirements for its attainment,

---

29. Malone, *Jefferson, The Virginian*, 101.

Voltaire on the evils of clerical oppression.... The pervasiveness of such citations is at times astonishing.[30]

From his Williamsburg days onward, Jefferson, this lifetime voracious reader of the classics as well as an acquirer of new ideas, continued to grow in his admiration of the Enlightenment. He sought to unseat the place of the strictures found in revelation in Scripture and its interpretation by the church that he believed had undermined Europe. In Jefferson's thinking, the adoption of these ideas by the American colonies in financial support of the church, for example, ran against every tenet of the Enlightenment scientific age and even of justice itself. He saw Christianity, especially the clerical interpretation of its implications for belief, as a distortion of the truth as taught and lived by Jesus. Jefferson's reaction against religion's hold on conscience culminated in his intent to replace it with a more rational and scientific explanation for political and moral action. This is why he expressed such great pride in his Bill for Religious Freedom in Virginia and included it as one of only three accomplishments for which he wanted to be remembered, carved forever in stone.

But what he believed about God or a god—that which is the really real—is a key component in anyone's worldview and for Jefferson, like in other places, it is not entirely clear. He was not simply an atheist as many would accuse him. Although not an orthodox Christian like Wilberforce, he did admire Jesus as he often stated in his defense. As he wrote to Adams regarding the ethical teachings of Jesus,

> [I]n extracting the pure principles which he taught, we should have to strip off the artificial vestments in which they have been muffled by priests, who have travestied them into various forms, as instruments of riches and power to them.... There will be found remaining the most benevolent code of morals which has ever been offered to man. I have performed this operation for my own use by cutting verse by verse out of the printed book, and arranging the matter which is evidently his, and which is easily distinguishable as diamonds in a dunghill.[31]

Jefferson was applying reason, not belief, to the biblical texts, especially those that contained Jesus' life and teachings, in order to ar-

---

30. Bailyn, *Ideological Origins of the American Revolution*, 27.
31. Cappon, *Adams–Jefferson Letters*, 384.

rive at a rational moral code of conduct he could support. "For the use of reason," he noted, "everyone is responsible to the God who planted it in his breast, as a light for his guidance."[32] This was the root of his faith. Seeing was believing; reason and science were the only ground for Jefferson's idea of the truth in which his faith was grounded—a faith that progress would one day extinguish slavery. In fact, he dispenses with the Christian notion of faith by saying were he to found a new sect, his basis would be "the reverse of Calvin's, that we are saved by our good works which are within our power, and not by our faith which is not within our power."[33] In contrast, Wilberforce's faith in the transcendent God found in Jesus was what fueled his sense of responsibility to God's love as well as his persistence in believing that his actions were not only guided but also supported by God.

THE EPICUREAN

There remains one other telling note from Jefferson's pen that reflects his beliefs, adding further clarity to how his worldview influenced his actions. Toward the end of his life, he wrote a letter to William Short, his former secretary where Jefferson reveals another all too rare glimpse into his beliefs:

> I too am an Epicurean. I consider the genuine, (not the imputed) doctrines of Epicurus as containing everything rational in moral philosophy which Greece and Rome have left us. . . . I have sometimes thought of translating Epictetus (for he has never been tolerably translated into English) by adding the genuine doctrines of Epicurus from the Syntagma of Gassendi and an abstract from the Evangelists of whatever has the stamp of the eloquence and fine imagination of Jesus.[34]

Jefferson was seemingly searching for a way to build a bridge between outright skepticism and Christianity without adopting a supernatural belief. Epicurus was attractive to him as a Greek philosopher whom Rome later took up among its privileged classes. He was attracted to this philosophy as it formulated a moral way of life leading to happiness on earth for it held this was all there is. Epicurus wrote during a

---

32. Gaustad, *Sworn on the Altar of God*, 29.
33. Ibid., 134.
34. Peterson, *Thomas Jefferson*, 1431.

time of war in Greece and the decline of Athens. He sought to formulate a way to live that did not embrace either Plato or Aristotle with their insistence on building a republic with a transcendent focus founded on virtue. Rather, Epicurus advocated a principled withdrawal as the most moral course, eschewing politics and immersing oneself in a life of moderated pleasure—not self-indulgence. Happiness, he said, was based on the truth that all was material—even human beings were made of atoms, devolving again to atoms once again upon death. If all was material, then death held no sway over one's mind and happiness was to be found in a good and virtuous life well lived. One can easily see in Jefferson's periodic withdrawals to Monticello this ambiguity between Epicurean belief in eschewing politics and his personal ambition to rid the country of governmental tyranny as the Enlightenment tenets held. He appears to lean more toward the side of the Epicureans in his last years.

At the end, as he wrote to Short, "My business is to beguile the wearisomeness of declining life, as I endeavor to do, by the delight of classical reading and of mathematical truths, and by the consolations of a sound philosophy, equally indifferent to hope and fear."[35] If he was a true Epicurean, death held no fear and Christianity no hope. Living in retirement in his beloved Monticello, eating of the fruits of its fields and drinking of the wines he introduced into Virginia, Jefferson was living out what he believed at his core despite the specter of bankruptcy in doing so.

LIVING IN THE FUTURE

In one sense, Jefferson was already living in the future as a way to accommodate the present, a strategy which ameliorated the latent sense of guilt over slavery's intractable hedgehog-like grip on the new nation. He saw America as the test bed for the Enlightenment and as the foundation for the perfect political and moral order, ordained by God in human reason, becoming an example to other nations of how tyranny's reign could be overcome—political and religious tyranny alike.

Ironically, this view of the American example was similar to that of the Puritan notion of America as the "light on the hill," selected by God as the Polaris to the world by living in belief and trust in God. This was the religious view Jefferson firmly rejected, substituting his own amalgamation of beliefs, although always including in his thinking the

---

35. Ibid., 1432.

future abolition of slavery—one day. He naturally expected it to occur first in Virginia, as its educated young men would rise up to denounce this moral perversion (by that time diffusion would have ameliorated its evils), having been trained to think thus at Mr. Jefferson's University. Yet in arriving at this understanding, he evidenced a lack of self-awareness in at least two critical places in his thinking.

CONTRADICTIONS

The first contradiction was that in many ways Jefferson did precisely what he accused the religious priests and their followers of doing by inserting his own faith into law, and by being paid to do so by the state. For example, his Bill for Religious Freedom, which ended state sponsorship of religion in Virginia, and his shaping of the Bill of Rights and even later Supreme Court decisions, rested on his "faith" in reason. He did not seemingly realize that ideas and worldviews are not neutral simply because they are based on reason rather than religion, as followers of the Enlightenment would contend. Thus Jefferson clung fervently to the faith that reason would be the engine for the abolition of slavery sometime after he ended his life's journey. This was a belief he held to just as doggedly as Wilberforce held to a faith in God that he would bring about emancipation which enabled him to persist in that work to the end.

The second contradiction in Jefferson's thinking concerned the presence of readily observable facts regarding what was occurring across the Atlantic. Jefferson did not have to wait for the grave to see the beginning of the end for slavery. Scientific observation, that foundation of knowledge revered by the Enlightenment, would show that it was possible to do what he rejected as being so and to accomplish it without bloodshed or chaos. Three years before his death, Parliament had already begun to take up the bill that would end slavery in England's colonies. The "impossibility" of slavery's demise was being debunked in his time. In fact, other countries had already abolished slavery, if not in their colonies, then internally, including his arch-nemesis, England, in 1772. Championed primarily by Christian activists in England, the slave trade itself had been abolished in every European country except Brazil (Portugal) before Jefferson died. Only seven years after Jefferson lay beneath his epitaph, the English colonies ended slavery itself, again soon followed by several other European countries. Yet it was not the Enlightenment ideas of the "rights of man" so much as Christian action which flowed from belief that contributed to these vast changes in the culture and practices of the day. All this was beginning in Europe and in its colonies in the Americas in Jefferson's lifetime.

The moral revulsion against slavery that Jefferson had predicted in subsequent generations in America did indeed occur within years of his death and followed the course of England and Europe decades earlier. The changes in American moral culture were not merely a result of advancements in science and education but stemmed more forcefully from the efforts of Christian abolitionists such as William Lloyd Garrison and Frederick Douglass. It was these activists and others who began to agitate for a host of changes in the national social order in America, including the abolition of slavery in all of the northern states. Ironically, an alternative interpretation of the Bible and Christian beliefs would be used to *justify* slavery's practice in the South. What we now see as a selective reading that human beings were meant to be unequal, with one race oppressed by their superiors, was put forward as a so-called biblical teaching that was eerily like Jefferson's views expounded from his scientific rendering of humanity's differences.

Jefferson's Enlightenment paradigm simply could not allow him to see that his own ideas were tantamount to those of a religion, for man cannot operate without beliefs in something, be it God or reason. Nor could he take into his worldview by simple observation what was already happening in England and Europe and was beginning to happen in America in a way he did not envision. If anything, once he began the shift to his mature "faith," he held more firmly to these beliefs as he grew older. For Jefferson's philosophical and political heirs, Madison and Monroe, a spiral toward war was all that remained.

In his Enlightenment worldview, Jefferson was indulging in what commentator Mike Metzger calls an unwitting form of addiction:

> The Enlightenment hooked us on a drug called *progress in this life*, which is why George Orwell said that futurism is the major mental disease of our time. . . . Boston University professor Peter Berger warns that whoever slurps up the Enlightenment ideas had better have a long spoon. He "will find his spoon getting

shorter and shorter—until the last supper when he is alone at the table, with no spoon at all and an empty plate." The empty plate is the crushing disappointment from failed visions.[36]

The ultimate failure of Jefferson's optimistic worldview came with the election of Abraham Lincoln in 1860. Lincoln put into action what Jefferson sought to avoid by inaction and self-deception: the great national hypocrisy of the coexistence of freedom and slavery could only be resolved by a strong national government. Lincoln understood what Jefferson's nemesis Hamilton did, as did Washington and Adams, although they, like Jefferson, never acted upon their beliefs: that liberty for all—a national *moral cause*—can only be secured by national unity in action. Preservation of the union meant that the great unresolved moral question could not be left to either individuals or the separate states. The three fig leaves—diffusion, moral progress through education, and forced emigration of black Americans—these hapless products of Jefferson's worldview, became exposed for what they were: optimism at best, hypocrisy at worst. It took a Civil War to prove that beyond all doubt.

However, the ultimate failed vision of Jefferson's and many others' Enlightenment optimism occurred six score years after his death. In the trenches of "the war to end all wars," followed in less than two decades by the Nazi Holocaust, there ended whatever dream remained of rational optimism ushering in a new day for humanity. Our day still seeks the answers.

KNOWING AND DOING

1. Jefferson shared a worldview with many of his time that man's moral progress would follow his scientific progress. How justified were they in that observation based on your own experience or your knowledge of history?

2. Do you think that Joseph Ellis's "impossibility" explanation or John Chester Miller's explanation of "concern for posterity" offers the best account of Jefferson's reluctance to have anything to do with the slavery question after 1786?

---

36. Metzger, "Rear View Mirrors, Part Two"; the statement by Berger is from his book *Rumor of Angels*, 22.

3. Was William Lloyd Garrison right in his assessment that Jefferson could have made the difference in averting the Civil War had he led the abolition effort or even lent his name to sponsoring the cause?

4. Jefferson stated that "diffusion" to the western states would ultimately be the paradoxical strategy for ending slavery. Is there any justification for how such a brilliant man could hold this view, or was it simply a case of massive self-deception?

5. How would you describe Jefferson's overall worldview? Is such a worldview still prominent today?

6. Many historians and philosophers believe that the Holocaust ended the Enlightenment Project by exposing the failure of man's moral progress in the gas ovens and other brutalities of World War II. Is this a correct assessment, or do some ideas of the Enlightenment still hold important moral sway today?

7. Do you agree that a person's worldview is ultimately determinative in shaping his or her decisions and behavior? Why or why not?

11

The Puzzle of Persistence

What man actually needs is not a tensionless state but rather the striving and struggling for some goal worthy of him. What he needs is not the discharge of tension at any cost, but the call of a potential meaning waiting to be fulfilled by him.[1]

—Victor Frankl

If Thomas Jefferson can be described as a sphinx, what might be an apt metaphor for William Wilberforce? Hedgehog might be a good fit, perhaps?[2] This obscure little animal relies upon one resolute, unyielding protective course for the survival of its species and maintains one daily focus for a source of food. The hedgehog is a model of single-mindedness. The life of Wilberforce, although not one of curling up and waiting for the tide to subside, is a conundrum like Jefferson's. We are puzzled about why he persisted in an almost single-minded manner against the forces arrayed against him for more than forty years. Like Jefferson's optimism about slavery's demise in the face of the intransigent opposition of slaveholders and his own ambiguities, Wilberforce's persistence leaves those who would understand him with similar questions of "why?" His example, like Jefferson's, is not like any written in the previous pages of history.

---

1. Frankl, *Man's Search for Meaning*, 166.
2. A hedgehog is characterized as being undersized but nevertheless undaunted. It is cute but almost impervious to attack, not because of its fierceness but owing to its spiny armor. When confronted, the hedgehog does one single thing very well—it rolls into a tight ball and refuses to budge. Hedgehogs likewise have a single-minded devotion to ridding the world of insects, which they do with great, daily diligence over their lifetime.

Although it is not easy to explain the anomaly of Wilberforce's persistence—the singularly rare trait to endure over an entire lifetime—he left clues for us. Here are the salient questions before us: What produced his almost unfailing, cheerful keeping on as he led the fight against slavery for decades? How could he keep going in the face of repeated failure and virulent opposition from even the highest office in the land, the king? Where did his willingness to sacrifice his reputation and public acclaim, as well as sacrificing his health and his wealth, come from?

As we near the end of the story of two lives, the answers begin to clarify themselves in ways that allow us to better see Jefferson and Wilberforce as their contemporaries perhaps could not yet comprehend—by seeing them in the light of each other. In some ways, having examined Jefferson's tortured on-again, off-again romance with slavery's end, we can better understand Wilberforce. To begin this comparison, it may be best to start with a story told by an observer who traveled to England from America.

A VISITOR IN COMMON

One of the many ironies that accompanies the comparison of these two men is that both were the subject of William Lloyd Garrison's personal entreaties for compassion on behalf of the Africans in slavery. Garrison, who had decried the loss of Jefferson's leadership on slavery in America, would later visit Wilberforce in England in 1833 shortly before the old campaigner's death. Thus it was that Garrison became the unwitting cause of Wilberforce's last earthly act on behalf of the slaves.

Garrison came across the Atlantic to tell Wilberforce, in person, that one of the multitudes of causes to which Wilberforce had lent his name, the American Colonization Society, was in fact a racist organization seeking to rid America of freed Negroes by using false promises to entice them to relocate to Africa. Garrison asked the aged former member of Parliament if he would help to withdraw formal British support for the ruse his government had unwittingly abetted—embarrassingly, at Wilberforce's behest. Despite being all but blind and in desperately failing health, Wilberforce was led to make inquiries, then satisfied himself that the case was indeed falsely sold to him, and owned up that he had been badly deceived. Characteristically, despite being quite feeble, he acted promptly in gaining the necessary signatures to mount an official British protest against the Society, including documents of support from his old friends of the Clapham Circle who by now were internationally respected: Thomas Buxton, Zachary MacAulay, and James Stephen, who took the redress on themselves for their old friend. Each had been mentored by Wilberforce and each continued as a colleague, although now they were luminaries in their own right. British support was hastily withdrawn—Garrison's mission with Wilberforce, unlike with Jefferson, was a success.

Garrison subsequently wrote about the three days he spent with the aged Wilberforce, marveling at the traits he observed in this heroic figure: "a dovelike gentleness, amazing energy, deep humility, and adventurous daring."[3] His searing disappointment at Jefferson's reticence to support emancipation in America was now counterbalanced by Wilberforce's forceful, immediate, and vigorous action at the very end of his life. One can only wonder whether Garrison longed for Wilberforce to have taken on advocacy on behalf of the slaves' cause in his homeland.

We also cannot ignore one final irony here. Had the American Revolution failed, Wilberforce and his colleagues would have ultimately been successful in peacefully freeing the slaves in the American colonies at the same time the slaves in the West Indies colonies were freed—in 1834, a full thirty-one years before the death toll of the Civil War ended. That irony would not have been lost on William Lloyd Garrison.

AN OLD WORLDVIEW

What were the differences in Thomas Jefferson's counterpart in England that Garrison saw so clearly? What engendered in the dying Wilberforce the energy, courage, and forceful, timely action right to the very end? In these answers and in those we have focused on throughout, worldview comes to play the most prominent part in both men's lives.

Wilberforce's story shows that belief became a sense of responsibility to act, not giving the deference to the future when the task might be easier. This was likely the key underlying trait that allowed him and his Clapham Circle to make a mark on history. If the Enlightenment sought to push aside the old in favor of the new, Wilberforce and the Claphamites embodied the belief that G. K. Chesterton often affirmed: "Nine out of ten of what we call new ideas are simply old mistakes."[4] The

---

3. Belmonte, *Hero for Humanity*, 321.
4. Chesterton, "Why I Am a Catholic."

new ideas and strategies of Wilberforce and his allies were political and tactical, but the foundation they built upon was an old one: the historical faith of the many generations before them. This was a faith that seemed long forgotten in the European rush to exploit the colonies' riches with African laborers.

BELIEVING IS SEEING—THEN ACTING

To fully understand Wilberforce as a leader, as a man, and above all as a politician with Christian beliefs, we must understand what he deeply believed in most passionately that caused his unusual commitments. These beliefs undergirded all of his political accomplishments, his leadership philosophy, and certainly his entire life. It is not enough to simply say that he was "religious." That label only allows us the distortion of our contemporary stereotypes, especially of religious politicians, and might cause us to dismiss the bedrock upon which the Claphamites built their transformation of British moral culture. This is perhaps best revealed, as with Jefferson, in Wilberforce's own writings.

In 1797, in what then and now was remarkable for a politician, Wilberforce published a book he had long been pondering, composing it in his mind, carrying it about on scribbled notes in his pockets, and stuffed elsewhere. Its purpose was neither to promote himself nor to advance his political agenda. Rather, his target audience was Britain's leaders, and his theme was directed at how their manners and morals shaped—or misshaped—the culture. This work was given the effusively worded title *A Practical View of the Prevailing Religious System of Professed Christians in the Higher and Middle Classes in This Country Contrasted with Real Christianity*. Today we shorten that title to *Real Christianity*, a more accurate rendering for a more general audience.

Like Jefferson, he had only one book in him and very modest publication goals. The initial printing of five hundred copies seemed an accurate assessment of the religiously skeptical market in the Age of Reason. Stunningly, it went through several reprints in England and then in America, becoming a best-seller in those countries and in many others when it subsequently was translated into a dozen or more different languages. Its reception was completely unforeseen by the author.

The context leading to the publication of this extraordinary book was directly related to Wilberforce's two great objects and likely arose from the lowest point in the battle. He had been at the business of abolishing the slave trade for a good ten years and had just experienced the heartbreaking failure in 1796 of unexpectedly losing the final vote when his colleagues chose the theater over duty. The well of despondency and time of reflection he fell into seem to have also become the crucible for birthing the long delayed book.

He saw by this time that it was the leaders of England—the upper classes—who had the primary responsibility for changing the culture and were the main roadblocks to change. Their leadership needed to be based upon the historic core beliefs that they had long ago been abandoned in favor of personal pleasure. Like Jefferson, the British upper classes had become great admirers of the Epicureans and particularly the Roman Lucretius in their devotion to living a good life of pleasure seeking, a life Wilberforce himself had eschewed after his great change (and one which Jefferson would not have been comfortable with either). He hoped to see the core, traditional beliefs recovered, he wrote, for the good of England. This he firmly held would lead to an end to the greatest societal woe he felt its leaders evidenced—not slavery but *indifference*.

By 1797, Wilberforce could have written with expertise about more popular subjects: his tell-all conversion from rake to moral leader, for example; or his own challenges in living out his faith as a politician with some seamy behind-the-scenes tales about his colleagues. Most likely, he would have been expected to write about the political issues for which he was famous and use the book to seek widened public support, particularly concerning ending the slave trade and caring for the neglected and exploited poor. Curiously he does none of this. Slavery is mentioned in the book only once in a favorable aside about the Moravians who were traders in the West Indies but who opposed slavery. His was a much larger vision, and he explained the book's purpose was to:

> promote the happiness of his fellow creatures to the utmost of his power . . . he who thinks he sees many around him, whom he esteems and loves, labouring under a fatal error, must have a cold heart, or a most confined notion of benevolence, if he could withhold his endeavors to set them right from an apprehension of officiousness.[5]

But he did not want to be misunderstood as playing "holier than thou" either.

---

5. Wilberforce, *Real Christianity*, 72.

As he further explained his purpose to John Newton, this was to become his credo not only for what he believed but also for how he would live as a politician and a Christian and what he aspired to for the change in British culture and religious practice:

> It is a great relief to my mind to have published what I may term my manifesto, to have plainly told my worldly acquaintances what I think of their system and conduct and where it must end. . . . It is the grace of God only however that can teach and I shall at least feel a solid comfort from having openly declared myself as it were on the side of Christ and having openly avowed on what my hopes for the well-being of my country ultimately become.[6]

MORAL COURAGE

We first need to see Wilberforce's decision to write such a book as a serious risk to his career:

> . . . the courage apparent in this work is far from being inconsiderable. The manner is mild, indeed; but the undertaking is bold and hazardous. The author, in attempting it, risked everything dear to a public man and a politician as such—consideration, weight, ambition, reputation. He exposed himself to all the misapprehensions and hostility which attach to so noble an avowal of the humiliating doctrines of vital Christianity in a corrupt age. But he writes as one who did it deliberately and advisedly.[7]

Like Jefferson when he wrote his *Notes*, Wilberforce wrote boldly about an unpopular topic, but the difference was he never walked away from the implications that he raised, knowing he was setting a high bar for himself to live up to and opening himself up for being called overly judgmental or a hypocrite. He argues that what he is about in this book is the particular realm of the politician—even more so than the cleric. His was a wholly unique view then and certainly now, connecting together as it did the vocation of the politician with extending the values of the Christian faith—seen as empathy and responsibility—into the national culture. The rise or decline of religious faith he sees as "intimately connected with the temporal interests of a society,"[8] which he held fell di-

---

6. William Wilberforce to John Newton, 1797, The Newton Project.
7. Ibid., Introduction by Rev. Daniel Wilson, viii-ix.
8. Ibid., 72.

rectly within the realm of his political calling. We should also note how Newton has now thoroughly convinced him of the connection between his faith and the grittiness yet importance of his political vocation.

Wilberforce, in the wake of ten years of failure, seems convinced that he must confront England's leaders now because he has seen how what today we call "cultural Christianity"—form not substance—has had such a deleterious effect. In his perspective, the "prevailing religious system" impinged on every aspect of society. Not only was there a lack of concern for the slave trade, but this watered down hull of religion also threatened to bring England down in all quarters to the depraved and anarchic level of France.

While slavery and neglect of the poor were among the *symptoms* he was concerned with, Wilberforce believed that as a politician he must address the underlying disease, *the root cause* of the lack of concern and action on many fronts. In his decision to publish this book in the wake of devastating political failure there may lie a key to unlocking the secret of Wilberforce's persistence as a political leader and as the man who transformed England under what he would describes as God's providence. His words and his life, his calling and his beliefs—these should be seen as one, a connected whole, in a way uncommon on the pages of history. His worldview was not the dualism of Jefferson, and in this book he draws a bright line between himself and the American president's beliefs.

CURING THE UNDERLYING DISEASE

Wilberforce's appeal to his peers in upper class society is one asking them to consider not so much a change in private piety or outward religious practice but instead a change of heart—for their own good and for the good of the country. He sets forth his argument in seven chapters. In the first four, he diagnoses the disease, which he says expresses itself in the symptom of selfishness of every stripe. He labels this national spiritual illness as a four-pronged case of what he terms "inadequate conceptions:" "of the Importance of Christianity;" "of Human Nature;" "of God and of Christian Behavior;" and "Concerning the Nature and Discipline of Practical Christianity." He then turns in chapter 5 toward positive solutions to these ills of indifference, setting forth what Christianity is *intended* to be. Here he sees Christian faith not as simply another form of intellectual attainment or, as many held at that time, reserved for a quiet, personal piety, but a genuinely "more excellent way" of influencing life choices. Then in the final chapters he presents some "Practical Hints" that shows Wilberforce as a man more attuned to faith and daily life than to ethereal theology.

At the heart of his indictment of contemporary religion is the observation that many professing Christians do not have any understanding of what real Christianity is all about—it has become at best a sham. By "real" he means the Christianity of the Bible that has been historically understood and handed down from the beginning, not that which the Enlightenment had rejected as incompatible with reason.

He says that this new philosophy influenced by the Enlightenment has begun to corrupt the historical beliefs of the Church of England, birthing a pablum called Unitarianism. Ironically, this was Jefferson's religious choice at the end of his life as he turned away from Anglicanism. So confident was Jefferson in its spread that he affirmed his "trust that there is not a young man now living in the U.S. who will not die a Unitarian."[9]

Wilberforce next expresses alarm at the future of the nation and of the upbringing of its children if they are being reared in a system of mere moral maxims that are winked at and have little connection to daily reality: "Let us beware before it is too late. Let us beware that, in schools and colleges, Christianity is almost—if not altogether—neglected. We cannot expect those who pay so little regard to this great object of education of their children to be more attentive to it in other parts of their children's conduct."[10] Here of course Wilberforce stands in direct contradiction to Jefferson's view of education seen in the design of his university." Jefferson at the same time was already formulating his retirement plans for education in Virginia where the removal of Christian teaching from the curriculum of the University of Virginia was to be an important change.

SENSE OF RESPONSIBILITY

Two central themes that run throughout Wilberforce's book form his core beliefs and ultimately his entire worldview. In these dual themes we begin to find another insight into a deeper understanding of why such persistence—what kept him keeping on. The first is that of responsibility.

9. Gaustad, *Sworn on the Altar of God*, 146.
10. Wilberforce, *Real Christianity*, 2.

Wilberforce sees in the teaching of the moribund church and hence in the beliefs and behaviors of the leaders of England a diluted and distorted view of Christianity and an eagerness to leave it in its "proper" place—in church, confined to Sunday. This neglect, this dualism, he holds, belies an understanding that man is born with a responsibility—to his Creator and to his fellow human beings. Such inadequate conceptions as he calls them divorces faith from the rest of life. Wilberforce observes that this plays out in the neglect to care for those in need by those who are responsible for public policy. One does not get the impression that he is hurling fiery darts from his redoubt high above his readers, but rather that his place is down in the valley with them, struggling with his own failures as he confessed so often, even at the end of life. He places the blame not so much on individuals as on a culture in which there is an inadequate understanding of the darkness which lies in all human hearts. Of this he speaks much like the prophets of old:

> . . . we shall discover too many lamentable proofs of the depravity of man. Indeed, this depravity becomes more apparent and less excusable (in a supposedly Christian country). For the advantages we enjoy only increase the obligations imposed on us. . . . Prosperity hardens the heart. Unlimited power is ever abused. Habits of vice grow up by themselves. Those of virtue are slow in formation.[11]

Wilberforce goes on to provide a forthright response about his own and others' reluctance to do good, speaking in the third person about such indifference:

> He is deeply aware of its power, having learned about its strength from self-observation and long acquaintance with the workings of his own mind. He will tell you that every day reinforces this conviction. Indeed, even hourly he sees evidence to deplore his lack of simplicity of intention, his weakness of purpose, his own low views, his selfish, unworthy desires, his backwardness in duty, his dullness and coldness in performing it.[12]

---

11. Wilberforce, *Real Christianity*, 13. Here Wilberforce echoes the prophet Hosea, whose imprecations on behalf of God came against the very leaders of Israel and its consequent demise: ". . . when they had grazed, they became full, they were filled, and their heart was lifted up; therefore they forgot me so I am to them like a lion; like a leopard I will lurk beside their way" (Hosea 13:6–7, English Standard Version).

12. Ibid., 14.

Such self-awareness is evidenced in a letter Wilberforce wrote to his fellow Claphamite, Thomas Babington. Here he says of himself, "I wish I had been as active as I ought about the poor slaves."[13] We see both his deep sense of responsibility and his equally profound humility. Despite what he had accomplished by 1797, the personal responsibility for falling short weighed heavily upon him, and this is made clear in his writing. He is not one to judge others and then leave himself unscathed. It is a process of self-awareness that somehow Jefferson could not or would not enter into in *Notes* or elsewhere.

AN IMPOSSIBILITY WITHOUT HOPE

Wilberforce is not, however, one to despair of the future, nor does he want others to lack the expectant perspective on life that the Gospel offers. He goes on to say in his letter to Babington, "However, the Blood of Jesus Christ cleanses from all sin and there is the comfort which combines the deepest Humiliation with the firmest Hope."[14] Herein lies his second core theme—unflinching hope. His sense of hope lay neither in himself nor in the rising spirit of the age that some—including Jefferson—believed would inevitably lead to human progress. Instead, he trusted in God's mercy. This is the seeming paradox Wilberforce lived with: deferring to God's grace yet taking responsible action; living with hope yet exhibiting humility even in eventual success. He seemed to understand by experience that in a fallen world all achievement would remain partial. His concern with the theme of hope was to make the biblical message of the Gospel clear to those trapped in a tepid cultural faith that gave rise to a *carpe diem* life of debauchery. He would go on to assure his readers that the implications of the Gospel were practical as well as theologically sound. A response in faith to the love of Christ would engender a loving response to those in need. This was nothing less than the Great Commandment in action. Such a "great change, Wilberforce said, rested not on purposeful determination or on further education (as Jefferson believed) but on internal transformation of the heart—a change he could attest to in his own life and that of many others.

That England remained mired in indifference, Wilberforce wrote, was due not to a paucity of truth, for it was declared every Sunday in the

---

13. Pollock, *Wilberforce*, 151.
14. Ibid.

Book of Common Prayer and in the Scripture readings. Rather, there was a discrepancy between reciting the biblical creeds on Sunday and the actions taken in the marketplace and Parliament on Monday. This disconnect emanated, he concluded, from a false idea that religious holiness was irrelevant to the "soiled" work of Monday through Saturday. "Thus in the minds of the crowd, religion appears to be wholly excluded from the business world and the vanities of life."[15] This sickness in the church and hence in the nation's purported leaders, he wrote, is one that has spread to the vast majority of the people, because it is the leaders who shape the nation's culture.[16] Truth in worship is set aside, he says, for a week at a time. Most people falsely believe that faith is impractical for the daily, gritty affairs of politicians or merchants:

> When the service is over, we dismiss them completely from our minds, until next Sunday, when once more we renew our periodic humility and gratitude. Noticing such lukewarmness, you may pardon the writer for such outright condemnation. We may allow such behavior, for those who, like the Unitarians, deny or explain away the distinctive truths of the Gospel. But for those who profess a sincere belief in them, this coldness is insupportable.... their joy and trust in Him cannot be expected to be very virile.[17]

For Thomas Jefferson, Wilberforce's moral solution to societal change would have been anathema, and vice versa. Like Wilberforce, Jefferson clearly saw human selfishness played out in the South's opposition to ending slavery lest a way of life be lost. Yet ironically, the key component of the great solution Jefferson foresaw to remedy selfishness was the removal of the supernatural from the new world order spawned by the Enlightenment, a world which was now to be governed by reason and advanced education with religious faith consigned to private expression.

In his correspondence with Adams, Jefferson candidly reflected on their joint belief that Dr. Joseph Priestley's new book, *The Doctrines of Heathen Philosophy Compared with Those of Revelation*, and Priestley's other works on the failings of Christianity would help put to rest once and for all the false superstitions surrounding the Christian religion, es-

---

15. Ibid.

16. For a recent perspective on the impact of leadership on culture, see Schein, *Organizational Culture and Leadership*.

17. Pollock, *Wilberforce*, 25.

pecially the Trinitarian doctrine.[18] This was a worldview that could not be more at odds with that of Wilberforce as expressed in *Real Christianity*.

THE CRUCIBLE OF POWER

As a long-time leader in England, Wilberforce knew very well what it meant to be tempted by the lure of power. In *Real Christianity* he took the issue head on, not with theory but with the voice of personal experience. He saw the desire for human admiration and the applause of the people as a particular trial for those in leadership, those with great resources, and even more so those who live a very public life such as he did. He called public admiration ultimately a potential temptation toward pride. Power and admiration test leadership, character, and often engender what the Greek philosophers called *hubris*. Such pride he saw as the most general passion and the most commanding authority of the human heart: the sin behind all other sins. Wilberforce would find cause to agree with C. S. Lewis's rendering on pride:

> Like a restless conqueror it seems not to spare age, nor sex, nor condition of man. It takes ten thousand shapes, the most artful of disguises, and winds its way in secret when it dare not openly assert itself. *It is often the master passion of the soul* (emphasis added).[19]

Wilberforce held that only the Gospel and reliance on God's goodness and grace can free one from the lure of pride and arrogance, of self-importance and selfishness. But there is an apparent difficulty here, for even if one is what Wilberforce refers to as a true Christian, doing good for others will always bring its accolades from some quarter. How then does a leader remain humble while receiving praise so often? Again, here is a practical issue Wilberforce has undoubtedly dealt with himself as he responds to his own query.

First, he says, be suspicious of any extreme praise, for you do not know why others flatter you. But second, if there is occasion for unsolicited and yet sincere praise, accept it "as given by Providence for a present comfort and a reward for virtue." Yet praise should be regarded as "subservient to the improvement and happiness of our fellow creatures, and thus be conducive to the glory of God."[20] In other words, the motive

18. Cappon, *Adams–Jefferson Letters*, 361.
19. Lewis, *Mere Christianity*, 61.
20. Wilberforce, *Real Christianity*, 65.

should be to serve the needs of others and to give God glory as a priority; yet, when praised, accept it as a gift but let it not become your purpose. We can see here how Wilberforce operated day to day: not to seek the approval of others but with an eye fixed on the purpose of slavery's end. Personal advancement and prominence were dimmed by these beliefs and their achievement.

OPPOSITION

For Wilberforce, the flip side to the virtue of humility is how leaders handle criticism and opposition. Again, we get another clue as to what lay behind his perseverance under withering opposition and criticism. Politics is the arena in which both he and Jefferson endured more opprobrium than most people ever do—passionate, nasty, and personal public denouncement; outright scorn; and in Wilberforce's case even physical assault. They reacted differently when under attack or when they severely differed with others. Whereas Jefferson withdrew or anonymously attacked his opponents, Wilberforce candidly speaks to how his beliefs shaped his attitude when under the lash of his enemies' tongues or pens and why he stayed in the arena despite severe discouragement at times. He says it is precisely when a leader has what he calls "an excessive evaluation of our worldly character" that there is an inroad for a reaction in kind to unjust criticism:

> When attacked we see hot resentment; when impaired or lost, we see that bitterness of suffering. We cannot dispute these emotions—they are too obvious. We cannot deny their existence—they are too well known. . . . Only one thing can exclude these evils—a generous spirit.[21]

The desire for a great reputation, even when deflected by feigned humility, can be seen when one is under attack: it exposes our deeper motives, he says, and emotional reaction is even "natural." But the spirit of a leader who is generous toward others, even when vilified, comes not from rigid self-control, or from withdrawal or play acting, but from a transformed heart. This is evidence of the strength outside oneself that works quietly on the inside to remove pride and self pity. We get an even deeper glimpse here into the inner workings of Wilberforce during the many years of failure and denouncement—many more lay ahead.

21. Ibid., 66.

PERSISTENCE

Wilberforce recognizes in *Real Christianity* that even for the best of people, continuing in something that is morally good is so very difficult when one is fiercely and continuously opposed or when failure constantly looms. He sees this failure to persist as arising from a false or "weak" benevolence that is exposed when the initial ardor fades—a transitory sympathy. Of such people Wilberforce writes: "They do not possess that strength and energy of character which, in the face of difficulties and dangers, produce readiness in service, vigor, and perseverance in action."[22] "Weak benevolence"—the failure to persist on a right course—arises out of a false religion, be it Christianity or another belief on which one relies instead, he says. True religion results in a change in the heart, a transformation into a new life, and only such a renewal can bring the perseverance of character to do good that endures the years and the repeated failures that Wilberforce experienced. Knowing as we do the times that he would have turned back, we know how hard this lesson came for him but how critical it was for his keeping on a forward path for the decades ahead. He pleads with his peers (and us) to understand this lesson well.

With more than thirty years of his life remaining, his beliefs voiced here would be sorely tested time and again. He knew already that only in motives which were properly anchored would the constancy to persevere prevail. Whether it was in the flush of temporary success or in the winds of opposition, especially when no final end was in sight, persistence was not based upon half-hearted caring, stage-managed for public consumption. Self-advancement by currying a reputation for goodness in the eyes of the people could only take a man so far. This was a lesson Jefferson also experienced in similar ways, yet he did not seem to come away with the same insights as did Wilberforce. "Weak benevolence," as Wilberforce understood it, is another way to possibly explain why Jefferson folded his tent on slavery early on and later dismissed his reticence to act as the task of the next generation. It seems clearer that while Jefferson used increasingly convoluted rationales for his inaction he also had a misplaced faith that time and education would produce something almost supernatural—which of course he did not believe in.

---

22. Ibid., 75.

THE IMPACT ON A NATION

For Wilberforce, the "grand malady" of nations was no less than the grand malady of individuals—selfishness. A society that turned inward to its own pleasures and ignored the needs of the "least of these" was a society headed for a fall. The opposite was what he advocated throughout his life—a "public spirit," a term he used that meant a concern for the larger issues of society stemming from a vital Christian faith. He called this form of public spirit the "great principle of public life," one that was active and vigorous for the good rather than, for example, turning inward to seek status in reelection. Wilberforce described such deference as true societal benevolence, which he defined as: "Moderation in temporal pursuits and engagements; comparative indifference to the issue of worldly projects; diligence in the discharge of personal civil duties; resignation to the will of God; and patience under all the dispensations of God's providence."[23] Here he recognizes that the moral decay of individual leaders is ultimately becoming a national political malady. Thus redress of such need for reform was an apt pursuit for a politician and a Christian who sought to form the "good society."[24]

SELF-DECEPTION

Wilberforce's last chapter is devoted to what he calls "practical hints for real Christianity." In one way it is a summary; in another it is intended to give priority to what the leaders to which this book is primarily addressed should focus on in their own lives so that England might progress morally and grow in strength to become a great nation that would endure.

All he has been saying, it seems, comes down to this: *the leaders of England, be they politicians, merchants, or clergymen, have been practicing a form of religion that is false. It is not real Christianity rooted in the ancient faith in Christ, but rather it consists of moral precepts distilled from modern thinking embodied in the Enlightenment and the modern, truncated interpretations of the Bible.* This is not unlike the aphorisms of the Jefferson "bible." The culprit in such thinking is *self-deception*.

---

23. Ibid., 109.

24. In *The Good Society*, Robert Bellah and his colleagues would subsequently write about the need in America and in the Western world to turn back from individualism and toward a sense of community and responsible civic engagement.

Wilberforce contends that such internal blindness arises out of a belief that has come more and more under the influence of reason alone as the source of ethical knowledge—Enlightenment thinking. The result is a clouding of moral insight, a selfishness that overrates one's good qualities, and a mind that is blind to its sins and failures with a disposition to accept the praises of colleagues and the approval of the public as determinative of one's successes in life. As this worldview guides life through youth to middle age and finally to old age, the conscience is steadily stifled and the opportunity to amend one's ways fades with one's energies. Perhaps this insight also helps us to understand Jefferson's gradual backing away from his earlier commitments.

The spirit of the age, Wilberforce felt, was producing not only so-called cultural Christianity but also a growing unbelief in the supernatural work of God. He encourages the skeptical people of his Enlightenment age to examine the writings of the men they all admire and read: Bacon, Milton, Locke, and Newton. Each of these revered authors made a deep examination of Christian beliefs and embraced them. These were, of course, the same writers and thinkers whose works occupied Jefferson's library shelves and were well known by him, amply quoted in his letters to Adams and others. Somehow Jefferson did not see that their thought emanated from the very faith he had tried to bring down to his own level of understanding through reason. His was a belief in which moral precepts supplanted the ancient Gospel truths, which were at best outdated superstition to his understanding.

Instead, these writers and others that Jefferson read so assiduously only produced in him the skepticism that, according to Wilberforce, bred a sense of moral superiority. Those individuals who dismiss faith as outmoded will find that this causes them to see older, traditional thinking as mere superstition in the modern era of science and reason. This was certainly true in Jefferson's case. Wilberforce described the mental progression in skeptics as beginning with initial belief in some fashion, but then slipping gradually into doubt, and finally ending in unbelief. It is what he called "the natural history of skepticism."[25] Although he went on to say that total unbelief does not always arise from such thinking, he felt that Unitarianism was likely where many skeptics would take their final refuge. It was almost as if the two men were having a debate from afar.

25. Wilberforce, *Real Christianity*, 128.

A PLEA FOR A NEW DIRECTION

Wilberforce closes his book by bringing the argument back to England itself and the implications for its future. With war against France looming as he wrote, revolution was in the very air they were breathing, and self-centeredness was likewise ascendant. He literally pleads for a turn in a new direction:

> We bear the marks only too plainly of a declining empire. . . . It may appear before the eyes of the world foolishness for real Christians so to pray; yet, we believe from Scripture that God will be disposed to favor the nation to which His servants belong. Boldly I must confess that I believe the national difficulties we face result from the decline of religion and morality among us. I must confess equally boldly that my own solid hopes for the well-being of my country depend, not so much on her navies and armies, nor on the wisdom of her rulers, nor on the spirit of the people, as on the persuasion that she still contains many who love and obey the Gospel of Christ. I believe their prayers may yet prevail. So let the prayers of the Christian reader also be offered up for the success of this feeble endeavor in the service of true religion. . . . May there be in this nation a place where the name of Christ is still honored and men see the blessings of faith in Jesus. May the means of religious education and consolation once again be extended to surrounding countries and to the world at large.[26]

ENCOURAGEMENT

Though Wilberforce did not write this book to be praised, it must have encouraged him that John Newton was so excited that a man in his political profession, especially, took the time and the care to write such an extraordinary book. In June of 1997, he wrote Wilberforce the following:

> I can converse with you as often as I please by your late publication, which I have now read through with increasing satisfaction a third time. I mean not to praise *you*, but I must and will praise the *Lord*, for your book, which I cannot doubt will be accompanied by a divine blessing, and productive of happy effects. I hope it will be useful to me, and of course to those who attend on my ministry. I have been near 50 years in the Lord's school, during

---

26. Ibid., 130–31.

this space He has graciously taught me many things of which I was once no less ignorant than the beasts of the field. He has made me a debtor to many ministers and to many books, but still I had something to learn from your book. You have not only confirmed but enlarged my views of several important points. One thing strikes me very much and excites my praise to the Lord on your behalf. That a gentleman in your line of life, harassed with a multiplicity of business, and surrounded on all sides with snares, could venture to publish *such* a book, without fearing a retort either from the many friends or the many enemies amongst whom you have moved so many years. The power of the Lord in your favour, seems to be little less than remarkable than in the 3 young men who lived unhurt and unsinged in the midst of the fire, or of Daniel who sat in peace in the den when surrounded by lions. It plainly shows that his grace is all-sufficient to keep us in any situation which his providence appoints us.[27]

At this time of recent failure, Newton's enthusiasm must have been a needed tonic for reigniting Wilberforce's energies and commitment.

In some ways, the process of writing his book may also have been an encouragement to Wilberforce to redouble his own commitment to his own now clearer beliefs and not to despair at a moment of great failure. He almost seemed to be urging on himself and his friends not to yield to the discouragement of the stifling and selfish ways they saw all around them and in the moribund church. In putting pen to paper, he might also have been able to overcome the strong temptation to withdraw that we know he considered for a time at this disappointing juncture. Hence, this book was neither a personal vilification of those who disagreed with him politically nor a means for advancing his political agenda. This publication was simply the expression of a man in public life who loved his people and his country and who could see no way forward other than the one he laid out therein: moral reformation of the nation leading to sweeping changes in manners—the culture of England. Slavery's end, he believed, lay within such a course, as did the larger cause of England's destiny. As we have seen, he was ultimately proven right. He did persist.

The Saints would continue for thirty-six more years after the publication of *Real Christianity*. Their anchor, as well as their north star, was the true

---

27. John Newton to William Wilberforce, June 7, 1797, The Newton Project.

faith they shared, not the man they followed or even their great cause. It was the faith that Wilberforce learned at John Newton's knee as a young boy. A wider gap could not be found than the worldviews that set apart Jefferson and Wilberforce. This juxtaposition of their deepest beliefs tells the tale better than any other explanation as the foundational reason for their differences in thought and in action, in results and in persistent and courageous engagement despite common fierce opposition. The guiding beliefs of each man guided their choices year by year and in these life orienting beliefs lie the ultimate explanation of what distinguished them most starkly; where they were truly at crossed purposes. Their core beliefs frame the most complete answer to our questions about the conundrum of the persistence of the one man and the failure of the other to continue the fight. Herein lies the story of how, on the one hand, optimistic faith in man's progress led not to freedom but to war, and how, on the other hand, a sense of responsibility coupled with hope produced hard-won victory. The lessons for our day are ones we need to lean forward to hear from their lives. We conclude our retrospective look at their lives by attempting to answer the three large questions we put before ourselves at the outset.

KNOWING AND DOING

1. How would you compare William Wilberforce's expression of Christian beliefs as a politician with how politicians do so today?

2. Do you agree that Wilberforce's worldview was what fueled his sense of calling, responsibility, and persistence vis-à-vis Jefferson's, or do you see other major factors in his story that also account for these differences?

3. Why do you think *Real Christianity* was so well received in England and America? Do you think a politician today could write such a book and gain similar popular approval here and abroad?

4. Imagine a conversation about slavery between Wilberforce and Jefferson in 1820 when they were old men. What would Wilberforce argue that might persuade his American counterpart to throw in his lot with the abolitionists as a leader before his life ended? What might Jefferson, seeking to demur, have argued as to the difficulty of the task and why he could not act?

5. Is it less appropriate in our day to speak so openly about one's faith, or were the challenges to such public expressions similar to ours two hundred years ago?

6. Are you able to speak openly at work about your beliefs or perhaps to winsomely challenge others as Wilberforce did from time to time?

7. Does your example comport with your words, as Wilberforce wrestled all his life to do in his vocation?

12

Lessons and Legacies

The sepulcher of famous men is the whole earth, not only the epigraph engraved on the columns in their own country, since also in foreign lands there dwells the unwritten memorial of them, graven not on stone but in the hearts and minds of men.[1]

—Pericles

The stories of these two lives, in the final analysis, provide lessons for those who would pursue a purpose, a calling, and possibly lead others in that quest as well. The legacies of Thomas Jefferson and William Wilberforce have remained to influence the course of events in the two centuries since their passing. So how in the end do we weave it all together into a story with lessons for our time and for our own life stories?

The beginning point to bringing these two stories to a conclusion must be that offers a perspective for ourselves and our age. The common thread is that each of us faces potential responsibilities that are placed upon the doorstep of our life, even as these two men did. Each age and each generation knows its has responsibilities to the next, and it lies within our power to act—or not.

Of George Washington and of Wilberforce, Steve Garber observed: "Both saw themselves as implicated in history, as responsible for history, for the way the world is and ought to be—and that commitment plainly grew out of a thoughtfully-framed understanding of faith and vocation, of creed and calling."[2] Garber's observation holds true for Thomas Jefferson as well.

1. Thucydides, *Peloponnesian War*.
2. Garber, "A Wound in My Heart Has Been Healed."

ON LEADERSHIP

The choice to act alone, to draw in others, or to withdraw is one each person makes throughout his or her days on earth. If Thomas Jefferson or William Wilberforce could sit down beside any one of us right now, we can safely predict that both men would agree on one important lesson they learned: we should act when there is a clear need; we should lead when the opportunity is presented. They might well differ on where to place our energies for the issues of our time—whether to advance ideas or to take action—but neither man would be content to have us seek a life of ease, of contemplation, of withdrawal, or to live so that there is no personal cost.

They would also have much to say about those we have chosen to lead our nations in this century and those who have put themselves forward as our political leaders. Although polite, they might not be so complimentary of those who came after them in governing our nation. We might expect a conversation with Jefferson about the encroachment of governmental tyranny; Wilberforce might review with us the toleration by the church and by our national leaders of the widening gap between the rich and the poor. Selfishness would likely be a common theme for them—at both the political and individual levels. They would have ideas about the failings of the church but likely not agree on what those were.

If they could speak now, they might also encourage us not to allow criticism to deter us in our purpose but to serve others in a way that is neither prideful nor tyrannical when placed in any position of minor or major prominence. Both men would likely advocate for leaders to be such *among* others despite times when they would counsel that good leaders must at times take the bit in their mouth and stand alone. They would have us see that in being leaders or in the important work of choosing leaders, we should see the task to which we elect them as one of service to others before self in a mutual commitment to a great purpose. Our statesmen, they would counsel, are not counted as those assuming a "rightful" or earned place of primacy, recognition, rank, or perquisites. Each man would pass on a similar lesson, one they shared about leadership despite their vastly different worldviews—to lead is to serve. In their own way, they would likely agree on a timeless principle, one that survived the "cut" to be included in the Jefferson Bible:

> You know that those who are recognized as rulers . . . lord it over them; and their great men exercise authority over them. But it is not this way among you, but whoever wishes to become great among you shall be your servant; and whoever wishes to be first among you shall be slave of all. For even the Son of Man did not come to be served, but to serve, and to give His life a ransom for many.[3]

Many have discovered as they did independently that this teaching is perhaps the single most important and most basic principle about life and about leadership, a principle that has stood the test of two thousand years' time—one that applies equally whether one has the title "leader" or "follower" or whether one is called "mom" or "dad." It is a principle many in our age of therapeutic individualism[4] have forgotten. Herein lies the origin of the term "servant leadership," which has some currency today. Some still find that it is true—pragmatically if for no other reason. Servant leadership "works" in all spheres of human endeavor. Both Wilberforce and Jefferson sought with differing degrees of success to model their lives on such a principle; both knew and understood that the Greek words for leader allowed a distinction between leader *over* and leader *among* others.

To draw on the lives of William Wilberforce and Thomas Jefferson is to have "experienced" their lessons for us, which is one of the functions of story. In doing so, they have served as "living" examples for us whether we are or will become leaders or whether we live simply as people challenged by our times. Both men were at the heart of a cultural transformation in their nations during a time of great complexity, danger, and ferment. They lived into those experiences over their long careers. The lessons they learned and lived—good and bad—are as valid for us today as they were to the generations that followed and the people that were mentored by them. Those who care about character and about

---

3. Mark 10:42–45, New American Standard Bible.

4. Smith, *Soul Searching*, 172–75. According to Smith, therapeutic individualism is a worldview, an unconscious "taken-for-granted set of assumptions and commitments about the human self, society, and life's purpose that powerfully defines everyday moral and relational codes and boundaries in the contemporary United States. . . . Therapeutic individualism defines the individual self as the source and standard of authentic moral knowledge and authority, and individual self-fulfillment as the preoccupying purpose of life. Subjective, personal experience is the touchstone of all that is authentic, right, and true" (175–76). See also Hunter, *Death of Character*.

a life well lived can learn from their lives through deeper reflection on these comparions.

With that backdrop on leadership and their stories in mind, let us allow these men, who altered their worlds as leaders and still influence our time with their legacies, to act as wise mentors for us and our times: both for those who will lead and for those who will select and follow leaders—which includes all of us. We seek their answers from two centuries before us to the three questions we set forth at the outset:

- How does one form or discover a life purpose that is worthy of giving oneself to until the end?
- What lessons can one learn for living such a purposeful and good life that persists to the end, overcomes great obstacles, and brings about profound change for the good of people?
- How does one finish the story well, leaving a good legacy behind for the next generation?

LESSONS FOR TODAY

Since we have taken a comparative look at the stories of these men, the legacies and lessons for our age flow from their stories and from our insights about them—by *comparison* particularly. Perhaps the ancient Proverb describes well what we can distill from their lives seen in parallel: "As iron sharpens iron, so one man sharpens another."[5] In a real sense, the story of one man sharpens the clarity of the other's story and how we derive meaning for our day.

Looking back, the answers to our three questions posed at the outset provide sharpened lessons that deserve to be underscored as among the more important for the twenty-first century, with the understanding that each person who has read their stories will also, appropriately, add personal "takeaways" as he or she hears and reflects upon them.[6] Consider these only a beginning point for yourself.

---

5. Proverbs 27:17, New American Standard Bible.

6. The author wishes to reiterate that over the course of using these two stories in teaching leaders and in informal conversations afterward, much of what has been learned is owed to the insights of others. Although memory does not allow direct attribution, I wish to acknowledge my debt here.

ON PURPOSE

The power of purpose that is rooted in serving others is the centerpiece for a good life. In large strokes, each man saw his life purpose as creating a good society and removing tyranny. How each discerned this purpose and the implications for personal responsibility and consequent action differed greatly, but the lesson concerning the power of purpose remains the same.

This may be the single most important lesson to draw from their lives, and it is a good place for any of us to begin our vocation or to reassess its course—certainly for anyone desiring to become a person of influence for the good of others. Answering the question, "What is my purpose in life?" is critical for any of us to ask ourselves and then to be clear about the answer as early in life as possible. It is also a reasonable test for selecting those who would lead us—what is their expressed and *lived out* purpose? Is it real or is it window dressing? Following are some good questions to ask yourself, implied from examining these two lives as we have done:

- Is there a North Star that guides your life?
- Can it be stated simply and clearly?
- Has that purpose possibly shifted with the winds of opinion, need for approval, or failure?
- How do you or will you translate that purpose into your own responsibility and action in the years ahead?

Wilberforce seemed again and again to come back to his "two great objects" as the animating compass point from which he chose his calling and the focus of his energies over a lifetime—to transform the moral climate of English society and to abolish slavery. He did not dissipate himself with careerism or delude himself that he could better accomplish his ends if he became a "great man." This we have seen. Yet the deeper purpose that undergirded his two "great objects" was his expressed belief and his trust in the one who called him to such responsibilities and gave him hope for completing his two tasks before the end of his life story. That this was his primary calling within the sphere of his life's work in politics he knew well—even when he wavered, perhaps especially when he wavered, he returned to this center.

As we saw, this calling had to be twice reinforced by his long-time mentor, John Newton. When failure brought him low enough to quit, it was Newton who reemphasized the need for Wilberforce to remain committed to his vocation and the work he had begun. In addition, Wilberforce was taught by Newton and by old John Wesley that *if* he was called, *then* the God who called him would be the one upon whom he could and should depend daily with confidence—most signally at the critical times of defeat or discouragement.

Wilberforce's thesis in *Real Christianity* is perhaps the best place to see him articulate how he understood his real purpose in life within a political career devoted to the good of others. It was not a passion of youthful idealism or personal ambition—those would have foundered well before the end. Rather, it was one honed in the mud pits of political life. Purpose gave him backbone in his persistence. His own writing showed this matured understanding when he described the dangers of shifting purposes to respond to the roar of the crowd or the siren call of one's own self-advancement. He saw these ends as doomed to fail in the long run. It is likely he drew this conclusion from the observations he had already made of his colleagues in Parliament enhanced by his reading of history. Yet he was brutally honest that both these temptations of self elevation were his, too; he was certainly not immune. That honest recognition served to keep him humble and to refrain from being overly judgmental of his colleagues.

Jefferson's life purpose is somewhat more difficult to identify, and we may not be able to improve on the judgments that many historians have rendered in seeking to understand what motivated this great man at his core. He himself probably came closest to expressing his purpose when he wrote to his daughter of his concern for the liberty of the individual and his opposition to tyranny. He, like Wilberforce, sought to create a good society that, for him, was based on an agrarian foundation, freed from the onus of government control and from the moneyed interests of banks and manufacturers. Early on, his purpose in ending tyranny included liberating the slaves, but as his life wore on that burning, early purpose faded and he declined to get personally involved in its resolution. His expression of opposition to slavery became more complex and nuanced, often being expressed as a fear of the consequences of either freedom or continuation of the practice of holding slaves. His thinking was preoccupied with the tensions between states' rights and the federal government's power to compel as the fault lines running between North and South deepened and as more parts of the Louisiana Territory petitioned for statehood. While the focus for his life was demonstrably more uneven than Wilberforce's singular commitment, overall it had a certain consistency as his personal aspiration for power wrestled with his belief that less government, less public religion, and more education were the keys to freeing man's mind to rise untrammeled toward moral elevation. Ultimately, these were ideas to which he devoted his energies, and as he grew older he neither sought to take the lead nor accepted responsibility for ending slavery. Instead, his last great work was the extraordinary effort at the end of his life to found the University of Virginia, in his own image, as a place where ideas would flourish unhindered by the biases of religion and advance the next generation's progress. It was a great work to be sure.

We also saw that Jefferson's purpose of eradicating all forms of tyranny took an unfortunate turn as his antipathy toward Hamilton and his followers rose and became a thinly disguised opposition to his former benefactors and mentors, Washington and Adams. Ultimately it led to his estrangement from those who had so greatly assisted his advancement. His decision to resort to questionable and often surreptitious political tactics to advance his purpose of eradicating Federalism's tyranny ultimately served to create severe enmity and distance, although he was hardly alone in using such tactics in the early American political scene. This struggle inevitably led to the two-party system we know today. Most would conclude this is a strength of American-style democracy but one bought at the price of periodic partisan conflict and the decision paralysis seen in our time. The close circle of those who followed Jefferson's lead were, like him, often slaveholders whose exploitation of fellow human beings was far more egregious than the contest of political philosophies of strong government versus the preeminence of states' rights. Open warfare between the states and the two cultures was the final consequence of the unresolved political conflict.

In Jefferson's case, an expressed, compelling purpose to serve others as an ideal did not result in a life resolute against all forms of oppression, nor did he live to see the transformative results for society that he desired in the agrarian model he espoused. His focus on opposing the Federalists at any cost led to unfortunate choices that hurt his main benefactors. The irony is that Jefferson's ringing language had far more impact on the generations that followed than they did on his own. It is the soaring words of the Declaration that perhaps best stand the test of time as his greatest legacy in framing a purpose for others to advance human life, liberty, and happiness.

ON PERSISTENCE

Perseverance may be the single most overlooked quality in a leader—or in a life well lived—yet it is the one most difficult to sustain over a life as age and circumstances take their toll. Both men showed a singular level of persistence in the face of opposition as they pursued their quests—with one exception.

It is not flashy, it is not easily detectable early on in a person's life, but without it, little can be accomplished—that is the nature of perseverance. Both Wilberforce and Jefferson did persevere with great energy, albeit in differing ways and with evolving emphases in Jefferson's case. Why some persist courageously against all odds while others take a more pragmatic course seems linked to the awareness of a life calling and the centrality of purpose, as observed earlier. In our two stories we saw that it was sustained by core beliefs and values that remained clear in the face of crisis, failure, and unpopularity. Humility is certainly an essential precursor. The foe of perseverance is less the opposition of enemies and more that of repeated or even anticipated failure and discouragement when faced with a seemingly insurmountable task. Perseverance does not hold out a lofty outcome as the inevitable result but requires faith that effort just might produce the desired results.

Of all the qualities that Wilberforce showed over a life, persistence stands out above the others as characteristic of his distinctiveness. Whether it was ill health, defeat after appalling defeat, or the opposition of friends, colleagues, the King, and the nation's leaders, he kept on keeping on for more than forty years until the final victory was at the door two days before his death. But even had he died without victory on slavery in sight, he would still have had the comfort of being part of leading a cultural transformation over those same years. What he and the Clapham Circle led in changing the national ethos guaranteed the moral conditions for slavery's end were in place. The lives of so many in the oppressed classes were the richer for his persistent efforts and the lives of the wealthier classes were freed from the tyranny of selfish and debauched habits of the heart.

That many others beyond the Clapham Circle persevered alongside him for those years is a rich testament to them and to Wilberforce as a leader. There was developed in those decades a core of tested leaders, a new generation he had helped to raise up, who would see the demise of slavery through to its end. Leaders beget leaders.

But, most importantly for him, he believed this work was God's will and would not be thwarted come what may, a lesson Newton instilled. Wilberforce could not turn aside from obedience to his calling. God would persevere for the slaves even if all men would not.

Jefferson had this insight on the importance of persistence in common with Wilberforce; yet for the American there was a cosmic fear that seemingly paralyzed him short of taking action. This does not mean that Jefferson was a man who lacked the capacity for courage or the will to persevere; it was seemingly more a case that he could not stomach direct, protracted opposition nor could he envision a way forward on slavery. At least he could not find hope in the same way he could in seeking an end to the Federalists' reign. He, too, had his share of personal hardships that would break many a man as he experienced the death of his dear, young wife and three of their children. Furthermore, he suffered the public humiliation of the accusation of being a coward in the face of the British attack, which left a deep, emotional wound. For many years he found himself thwarted at every turn in his political vision of a more limited American government by the brilliant young upstart, Alexander Hamilton, whose broader dream for the new government was embraced by Washington and then Adams. The years of public thrashing Jefferson took from Federalist newspapers and pamphlets, often at Hamilton's behest, left him bitter and at least temporarily deterred on three occasions.

Jefferson's approach to opposition was not to keep at the game and let the criticisms roll off his back, as did Wilberforce. His tactic was to withdraw and to work behind the scenes on his political agenda. The result was that ultimately his more limited view of government and of the presidency did prevail for a long season, removing what he saw as government tyranny over the states and the people. He would be able to say that he ushered in a second revolution—an era dominated by Jeffersonians led by his protégés Madison and Monroe. At the end of his life, it was his personal vision, plans, actions, political acumen, and certainly perseverance that led him to see the great university he had so long envisioned established in Virginia. It may have been his finest hour.

Nevertheless, on slavery, he completely withdrew from the field, seemingly because he concluded that to focus on its end would be inimical to his political aspirations and would only bring about a worse end. Nor did his worldview allow envisioning a national solution of some form of government coercion of any kind. He certainly did not seek providential favor upon this difficult work as he saw it as the role of man, alone. Hence, for all of his great intelligence, he simply did not have the vision or the confidence that this dilemma could be resolved in his generation. Although many thought he would lead the charge against slavery after the American bill to end the slave trade passed in 1808, he did not. This reluctance to continue forward on slavery is what primarily sets him apart from Wilberforce.

Jefferson believed that ideas, not necessarily people, would persevere, grow in influence, and ultimately triumph. He was not without faith as some claimed: he possessed the Enlightenment faith in human progress. However, this form of faith, this worldview, lacked what Wilberforce's belief required—a trust that God's actions would support justice for African slaves using common political clay. The avenging God of Jefferson's nightmares was not one who would rescue white and black alike from this folly, but one who would descend one day on the white masters and destroy the newfound nation for its moral depravity. Jefferson's worldview did not allow for the possibility of colaboring with the gracious God Wilberforce believed in. In that sense, Jefferson's way of viewing the field of battle and his conclusion about the impossibility of ending slavery were accurate. He did not have the eyes to see it. Yet he was right that ideas have consequences. It was his expressed ideas on equality that eventually gave voice to emancipation under Lincoln's fixed purpose, but at a terrible price. What might have happened had Jefferson put his name and reputation behind abolition anytime from 1800 on we will never know.

There is one final note on perseverance. In its worst dress, it can simply be stubbornness born out of pride, not wanting to face defeat or even make a strategic retreat. C. S. Lewis saw this in the political leaders of his day during and after World War II.[7] Wars are a specific case in point where objectives often are long out of reach, but the nation's leaders plow ahead for the sake of "honor." Certainly the French did so in the nineteenth century until they fell exhausted under Napoleon's failure at

---

7. Lewis, *Mere Christianity*, 110.

Waterloo. Vietnam for both France in the 1950s and the United States in the 1960s and 1970s is another textbook case of personal and national pride leading to stubbornness and failure. David Halberstam, among others, showed how "the best and the brightest" leaders, that great collection of Ivy League sheepskins, continued on in Vietnam even after it was apparent that the ill-fated strategy and the will of the people were not up to the task.[8] To make matters worse, these intellectually gifted American leaders all but duplicated the well-documented lessons of the French just a few short years before.[9] America's experience in Vietnam belied the old admonition, "When you're in a hole, stop digging."

ON FINISHING WELL

Finishing well involves running the course toward one's purpose in life and persisting in it to the end, but there is one thing more: doing so with your integrity intact. Integrity is the inherent connection between word and deed, between belief and action, between knowing and doing. It makes the crucial difference in the legacy of a life well lived. We know this in part because if integrity is lacking, everyone knows even if they will only talk about it privately. Comparing the lives of these two men bears out this conclusion. Wilberforce could not but act on his beliefs—in his worldview, he was responsible—whereas Jefferson could defer action on his beliefs into the future with faith in progress.

Wilberforce's belief in and dependence upon a transcendent God who guided his responses to the small and large affairs of men captured his life's energies from the time of his "great change." That commitment added to his natural and developed personal strengths and ambitions. It seemingly enabled remarkable persistence and bred integrity of purpose which aligned with his life choices—a life unfragmented and unfeigned. It was the quality that by the end brought applause from friend and foe alike.

Jefferson was also seized with an animus toward tyranny that became his central vocation, first expressed as he stood against slavery in 1769, but then was adjusted over the years. For him, however, there was growing consternation between his belief in a small, secular, central government and the necessary federal solution to slavery's end fueled by a

---

8. Halberstam, *The Best and the Brightest*.
9. See particularly the writings of Bernard Fall, e.g., *Street without Joy*.

moral imperative. It seems that this growing realization of the terrible choices before him left an ethical dislocation except for fanciful, theoretical solutions. Hence, his ultimate conclusion that moral progress fueled by advancing education and also demographic diffusion of slavery was his redoubt on the only ending he could speak of. These were thin reeds that defended him from history's charge of hypocrisy and moral cowardice.

Nevertheless, despite a very clear case study from which to draw upon, in today's culture Wilberforce's ethical beliefs about political leadership are seen by Western culture as best confined to the domain of churches and to the backwaters of religious idealism or zeal. Today it is awkward to even discuss such a degree of faith openly in the public square or the marketplace even when clearly moral choices are before us. In a nation where the vast majority of people say they believe in God like ours, or in a nation that has a long religious tradition such as that of England or Germany, it should not be embarrassing to point out that fragmentation of life—inconsistency between belief and behavior (not walking the talk as we now say)—has had consequences.

Wilberforce, if he was in office today, would ask us, even as he did those who believed the Enlightenment faith of his day, why should only *religious beliefs* be separated from public actions? In truth, all would be named as hypocrites who would divorce their beliefs from their actions—public or private. It simply is not possible to do so with any integrity. In the twenty-first century, it is ironically Jefferson whom our culture cites as the exemplar for drawing a bright line between the public and the private. But as we have seen, even he could not separate his beliefs in the efficacy of time and reason from his choices in office or out.

Thus, the arguments of the Enlightenment worldview of Jefferson and the Christian worldview of Wilberforce remain in stark contention right into the twenty-first century. To separate the truth that derives from tradition and revelation from the truth that is derived by reason alone, as the Enlightenment did, is a false dichotomy, especially if we use a test that science advocates: experience. If we conduct an honest examination of the actions of several revered American leaders, we see that they too demonstrated a consistency in their belief in God, in the words they spoke, and in their actions, however cautious they were in invoking them on others:

- George Washington introduced the precedents for governing an entirely new nation, describing it as being birthed and sustained by what he called Providence.
- Ulysses S. Grant and Robert E. Lee presided over vast opposing armies and heartbreaking bloodshed; nevertheless, each commanding general, North and South, attributed the future outcome, win or lose, to Almighty God—and sustained that belief in victory and defeat.
- Abraham Lincoln repeatedly called upon the nation to pray and fast so that God's guidance and mercy might end the war of brothers and free those unjustly enslaved.
- Harriet Tubman heard God calling her to lead her people out of bondage even as Moses did, and she risked her life time and again relying, she said, on prayer and heavenly courage to bring hundreds of slaves north to freedom
- Martin Luther King, Jr., invoked the prophet Amos that God's justice would roll down like a river not only for the good of the descendants of African slaves but also for those who retained deep prejudice, so that both might finally be free to be brothers and sisters as they were created to be.
- George Marshall, first among equals in World War II, presided over the greatest war ever fought and stood as a tower of unquestioned integrity, not only guiding a victorious outcome, but also forming the plan that would bear his name to bind up the wounds of former enemies. He rested his case on his quiet faith in what was right and just.

Perhaps we already know these stories, but sometimes we tell them with a reticence to recognize the faith that each of these and many other leaders possessed, explaining away what they themselves would not have. They lived lives of integrity precisely because of their beliefs. Although they would not always express their beliefs in the language of what in our time is called evangelical faith, nor would they use a trumpet to call attention to it, each of them recognized the reality of their dependence on God and his providence. Whether in success or failure, they spoke or wrote of it often quietly but at times publicly as well, and it did not compromise their capability or the trust of their followers.

The difference in finishing what each man began as neophyte politicians was the connection each man made between his distinct faith's expression and his political calling. Wilberforce privately and sometimes publicly acknowledged that he and his colleagues could not accomplish the difficult tasks of abolition and emancipation without God's help. But that also allowed him to keep his commitments unchanged and to finish the race with faithful action right up until the last. Jefferson, on the other hand, did not believe, as far as can be seen, that God acted in response to prayer for the day-to-day challenges he faced as he wrestled with his conscience over slavery. Rather, Jefferson conceived of God as a watchmaker, observing the ticking and the movement of the hands of time, rarely if ever intervening, and definitely not acting in response to the prayers of mere men. Thus Jefferson could not call upon God to help end slavery except in wrath against the slave owners. This was another place where Jefferson parted company with his early mentor, Washington, whose private prayers revealed a man deeply dependent on God during the course of the Revolutionary War and in the inaugural American presidency.[10] As the burden of slavery's end rested ever more heavily on Jefferson, it would appear he came to a point where he could no longer carry the load alone lest he risk failure in the task and failure in the wider game as the nascent American experiment in democracy transitioned from the Federalists to the Jeffersonians.

In expressing his own faith, Wilberforce was careful to live with the integrity he advocated in *Real Christianity* for all leaders. He regularly examined both his actions and his motives at the end of the day and recorded his assessment in his journals. His actions generally spoke what he believed, as did those of the Clapham team. At appropriate times, he gave credit where he believed it was due, anchoring justice for his African "brothers" in the belief that God created all people in his own image, and he voiced a personal responsibility to the God who watched over the affairs of all men. The marker Wilberforce laid down with his book left no doubt about what he believed, and his prior and subsequent actions did not diverge from what appeared on the written page. Yet he never "used" his faith in a political sense for any advantage (even if he could have done so).

The disconnect between faith and vocation today be it politics, business, or any field, is a product of a similar but reversed separation prac-

---

10. Michael and Jana Novak, *Washington's God*.

ticed in many churches, where speaking of the day-to-day grist of market capitalism or political disputation is often avoided. As long-time teacher of preachers, Haddon Robinson, has observed of the best sermons, "*The line of penetration is from the pulpit to the pew to the pavement.*"[11] Yet the reigning assumption even in today's religious culture often seems to be the same as Wilberforce's early presumption about leaving politics for the ministry—that real faith is primarily found in "religious" vocations; those who pursue careers in business or law or government are acting religiously only when they worship or meet in small groups or use their money for the needs of the church or the poor. When they work to make money or negotiate compromises, it is not seen as the domain of worship. The marketplace and the public square are simply too tainted. This assumption may be an even greater danger to living a life of integrity in faith and vocation if it is left unchallenged. Fortunately, John Newton forcefully taught a young Wilberforce that there was ample opportunity for living with integrity in *every* sphere of life, not just on Sunday.

We lose an opportunity to transform our own world when we assume, like Wilberforce did for a time as a young man, that our chosen careers are not as valuable in serving others if they involve the rough and tumble of politics, the swings of the financial industry, the glamorous entertainment world, or the impenetrable domain of the language of lawyers. If Wilberforce had followed the course he was about to choose when his faith came alive, he would not only have divided his newfound faith from his vocation, but he would also have disconnected his vocation from influencing the corrupt English culture that the Anglican Church had sadly neglected for decades. As Steve Garber once again reminds us, "*The reality [is] that faith always shapes vocation which always shapes culture.*"[12] This is among the deepest lessons of a life well lived to the end such as the life of William Wilberforce. We err greatly if we follow the presuppositions of the Platonic two-tiered world of spirit and flesh that invaded the church's doctrine, practice, and daily life itself, equally influencing the dualism of the marketplace and the public square.[13]

We similarly err by unwittingly adopting the Enlightenment "faith" of Jefferson, who held that religious expression was a danger to reason

---

11. Robinson, in an endorsement of Heatley's book, *The Gift of Work*.

12. Garber, in an endorsement of Tchividian's book, *Unfashionable*.

13. See, for example, Witherington, *Work* and the earlier classic by Sherman, *Your Work Matters to God*.

and must be kept separate from the state. When Jefferson took this erroneous path to relegate faith only to private matters and supplanted it with reason in public affairs, many others after him followed the same path and many continue to do so in observing that precedent. The results of such beliefs were not only seen in the horrors of the Civil War, but they have also quietly entered as presuppositions into every sphere of our own political and social culture long after the Enlightenment Project failed.

The choices that faced these two men and the ideas by which they were influenced remain floating in the very air we breathe today, whether we worship in a church or on a golf course. Wise mentors like John Newton continue to be in great demand to show us a better way than an artificially partitioned life. An integrated life is one of integrity—and of freedom—to do what we are called to do, to act on what we believe, and to know that we do not need to apologize when we have done our best when belief and action align for all of life. An integrated life draws upon grace, not human accomplishment; it is one without regret at the end and anticipates a "well done" as the reward.

Someday, like William Wilberforce and Thomas Jefferson, our lives will end and the assessment will be made concerning what we left behind. We have only to look around us to know that this is inevitable: people thrive, grow old, and then die—some sooner, some later. Before then, we will all likely make our own assessments in some measure by asking ourselves if the world is a better place for our having lived in it. Most of us take stock from time to time, whether it is to understand what our purpose might be or to see if our youthful purposes have been fulfilled. We each ask ourselves in reflection, more often than we realize, whether there is more to do; whether we need to change course; whether it is simply time to put our feet up and reminisce.[14] Were we good stewards of the gifts and callings we were entrusted with? Did we take responsibility for leading when the opportunity was placed before us? How are we using our nonrenewable time on earth? These are good questions to ask

---

14. So-called adult day camp is a more recent phenomenon, whereas living life as best one can until the end has been the prevalent choice until this time of greater longevity and more choices for living out the end of life.

ourselves wherever we are in life as we draw the stories of these two men and their legacies and lessons to a close.

We all leave something behind much like a boat leaves its wake to ripple outward. Every one of us passes on something that impacts the next generation. For those who have led and served well, the heritage is most often left in the lives of others. We are judged by our beliefs and by the consequent actions together, although much of what we have done may remain far more obscure than the legacies of the two men we have spent time with here. We may never know how many others have benefited from our lives or how many have been harmed by our indifference, lack of action, or outright enmity. In short, there is little that separates us from Wilberforce and Jefferson, for we are all human beings: created equal, yet fallen, with the hope of redemption still, despite ourselves. We all must come to the point, as Wilberforce did, where we have the opportunity to learn that we are completely dependent upon God and everything else is an illusion. We may think it all turns on our doing as Jefferson did and turn aside when we are overwhelmed by the implications. In reality, if these two stories allow us to conclude anything it is that it all turns on God's freely doing what we cannot in the end. The word for that is grace.[15]

The poet Shelley reflects on this truth through his insightful poem, "Ozymandias," observing that each one of us, great and small, leave behind what we have built with our lives. Despite all that we might erect for posterity to take note of, little is there to see, and that diminished almost entirely, for those who would build monuments to themselves:

> Nothing beside remains. Round the decay
> Of that colossal wreck, boundless and bare
> The lone and level sands stretch far away.

Shelley understood, as he reflected on the ancient, decayed edifice he discovered in the desert, that we each have a choice to build a monument to ourselves or to build into others' lives through acts of service that remain after we are gone. We can take up the responsibility to assist others or to stand on top of their prone bodies in our ascension to the temporary heights of accomplishment.

But Wilberforce understood even more fully, as Shelley did not and as Jefferson apparently could not, that others would the best ones to

---

15. Andrews, *Kingdom Life*, 51.

write our epitaph; that our legacies are really work we have had prepared already for us to do by our Creator and which are also enabled by him.[16] The wisdom of the ages tells us that it is an ephemeral undertaking to attempt to lord it over others in death as we may have sought to do in life because, at the end of the day, nothing will remain. We may write our own epitaphs, but time will erase them and substitute truth.

We may seek great things for ourselves, we may aspire to be great leaders or recognized experts or even good neighbors, but the voice of the universe tells us that Jesus was right in his lessons that dwelt on serving others. This course, paradoxically, marks the road to servant leadership and lasting success—even as we are told by the stories of these two men. At the end of time, the very best accolade we can ever imagine will recognize how well we have been stewards of the gifts we have been given and the opportunities and challenges we have faced, whether as leaders or as followers. It is in faithful persistence in the tasks and the responsibilities that are our calling that we can know at the end of the day we have used our gifts and opportunities well and have accomplished our purpose on this earth.[17]

KNOWING AND DOING

1. This may be a good time to take stock of your life. Even if you are young, there is already a good body of knowledge that you have about yourself: your purpose, your goals in life, and your discipline in persisting day by day. If you are near the end, it is also a good time because as long as we are alive we have a calling. Don't use this as a time to lament what you have not done, but focus upon thankfulness for what has been done through you and for the gifts and purpose and opportunities you have still.

2. If these lessons and legacies from the lives of Wilberforce and Jefferson are virtues and principles that have merit, try using these as a mirror for your own life and as a way for God to search you

---

16. "We are his workmanship, created in Christ Jesus for good works, which God prepared beforehand, that we should walk in them." Ephesians 2:10, English Standard Version (ESV).

17. The essence of this understanding comes from the parable of the talents where Jesus says to those who steward their gifts wisely: "Well done, good and faithful servant. You have been faithful over a little; I will set you over much. Enter into the joy of your master." Matthew 25:23, ESV Study Bible.

and know your heart and your thoughts so that he might lead you deeper into your story and to results that will last.[18]

3. What other "lessons and legacies" have you drawn from the stories of these two men? For yourself? For our nation's leaders?

4. What may have been your one biggest "Aha!" from these stories?

---

18. This principle is one David, the greatest king in Israel's history, used as a prayer but perhaps also as a periodic way to assess his own life and leadership. Psalm 139:23 in the New Living translation renders it: "Search me, O God, and know my heart; test me and know my anxious thoughts. Point out anything in me that offends you, and lead me along the path of everlasting life."

Epilogue

Wilberforce, Jefferson, and the End of the Story

On December 3, 1861, Abraham Lincoln delivered his first State of the Union address to Congress. It was a watershed in American history. He sought to glue back together the broken nation while simultaneously eliminating the root cause of the violent parting of North and South that had occurred in the months before he took office. As he laid out his priorities for the divided nation, the two armies were already engaged in the great Civil War that would dominate every day of Lincoln's time in office until his tragic death in 1865. On this day early in his presidency, he took an unprecedented step that no president before had taken: he proposed to give diplomatic recognition to two countries whose populations consisted primarily of freed black slaves, Haiti and Liberia, thus breaking with every president before him, beginning with Thomas Jefferson. Although it may have seemed innocuous in light of everything else he addressed, it only confirmed, for some, the reckless and divisive course he had charted. For others, it marked the beliefs he would hold to in the darkest days ahead.

The backdrop for Lincoln's decision was that Haiti had been freed from the dominion of its French overseers in 1801 by a revolution of African slaves. The Adams administration had begun the process of giving diplomatic legitimacy to Haiti, recognizing the kinship of their countries' births. But when Thomas Jefferson came to the presidency, things quickly changed. He refused to receive the credentials of Haiti's chargé d'affaires; then he proceeded to scuttle America's diplomatic recognition entirely. Napoleon soon tried to retake the island by sending forces under his brother-in-law, Charles Leclerc. Incredibly, Jefferson secretly worked with Napoleon to help restore French rule—and reinstitute slavery.¹ It was destined to be a miserable failure—for the French.

Similarly, Liberia had been founded by freed black slaves from the United States. They were later to be joined by other free blacks who wanted to become U.S. citizens but were coerced by the American Colonialization Society to relocate there much as Jefferson and others had advocated as the solution when slavery ended. The driving force behind this geographical transfer was not as benign as it might appear, fostered as it was by the racist view that blacks and whites could not live together due to blacks' inferior capacities. (The Colonization Society was the same one that Wilberforce had been deceived into sponsoring shortly before his death, but which he recanted when he learned the truth during William Lloyd Garrison's visit.) In 1847, Liberia put forth its own Declaration of Independence, charging the United States with oppression that had forced the former slaves to make new lives in a land other than the one that had become their own. Quickly recognized diplomatically by Britain and several other European countries, Liberia was refused recognition by the United States as Haiti had been. A national policy of nonrecognition of nations comprising former slaves had been in place since Jefferson's presidency.

Lincoln knew he risked severe disapproval from the wavering border states, whose support he badly needed in this great struggle. Many others, some from the North and the entire South, would disagree vehemently with his decision, yet his stated rationale was simple, resting as it did on justice and fairness long overdue:

> If any good reason exists why we should persevere longer in withholding our recognition of the independence and sovereignty of Hayti and Liberia, I am unable to discern it. Unwilling, however, to inaugurate a novel policy in regard to them without the approbation of Congress, I submit for your consideration the expediency of an appropriation for maintaining a chargé d'affaires near each of those new States. It does not admit of doubt that important commercial advantages might be secured by favorable treaties with them.²

In proposing this change in policy with disarming forthrightness, Lincoln redressed decades of discrimination against former slaves who had taken the very same steps as the United States in separating from

1. Oakes, *The Radical and the Republican*, 156.
2. "State of the Union Addresses."

England. For Lincoln, the issue was both ethical and pragmatic—we might gain economically as well as in moral standing.

Once again we are left with questions: Why did Jefferson not follow Adams's lead and recognize Haiti? Why would he secretly conspire to overthrow the nascent country in league with France? Why did this precedent lead later administrations to adopt this policy and fail to recognize Liberia? These unsettling queries only add further consternation to an already unclear record regarding slavery set against his oft-stated beliefs. Ironically, Jefferson had clearly voiced a view of the benefits of rebellion against tyrannical governments that would seem to place him on the side of former slaves' quest for liberty and a new nation of their own:

> God forbid we should ever be twenty years without such a rebellion. The people cannot be all, and always, well informed. The part which is wrong will be discontented, in proportion to the importance of the facts they misconceive. If they remain quiet under such misconceptions, it is lethargy, the forerunner of death to the public liberty. . . . And what country can preserve its liberties, if its rulers are not warned from time to time, that this people preserve the spirit of resistance? Let them take arms. . . . What signify a few lives lost in a century or two? The tree of liberty must be refreshed from time to time, with the blood of patriots and tyrants. It is its natural manure.[3]

Consistency of practice with belief should have produced in Jefferson an eagerly outstretched hand to Haiti rather than a cold shoulder.

In a second break with the past, Abraham Lincoln again acted in opposition to Jefferson's precedent when he decided to actively enforce the laws against slave trading that dated back over fifty years. He soon sent out U.S. ships to confiscate five slave-carrying vessels that were flying the British flag in order to practice their dirty business undeterred. Up until then, they had been successful. Lincoln's decisive action resulted in the freeing of hundreds of slaves as the first American execution of a ship's captain for illegally transporting slaves was swiftly completed. Surreptitious American slave trading came to an abrupt halt.

Then Lincoln, with William Seward, his secretary of state, had a treaty drawn up with Britain for mutual suppression of the slave trade. This was the very treaty Wilberforce had urgently proposed to Jefferson in 1808, in response to which he had received only silence.[4] Lincoln was thus able to report to Congress that for the first time in U.S. history,

3. "Thomas Jefferson Quotes."
4. Oakes, *The Radical and the Republican*, 157–158.

"So far as American ports and American citizens are concerned, that inhuman and odious traffic has come to an end."[5] The last vestiges of American slave trading had ceased. The formal diplomatic recognition of Haiti and Liberia followed immediately thereafter.

THE DECLARATION'S IDEAS EMBODIED

If there was an American political leader whose life and vocation can be compared with the life of Jefferson in his facility with the written word and in his passionate expression mounted against the offense of slavery on the soul of the nation, it was Lincoln. Time and time again in public speeches, both before and after he assumed the presidency, Lincoln went back to the writing of the founding fathers. He particularly favored Jefferson's words while enlarging them with his own, drawing upon not only the Declaration of Independence but also other statements Jefferson had written on slavery and human freedom. Lincoln used these words to cement the continuity of his actions with the founding principles, framing these precedents as support for his course and that of the unity of the states.

He voiced, for example, that the North's primary purpose in fighting was to keep the Union intact while maintaining the core values of his predecessors. In that sense, he was the linear descendant of Jefferson's thinking more than any man who held the office before him, even though Lincoln's scholarly preparation was bereft of Jefferson's classical advantages. The only books Lincoln read for many years as a youth were the Bible and *Robinson Crusoe*, and their soft echoes resonate throughout his writings and speeches.

Lincoln used two posts, as it were, to support the door to freedom for the enslaved. The first was his belief in the importance of continuity with the founding principles of America. This continuity, he averred, could occur only if the Union was restored in accordance with the original vision for one nation. The second post supporting Lincoln's door to freedom was an often-used quotation of Jefferson, which ironically tied Lincoln more closely to Wilberforce: "I tremble for my country when I remember that God is just."[6] In bringing back those words to fuel his own course, Lincoln revealed what lay at the center of his own awe-inspiring persistence—his growing awareness of God's justice for the oppressed and his own responsibility for redressing this wrong as the leader of the

---

5. Ibid., 159.
6. Trueblood, *Abraham Lincoln*, 84.

country whose core values he would uphold come what may. More and more it seems to have become Lincoln's vocation, his calling, that he must take up abolition as God's instrument and persist in it until the end: "I expect to maintain this contest until successful or until I die, or am conquered, or my term expires, or Congress and the country forsake me."[7] In this statement we can hear the tones of Wilberforce before Parliament that he would not back away until slavery's end.

THE POWER OF A LIFE STORY

In many ways, it was Wilberforce's story as much as Jefferson's words that energized Lincoln's persistence against opposition. As Lincoln observed in his campaign for election:

> I have not allowed myself to forget that the abolition of the Slave-trade by Great Britain, was agitated a hundred years before its final success; that the measure had its open fire-eating opponents; its negro equality opponents; its dollar and cent opponents; its inferior race opponents; its stealthy "don't care" opponents; its good order opponents; that all these opponents got offices and their adversaries got none. But I have also remembered that though they blazed like tallow-candles for a century, at last they flickered in the socket, died out, stank in the dark for a brief season, and were remembered no more even by the smell. Schoolboys know that Wilberforce and Granville Sharp helped that cause forward; but who can now name a single man who labored to retard it?[8]

Wilberforce passed on to Lincoln lessons of persistence and moral courage, perhaps even the importance of faith that increasingly marked Lincoln's few years in office, particularly from 1862 on. As the war dragged on with its rivers of blood and untold heartache, Lincoln's sorrows grew even as he persevered almost alone. These virtues of Wilberforce's character could be seen in Lincoln's dogged pursuit of the presidency and then in his moral opposition to tolerating slavery in a country that recognized God as the author of equality.

It was particularly in the darkest hours of the war that Lincoln began anew to recognize God's providence in the affairs of men; here he came, almost reluctantly, to the deeply held beliefs of William Wilberforce, breaking with the philosophy of human self-determination that he had long embraced much as Jefferson had. In 1862 he made a vow, not unlike that of Wilberforce and The Saints, that he would follow the leading he

---

7. Ibid., 37.
8. Lincoln, "Speech Fragment Concerning the Abolition of Slavery."

felt to end man's oppression of other men, yet he would yield himself to the outcome God would bring about—whatever it might be. The same worldview to which Wilberforce held helped engender Lincoln's persistent quest to end slavery while he still submitted to God's providence in the timing. This lesson seemed to animate Lincoln's own response ever more as the nation sank deeper and deeper into the horrific war. If Lincoln had not found comfort in a God of sovereign providence, he might well have broken or given up to let another generation try its hand.[9] For many of us, this is not the Lincoln we thought we knew. His was an uncommon faith, uncommonly expressed not often written of. How this occurred is a fascinating but little recognized part of his life.

A SECOND "GREAT CHANGE"

In the dark days following his four-year-old son's death in 1862, the Christian faith and worldview that changed William Wilberforce also caused Lincoln to quietly and gradually undergo *his* "great change" as he struggled with the loss of his dear Eddie. He could not grasp what the death of the innocent child could possibly mean amidst the thousands of mounting war dead. In quiet, private encounters with a pastor who came to console him, Lincoln began to see that in suffering there could also be meaning and that a God of providence stood behind it all with purposes that were unfathomable yet at the same time undergirded by a love deeper than could be fully known. A slowly dawning belief began to give Lincoln new certainty in his calling and growing acknowledgment that his dependence upon God was what would sustain him through the remaining dark years of war and bloodshed. This belief was neither Jefferson's Enlightenment principles of the rights of man nor the philosophy that widespread education would lead to progressive cultural morality. Lincoln's beliefs, however, were not expressed in Wilberforce's evangelical Christian language either.

Although Lincoln would not express his own transformation in the words used by The Saints, it was his often expressed faith in divine Providence and in the belief that he must persist in doing what was right that kept him going through all the setbacks over the course of his four plus years in office. The hardships, fears, and opposition he experienced in his brief time must have seemed like a compression of all those that

---

9. I am indebted to Elton Trueblood for this deeper understanding of Abraham Lincoln in his incredibly rich small book, *Abraham Lincoln: Theologian of Anguish*. Regrettably, the book is out of print, but used copies can still be purchased.

Wilberforce faced for more than forty years. During those dark hours, Lincoln called on nine different occasions for an official national day of prayer and fasting—far more than any president before or since—and inaugurated the national observance of Thanksgiving.[10] This was a practice Jefferson studiously avoided, as did his protégé Madison after him. For Lincoln, his promise to God when he took the oath of office now bore down on him with new meaning. The recognition of what he had vowed was also the precursor to the courageous decision to issue the Emancipation Proclamation that forever changed the face of the country. Lincoln expressed the burden of his presidential oath when he spoke directly to the seceding states in his First Inaugural Address on March 4, 1861:

> In your hands my dissatisfied fellow countrymen, and not in *mine*, is the momentous issue of civil war. The government will not assail *you*. You can have no conflict, without being yourselves the aggressors. *You* have no oath registered in heaven to destroy the government, while I shall have the most solemn one to "preserve protect and defend" it.[11]

Elton Trueblood argues that from the day Abraham Lincoln took that oath, he began the journey from a politician to becoming the "theologian of anguish," whose struggle became less and less one of politics and ever more one raised to "the level of the holy." This became more publicly evident as Lincoln met with his cabinet in the wake of the successful battle at Antietam. At this meeting, he explained why he was about to issue the Emancipation Proclamation to free the slaves in the South in 1863: "I made a solemn vow before God, that if General Lee was driven back from Pennsylvania, I would crown the result by the declaration of freedom to the slaves."[12] Gideon Welles, secretary of the navy, confirmed this in his diary and added that Lincoln said that God "had decided this question in favor of the slave."[13]

THE END

In a real way, Lincoln and Wilberforce joined arms that day as each man saw his calling to free the slaves as being from the Creator of men: each had vowed to follow that call where it led; each could do nothing but continue until the end; and each had seen the unimaginable outcome

10. Ibid., 93.
11. Ibid., 24.
12. Ibid.
13. Ibid., 25.

as resting wholly on a God of providence and of grace who favored the weak over the strong. One saw the end of slavery won in the "peace" of legislative battles of more than forty years before he died in bed, in a home not his own; the other saw slavery end in an exhaustion of a war he presided over for nearly five years of uncountable deaths and unimaginable anxiety before he died in a strange bed, the victim of an assassin's bullet.

The man who finally led an end to slavery in America was a profoundly humble, steel-centered leader—perhaps the greatest president ever to hold the office. Lincoln was a man who believed in Jefferson's words of the equality of man, then acted upon Wilberforce's example of action rooted in beliefs about what it actually meant to be a man and a brother. In that sense, the paths of Lincoln's two predecessors were the sources for his inspiration which finally crossed then joined together to complete the unfinished journey.

An Exhausted Abraham Lincoln, Days Before His Assassination

Jefferson decried to the end of his days the unjust captivity practiced in America, yet he could not come to the place where he would risk giving up his plantation, freeing but a handful of his slaves upon his death.

Wilberforce, on the other hand, gave up his health, wealth, energies, and ambitions because he believed he could not rest or deviate from his call but must persist until the end. Lincoln would also persist through repeated failures and disappointments his entire life. He had thought his goal in life was to achieve the highest office,[14] only to find that his real call was the same terrible one that came to Wilberforce. He, too, would give up his health and his energies and the approbation of great office so that others could find life and liberty and pursue happiness as free men. It has been well said, "Greater love has no one than this, that someone lay down his life for his friends."[15] Am I not a man and a brother? Two men answered "Yes" to that question, and in so doing gave up their lives.

As Lincoln lay fatally shot behind the left ear in a bed in tailor William Peterson's house, his pulse slowly flickered and, at 7:22 a.m. on April 15, 1865, stopped. At that, the attending physician said simply, "He is gone." Everyone attending him then knelt, placing their hands on the bed as a minister present asked that God would accept his humble servant into his kingdom. As they knelt in silence, Secretary of War Edwin Stanton quietly said, "Now he belongs to the ages." He had fought the good fight and persisted in it; he had kept the faith. Although the last page of his story was now written, his legacy to future generations was just beginning. It was a legacy that helped bring together William Wilberforce and Thomas Jefferson in spirit and intent and one that would carry forward to be taken up by Rev. Martin Luther King, Jr., in his own quest to lead the descendants of African slaves to their final freedom.

It is a story of oppression, courage, and persistence that will likely keep recurring in one form or another until all men love their neighbors as themselves. Each generation until then will have the legacies of these great leaders upon which to draw and the source of their strength to endure will sustain them as well. This might be your story.

---

14. As Lincoln aptly said for all who would aspire to the top of the ladder: "Nearly all men can stand the test of adversity, but if you really want to test a man's character, give him power."

15. John 15:13, English Standard Version.

Appendix

Comparative Life Timelines

Jefferson			Wilberforce
Born, April 13, Shadwell, Virginia	1743		
Father dies	1757		
		1759	Born, August 24, Hull, England
Enters William & Mary; Wm. Small mentors	1760		
Reads law with mentor George Wythe	1762		
		1768	Father dies; John Newton mentors
Elected to House of Burgesses: Virginia slavery abolition bill defeated	1769		
		1772	Slavery abolished on English soil
Drafts Declaration of Independence	1776	1776	Enters Cambridge
Virginia Governor: flees British army	1780	1780	Elected to Parliament from Hull
Beloved wife Martha dies	1783		
Minister to France	1784	1784	Elected from prestigious Yorkshire
Notes on State of Virginia republished	1786	1786	"Great change;" Newton: "do it"
		1787	Societies for Reformation of Manners
First U.S. Secretary of State	1789		
		1791	First slave trade bill defeated
		1792	Moves to Clapham

248

Returns to Monticello	1794		
Vice President to Adams	1797	1797	Publishes Real Christianity
Returns to Monticello	1798		
Elected President	1801		
Louisiana Purchase	1803		
		1807	Slave trade bill finally passes
Slave trade bill passed	1808		
Returns to Monticello last time	1809		
Renewal of Adams correspondence	1812	1812	Steps down to represent Bramber
Edward Coles seeks abolition support	1814		
University of Virginia launched	1817	1817	Europe slave trading agreement
Lafayette returns: rebukes slavery	1821		
		1823	Abolition bill introduced by Buxton
University of Virginia opens	1825	1825	Retires from Parliament
Dies July 4th: bankrupt	1826		
		1830	Goes to live with sons: bankrupt
		1833	Dies July 29th; abolition bill passes
		1834	Slaves free in English colonies, July 31
Lincoln elected President; slave trade end enforced; Civil War	1860		
Emancipation Proclamation	1863		
Civil War ends; Lincoln assassinated; 13th Amendment abolishes slavery	1865		

Bibliography

Aitken, Jonathan, *John Newton: From Disgrace to Amazing Grace*, Wheaton, IL: Crossway Books, 2007
———, "Newton, Wilberforce, and the Spirituality of Abolition," *Implications* online journal of the Trinity Forum, March 12, 2007.
Andrews, Alan, General Editor, *The Kingdom Life: A Practical Theology of Discipleship and Spiritual Formation*, Colorado Springs, CO: NavPress, 2010.
Bailyn, Bernard, *The Ideological Origins of the American Revolution*, Cambridge: The Harvard University Press, 1967.
Bellah, Robert, et al, *The Good Society*, New York: Alfred Knopf, 1991.
Belmonte, Kevin, *Hero for Humanity: A Biography of William Wilberforce*, Colorado Springs, CO: NavPress, 2002.
Berger, Peter L., *A Rumor of Angels*, Garden City, NY: Doubleday, Anchor, 1970.
Bernstein, R.B., *Thomas Jefferson*, New York: Oxford University Press, 2003.
Bonhoeffer, Dietrich, "After Ten Years," *Who Stands Fast?* McLean, VA: Trinity Forum, 2009.
Buxton, Charles, Ed., *The Memoirs of Sir Thomas Foxwell Buxton*, 4th ed., London: John Murray, 1850.
Capon, Lester J. Ed., *The Adams-Jefferson Letters: The Complete Correspondence Between Thomas Jefferson and Abigail and John Adams*, Chapel Hill: The University of North Carolina Press, 1987.
Chadwick, Bruce, *I Am Murdered: George Wythe, Thomas Jefferson and the Killing That Shocked a New Nation*, New York: John Wiley & Sons, Inc., 2009
Chesterton, G. K., "Why I Am a Catholic" Free Republic.com, http://www.freerepublic.com/focus/f-religion/2645606/posts.
Collins, Jim, *Good to Great: Why Some Companies Make the Leap and Others Don't*, New York: Harper Collins, 2001.
Crawford, Alan Pell, *Twilight at Monticello: The Final Years of Thomas Jefferson*, New York: Random House, 2008
Cunningham, Noble E. Jr., *Jefferson and Monroe: Constant Friendship and Respect*, Chapel Hill, NC: University of North Carolina Press, 2003.
Durant, Will and Ariel, *The Age of Reason Begins: A History of European Civilization in the Period of Shakespeare, Bacon, Montaigne, Rembrandt, Galileo, and Descartes: 1558 to 1648 (the Story of Civilization, Part VII)*, New York: Simon and Schuster, 1961.
Ellis, Joseph, *American Creation: Triumphs and Tragedies at the Founding of the Republic*, New York: Random House, 2007.
———. *American Sphinx: The Character of Thomas Jefferson*, New York: Vintage, 1998.
———. *His Excellency, George Washington*, New York: Alfred Knopf, 2004.

Fall, Bernard, *Street without Joy: The French Debacle in Indochina*, Mechanicsburg, PA: Stackpole Books, 2005.
Garber, Steve, "A Wound in My Heart Has Been Healed: On Kenya, Kazakhstan and K Street, Too," The Washington Institute website, http://www.washingtoninst.org/168/a-wound-in-my-heart-has-been-healed-on-kenya-kazakhstan-and-k-street-too/.
———. "Making Peace with Proximate Justice," *Comment*, December 2007.
———. *The Fabric of Faithfulness: Connecting Belief and Behavior*, Wheaton, IL: IV Press, 2010,
Gaustad, Edwin S., *Sworn on the Altar of God: A Religious Biography of Thomas Jefferson*, Grand Rapids, Wm. B. Eerdmans, 1996.
George Wythe College Website, "Building Statesmen," http://www.gw.edu/about.
George, Bill, *True North*, San Francisco: Jossey-Bass, 2007.
Hague, William, *William Wilberforce: The Life of the Great Anti-Slave Trade Campaigner*, New York: Harcourt, Inc, 2007.
Halberstam, David, *The Best and the Brightest*, New York: Ballantine Books, 1993.
Holladay, J. Douglas, "A Life of Significance," *Character Counts*, Os Guinness, ed., Washington, D.C.: The Trinity Forum, 1999.
Homer, *The Odyssey*, Robert Fagles, trans., New York: Penguin books, 1996.
Howse, Ernest Marshall, *Saints in Politics: The Clapham Circle and the Growth of Freedom*, London: George Allen and Unwin Ltd., 1971.
Hybels, Bill, *Descending Into Greatness*, Grand Rapids, MI: Zondervan Publishing House, 1993.
International Justice Mission, http://www.ijm.org/ourwork/injusticetoday.
Isaac, Robert and Wilberforce, Samuel, *The Life of William Wilberforce*, vol. 3.
Heifitz, Ronald A. and Lipinski, Marty, *Leadership on the Line: Staying Alive through the Dangers of Leading*, Boston: Harvard Business School Press, 2002.
Hunter, James Davison, *The Death of Character: Moral Education in an Age without Good or Evil*, New York: Basic Books, 2000.
Katzenbach, Jon R. and Smith, Douglas K., *The Wisdom of Teams*, New York: Harper Collins, 1993.
Kelling, George L. and Wilson, James Q., "Broken Windows," *The Atlantic*, March 1982.
Kennedy, Roger, *Mr. Jefferson's Lost Cause: Land, Farmers, Slavery and the Louisiana Purchase*, London: Oxford University Press, 2003.
Koch, Adrienne, *Jefferson and Madison: The Great Collaboration*, Old Saybrook, CT: Konecky and Konecky, 2004.
———, and Peden, William, eds., *The Life and Selected Writings of Thomas Jefferson* New York: Random House, 1944.
Kuhn,Thomas, *The Structure of Scientific Revolutions*, Chicago: University of Chicago Press, 1996, 3rd Edition.
Lean, Garth, *God's Politician: William Wilberforce's Struggle to Abolish the Slave Trade and Reform the Morals of a Nation*, Colorado Springs, CO: Helmers & Howard, 1987.
Lewis, C. S., *Mere Christianity*, San Francisco: Harper, 2001.
———. *Prince Caspian*, New York: Harper Collins, 2004.
———. *The Abolition of Man*, New York: HarperOne, 2001.
Library of Congress, Stowage of the British Slave Ship Brookes under the regulated slave trade act of 1788, http://memory.loc.gov/cgi-bin/query/r?ammem/rbpe:@field(DOCID+@lit(rbpe28204300).

Malone, Dumas, *Jefferson and His Time, The Sage of Monticello*, Boston: Little, Brown, 1967.

——. *Jefferson, The Virginian*, Boston: Little, Brown and Company, 1948.

McCall, Morgan W. Jr., Lombardo, Michael, and Morrison, Ann M., *The Lessons of Experience: How Successful Executives Develop on the Job*, New York: Lexington Books, 1988.

McCullough gieheadtilt.com/mirrors-two, David, *John Adams*, New York: Simon and Schuster, 2001.

Metaxas, Eric, *Amazing Grace: William Wilberforce and the Heroic Campaign to End Slavery*, San Francisco: Harper Collins, 2007

Metzger, Michael, "Rear View Mirrors, Part Two," Doggie Head Tilt Blog, http://wwwdog. /#more-168.

Miller, John Chester, *The Wolf by the Ears: Thomas Jefferson and Slavery*, New York: The Free Press, 1977.

Novak, Michael and Jana, *Washington's God: Religion, Liberty and the Father of Our Country*, New York: Basic Books, 2006.

Oakes, James, *The Radical and the Republican: Frederick Douglass, Abraham Lincoln and the Triumph of Antislavery Politics*, New York: W.W. Norton & Company, 2007.

Peterson, Merrill D., ed., *Thomas Jefferson: Writings*, New York: Penguin Putnam, Inc., 1984.

Pollock, John, *Wilberforce*, London: John Constable, 1977.

Rouse, Marylynn, ed., unpublished letters between John Newton and William Wilberforce, The Newton Project.

Ryken, Leland, *Realms of Gold*, Portland: Shaw Books, 2000

Schein, Edgar, *Organizational Culture and Leadership*, San Francisco: Jossey-Bass, 2004.

Sherman, Doug *Your Work Matters to God*, Colorado Springs: NavPress, 1990.

Smith, Christian, *Soul Searching: The Spiritual Lives of American Teenagers*, Oxford: Oxford University Press, 2005.

The Armed Forces Officer, http://www.au.af.mil/au/awc/awcgate/usmchist/officer.txt.

The Avalon Project, Yale Law School, http://www.yale.edu/lawweb/avalon/presiden/inaug/jefinau1.htm, 1996.

The History Place: A Nation Divided--The U.S. Civil War, 1861-1865, http://www.historyplace.com/civilwar/.

The Papers of Thomas Jefferson, Princeton University, electronic version, http://www.princeton.edu/~tjpapers/declaration/declaration.html

Thucydides, *The Peloponnesian War*, Book II, chapter 43, section 3, All Experts website, http://en.allexperts.com/q/Greek-2004/2009/3/Pericles-1.htm.

Trueblood, Elton, *Abraham Lincoln: Theologian of American Anguish*, New York: Harper & Row Publishers, 1953.

Turner, Steve, *Amazing Grace*, New York: Harper Collins, 2002.

Weaver, Richard, *Ideas Have Consequences*, Chicago: University of Chicago Press, 1948

Wilberforce, William, *Real Christianity Contrasted with the Prevailing Religious System*, abridged, Portland: Multnomah Press, 1982.

——. *A Practical View of the Prevailing Religious System of Professed Christians in the Higher and Middle Classes in This Country Contrasted with Real Christianity*, Boston: Crocker and Brewster, 1829.

Witherington, Ben III, *Work: A Kingdom Perspective on Labor*, Grand Rapids: Wm B. Eerdmans Publishing Co., 2011.

Subject/Name Index

T. J. refers to Thomas Jefferson.
W. W. refers to William Wilberforce.
Page numbers followed by "f"
indicate illustrations.

Abingdon, Lord, 72
abolition. *See also* Clapham Circle; emancipation; slavery
    antislavery petition from Maidstone, 161–63
    on English soil, 66–67, 71
    as impossibility in U.S., 183–85
    passions against, 12
    T. J.'s failed legislation on, 22–23
    W. W. and, 33–35, 70–72, 111–27, 224–25
    in West Indies, 153–55, 163–66
Abolition of Slavery Act (England), 3
Adams, Abigail, 95–96, 98
Adams, John
    Alien and Sedition Act and, 119
    as Continental Congress delegate, 42
    death of, 2, 143–44
    on "diffusion," 184
    T. J. and, 90, 95–98, 109, 141–43, 182
Adams, John Quincy, 2
African Diaspora, 5. *See also* slave trade
African Institution, 149–50
Age of Reason, 188
Aitken, Jonathan, 27–28
Albermarle Academy, 131
alcoholism, 78
Alexander, Tsar of Russia, 150
Alien and Sedition Act (U. S.), 119
Amazing Grace (movie), 27, 169

American Colonialization Society, 201, 240
American Philosophical Society, 7
Anglo-American agreement (proposed) to enforce anti-slave trade laws, 126
antiperistasis, 35, 35n
Anti-Slave Society for the Mitigation and Gradual Abolition of Slavery Throughout the British Dominions, 155
An Appeal on Behalf of the Slaves in the West Indies (Wilberforce), 155, 158
apprenticeship program for freed slaves in West Indies, 162–63
A Summary View of the Rights of British America (Jefferson), 41–42
Autobiography (Jefferson), 181–83

Babington, Thomas, 66, 69, 73, 209
Bacon, Francis, 215
Bailyn, Bernard, 192–93
Banneker, Benjamin, 179–80
Barbados slave revolt, 154
Barbary pirates, 127
Battersea Rise, 65
Berger, Peter, 197
Bernstein, R. B., 174
Beyond Good and Evil (Nietzsche), 111
biblical justification of slavery, 38, 197
Bill for Religious Freedom in Virginia, 193, 196
Bill for the More General Diffusion of Knowledge (1778), 46
Bill of Rights, 56, 196
Bonaparte, Napoleon, 239

"broken windows" anti-vice strategy, 82
Burke, Edmund, 114
Burr, Aaron, 90, 98, 98n
Buxton, Thomas, 156–58, 162–63, 202

Callender, James, 96
Castelreagh, Lord, 150
Catholic church, 189–90
Central College, 131
charitable societies, 80–84
Charlotte, Queen of England, 80
chattel, 5
Chesterton, G. K., 202
child labor, 78
Christianity
  cultural, 206
  hypocrisy of, 79
  justification of slavery, 197
  T. J. and, 188–94
  W. W. and, 30, 188–91, 203–18, 225, 231, 233
Church of England, 10, 81, 189–90, 207
Church of Scotland, 190
Civil War (U.S.), 105, 168, 184, 198, 202, 235, 239, 245
Clapham Circle
  African Institution and, 149–50
  antislavery strategy of, 70–72
  artful propaganda of, 74–77
  charitable societies of, 80–84
  founding of, 64–66
  king's involvement in, 79–80
  members of, 66–69, 74f
  social reform and, 77–79
  taught by their cause, 72–73
  teamwork in, 66–69
  W. W. as leader of, 69–70
Clark, William, 104
Clarkson, Thomas, 66–69, 72–73, 118, 120, 151, 155, 170
Clay, Henry, 20
Cobbett, William, 158
Coles, Edward, 136–39, 137n, 181
Condorcet, Marquis de, 180
Constitution, U.S., 21, 49, 53–56
Continental Congress, 21, 40–42, 49, 56, 123

Corps of Discovery, 104
Cosway, Maria, 136
Court of Directors for the East India Council, 68
Cowper, William, 76–77
criticism, handling of, 212
cultural transformation. *See* moral reform and progress

Declaration of Independence, 2, 42–46, 45f, 52, 145, 169, 176, 226–27, 242–43
Democratic Republican Party, 18, 97, 99, 109
Descartes, René, 18, 188
"diffusion" of slaves, 143, 143n, 181, 183–86, 196, 198, 231
dissections, 78
The Doctrines of Heathen Philosophy Compared with Those of Revelation (Priestley), 210
Dolben Act (1788), 75, 114
Douglass, Frederick, 127, 197
Dunglinson, Robley, 1

East India Company, 68
Ellis, Joseph, 60, 183–85
emancipation. *See also* abolition; slavery
  Registry of Slaves Bill, 153–54
  T. J. and, 59–60, 137–38, 142, 148, 176–78, 180, 182–87, 202, 229
  W. W. and, 81–82, 149, 153–58, 160–66, 196, 202, 233
Emancipation Proclamation, 245
the Enlightenment, 11, 13, 16–18, 23, 188–98, 207, 215, 231
"Enthusiasts," 10, 25–27, 63, 151, 190
Epicurus, 194–95
An Essay on the Treatment and Conversion of African Slaves in the British Sugar Colonies (Ramsay), 68
executions, public, 78

faith, 230–35
Fauquier, Francis, 16–18, 23
federalism vs. states' rights. *See* states' rights vs. federalism
Federalist Papers, 54, 89
Federalists, 26, 46, 54–55, 96–99, 186–87, 228, 233
finishing well, 230–37
Foreign Slave Bill (1807, England), 124
France, slave trade in, 150
Frankl, Victor, 200
Franklin, Benjamin, 4, 131n, 192
French Revolution, 54–55
Freneau, Philip, 91
futurism, 197

Garber, Steve, 121, 220, 234
Garrison, William Lloyd, 187, 197, 201–2
George III, King of England, 41–42, 43–44, 79–80
Gisborne, Thomas, 66, 69, 73
God's providence. *See* providence
Grant, Charles, 66, 68–69
Grant, Ulysses S., 232
Grenville, Lord, 123–24

Haiti, 239–42
Halberstam, David, 230
Hamilton, Alexander
  Burr and, 90, 98, 98n
  as Constitution defender, 49
  death of, 90, 98, 98n
  federalism vs. states' rights and, 91–93
  Federalists Papers and, 54
  rivalry with T. J., 61, 87–94, 96–98, 109, 115, 142, 182, 184, 226, 228
Hannah and Her Sisters (movie), 68
"happy slave" argument, 71–72
hedgehogs, 200, 200n
Henry, Patrick, 55
Homer, 15
hope, 209–11
Howse, Ernest Marshall, 69

human trafficking, modern, 169–70
humility, 211, 227

impossibility argument of abolition in U.S., 183–85, 196
India, humanitarian issues in, 68, 153
inferiority, racial, 174–81, 240, 243
integrity
  T. J. and, 97, 108, 230–35
  W. W. and, 230–35
  Washington and, 21, 24, 87
  Wythe and, 21
International Congress of Vienna, 150–51

Jay, John, 127
Jefferson, Jane, 7
Jefferson, Martha, 47–48, 50
Jefferson, Peter, 7
Jefferson, Thomas. *See also* the Enlightenment
  Adams, final break with, 95–97
  Adams, reconciliation with, 98, 109, 141–43
  Anglo-American agreement (proposed) to enforce anti-slave trade laws, 126
  antislavery legislation of, failed, 22–23, 37
  Autobiography of, 181–83
  background and education of, 7–8
  birth of, 6
  on Christianity, 210–11
  comparative life timeline, 247–48
  Constitution and, 53–56
  as Continental Congress delegate, 42, 49
  contradictions in, 196–97
  death of, 1–2, 143–44
  death of father, 2, 14
  death of wife, 47–48, 50
  elected president 1800, 97–99
  emancipation and, 59–60, 137–38, 142, 148, 176–78, 180, 182–88, 202, 229

Jefferson, Thomas–continued
  as Epicurean, 194–95
  epitaph of, 129, 145
  fear of slave revolts, 106, 176n, 180, 183
  finishing well, 230–35
  Hamilton, rivalry with, 61, 87–94, 96–98, 109, 115, 142, 182, 184, 226, 228
  in House of Burgesses, 22, 39–41
  integrity and, 97, 108, 230–35
  last words of, 144
  leadership style of, 40–41, 139, 183–87, 221–23
  life purpose of. *See* tyranny
  living in the future, 195–96
  Madison and, 49–56, 61
  mentors of, 15–24
  as minister to France, 49–50
  Missouri Compromise and, 139–41
  Monroe and, 20, 22, 49, 56–58, 61
  optimism and, 173–98
  persistence and, 135, 172, 227–30
  portrait of, 45, 100f
  presidential inauguration of, 99–103
  on public education, 173
  on racial inferiority, 174–81, 240, 243
  on rebellion, necessity of, 59
  in retirement, 129–46
  as Secretary of State, 60–61, 86–93
  slavery and, 102–8, 135–39, 147, 182–88, 247
  times of, cultural and political, 10–13
  treason accusation against, 47–48, 228
  in Virginia House of Delegates, 46
  Virginia laws, revision of, 46
  vocation of, 39–40, 220, 230
  Washington and, 87–97, 182
  worldview of, 22, 40, 173–98, 218, 229–31
Jefferson and Madison (Koch), 37
Jeffersonianism, 18
John the Baptist, 156

Kennedy, Roger, 94, 222, 222n
King, Martin Luther, Jr., 155n, 232, 247
Koch, Adrienne, 37
Kuhn, Thomas, 179

leadership
  author's thoughts on, 168–72, 169–70n
  in colonial Virginia, 22
  Marshall, S. L. A., on, 168
  moral, 149, 169, 171
  servant, 222, 237
leadership styles
  of T. J., 40–41, 139, 183–87, 221–23
  of W. W., 63–64, 151–53, 203–4, 221–23, 231
  of Washington, 90, 123
Leclerc, Charles, 239
Lee, Robert E., 41n, 232
Lewis, C. S., 187, 229
Lewis, Meriwether, 49, 104
Liberia, 239–42
Lincoln, Abraham, 182, 198, 229, 232, 239–47, 246f, 247n
Locke, John, 18, 215
Louisiana Purchase, 57, 99, 103–5
Louisiana Territory, 103–5, 109, 184, 225
Lucretius, 204

MacAulay, Tom, 163
MacAulay, Zachary, 66–68, 72–73, 124, 151, 163, 202
Madison, James
  Callender and, 96
  Constitution and, 53–56
  Enlightenment and, 189
  federalism vs. states' rights and, 91–93
  in House of Burgesses, 22
  on *Notes on the State of Virginia*, 59–60
  portrait of, 52f
  T. J. and, 49–56, 61
  University of Virginia and, 130–31, 134

Malone, Dumas, 191–92
"A Man Who Changed His Times" (Pollock), 62
market capitalism, 4–5
Marshall, George, 232
Marshall, John, 20
Marshall, S. L. A., 168, 171
Mason, George, 55
Maury, William, 3
McCullough, David, 96
Melville, Lord, 123
mentors
  importance of, 171
  of T. J., 15–24
  of W. W., 9, 27–28, 34–36, 70, 224–25
Metaxas, Eric, 82
Methodism, 9–10, 25
Metzger, Mike, 197–98
Middle Passage, 4–5, 28, 35, 68, 71, 103, 113, 125, 169
Middleton, Lord, 123
Miller, John Chester, 102, 105, 185–87
Milner, Isaac, 30
Milton, John, 215
Missouri Compromise, 139–41, 181, 186
Monroe, James
  Anglo-American agreement (proposed) to enforce anti-slave trade laws, 126
  Callender and, 96
  Enlightenment and, 189
  Missouri Compromise and, 139–41
  portrait of, 58f
  slavery and, 58
  T. J. and, 20, 22, 49, 56–58, 61
  University of Virginia and, 130–31
Monticello, 8
moral courage, 171, 205–6
moral decay, 214
moral leadership, 149, 169, 171
moral reform and progress, 18, 33–34, 77–83, 160
More, Hannah, 66, 68

Negro inferiority, 174–81, 240, 243
"The Negro's Complaint" (Cowper), 77
Nelson, Admiral Lord, 70
Newton, John
  Christianity and, 215
  death of, 124
  on end of slave trade, 122
  Enlightenment and, 18
  portrait of, 32f
  on *Real Christianity*, 216–17
  W. W. and, 30–32, 113, 120–21
Nietzsche, Friedrich, 111
North-South compromise, 107
Northwest Ordinance of 1785, 140
Notes on the State of Virginia (Jefferson), 59, 174–81

Odyssey (Homer), 15
opposition, handling of, 212
Orwell, George, 197

Paine, Thomas, 117
Pericles, 220
perseverance, 162
persistence
  Lincoln and, 242–43, 247
  T. J. and, 135, 172, 227–30
  W. W. and, 64, 80, 157, 172, 194, 213, 227–30
  Washington and, 123
Pitt, William
  death of, 123
  slavery and, 62, 112, 122
  social reform and, 80
  Treason and Sedition bills and, 119
  W. W. and, 29, 30–32, 34, 63, 86, 116–17, 122, 152
politics of personal destruction, 98, 159
Pollock, John, 62, 148
Porteus, Bishop, 79–80
Presbyterian Church, 190
Priestley, Joseph, 132, 210
Prince Caspian (C. S. Lewis), 187
Proclamation of the Encouragement of Piety and Virtue (1787), 79–80

prostitution, 78
Protestant reformation, 189
providence, 14, 83, 206, 211, 214, 232, 243–44, 246
proximate justice, 121
public executions, 78
public spirit, 214
purpose, 224–27

racial inferiority, 174–81, 240, 243
Ramsay, James, 66, 68
rationalism, 188–89
Real Christianity (Wilberforce), 203–18, 225, 233
Registry of Slaves Bill, 153–54
religious beliefs, 230–35
responsibility, 207–9
revelation, 17, 188–93, 231
Robinson, Haddon, 234

Saint-Domingue slave revolt, 117
"The Saints," 63–66
self-advancement, 213
self-deception, 214–15
selfishness, 214
servant leadership, 222, 237
Seward, William, 241
Sharp, Granville, 66, 124, 243
Shelley, Percy Bysshe, 236
Shore, John, 66, 68
Short, William, 49, 195
skepticism, 188–89, 215
slave revolts
    Barbados, 154, 155
    Saint-Domingue, 117
    T. J.'s fear of, 106, 176n, 180, 183
    in West Indies, fear of, 11, 117
slavery
    biblical justification of, 38, 197
    compensation for slave owners in West Indies, 162
    in deleted passage of *Declaration of Independence*, 44–45
    "diffusion" as solution to, 143, 143n, 181, 183–86, 196, 198, 231
    in District of Columbia, 106
    economics of, 3–5, 72
    emigration to Africa and, 177, 198, 201–2, 240
    end of, England, 3
    end of, U.S., 246–47
    Hamilton and, 89, 91
    "happy slave" argument, 71
    ignorance about, 71–72
    immoral nature of, 71
    impossibility of abolition in U.S., 183–85, 196
    Missouri Compromise, 139–41
    modern human trafficking, 169–70
    Monroe and, 58
    in *Notes on the State of Virginia*, 174–81
    perspectives of, 11–12, 38
    racial inferiority and, 174–81, 240, 243
    as states' rights issue, 54–55, 91–93
    T. J. and, 102–8, 135–39, 148, 183–88, 247
    T. J./Adams correspondence on, 141–43
    W. W.'s first exposure to, 28
    western expansion, impact of, 104–5
slave ships, cutaway views of, 75–76, 76f
slave smuggling, 126–27
slave trade
    in Charleston, South Carolina, 107
    economics of, 4–6
    end of, England, 64, 123–27
    end of, U. S., 106–8, 125–27
    enforcement of laws against, 125–26, 149–51, 241
    in France, 150
    internal, U.S., 127
Small, William, 8, 16–18, 23, 28
Smith, Adam, 4–5
smuggled slaves, 126–27
social reform. *See* moral reform and progress
Societies for the Reformation of Manners, 79

Subject/Name Index   261

Societies for the Suppression of Vice, 80, 112
Stanley, Lord, 162
Stanton, Edwin, 247
states' rights vs. federalism, 54–55, 87–95, 109, 142, 154, 185–86, 225–26
Statute for Religious Freedom (1777), 46, 53
Stephen, James, 66, 68, 124, 202
Stockdale Paradox, 82, 82n

therapeutic individualism, 222, 222n
Thornton, Henry, 64–65
Thornton, John, 26–27, 30, 33, 64
transport slavery. *See* slave trade
Treason and Sedition bills (England), 119
Trueblood, Elton, 245
Truman, Harry S., 125, 185
Tubman, Harriett, 232
tyranny
   political, economic and religious, 11, 13, 18, 46, 169, 172, 173
   of slavery, 109, 117, 184–86
   T. J. and, 2–3, 22, 24, 33, 40–41, 46, 61, 87, 90, 96, 99, 142, 191, 195, 221, 224–28, 230

Unholy Triangle, 3–6, 36, 60, 124–25, 150
Unitarianism, 207, 215
University of Virginia, 130–35
U.S. Constitution. *See* Constitution, U.S.

Venn, John, 33, 65
Virginia House of Delegates, 46
Virginia planters, 22
vocations
   Lincoln's, 242–43
   T. J.'s, 39–40, 220, 230
   W. W.'s, 33–35, 120, 205–6, 220, 224–25, 233–34

Washington, George
   death of, 109
   Garber on, 220
   as honorary citizen of France, 117
   integrity and, 21, 24, 87
   leadership style of, 90, 123
   persistence and, 123
   providence and, 232
   as slaveholder, 107n
   T. J. and, 87–97, 182
"weak benevolence," 213
The Wealth of Nations (Smith), 4–5
Wedgwood, Josiah, 74–75
Welles, Gideon, 245
Wells, H. G., 1
Wesley, John, 9–10, 70, 121
Whitefield, George, 9, 27
Wilberforce, Elizabeth, 9
Wilberforce, Hannah, 9, 25
Wilberforce, Robert, 9, 25
Wilberforce, William
   abolition and, 33–35, 70–72, 111–27, 224–25
   Anglo-American agreement (proposed) to enforce anti-slave trade laws, 126
   antislavery petition from Maidstone, 161–63
   background and education of, 8–10, 28–29
   birth of, 6
   Clapham Circle and, 69–70
   comparative life timeline, 247–48
   on crime and vice, 81–82
   criticism, handling of, 212
   death of, 3, 163
   death of father, 6, 14, 25
   early political career of, 29–33
   elected MP from Bramber, 153
   elected MP from Hull, 27, 29
   emancipation and, 81–82, 149, 153–58, 160–66, 196, 202, 233
   as "Enthusiast," 25–27
   epitaph of, 165–66
   family life of, 152
   finishing well, 230–35

Wilberforce, William–continued
  first exposure to slavery, 28
  first slave trade bill defeated, 34–35, 37
  Garber on, 220
  "great change" of, 28–33, 63
  health issues of, 152, 160
  on hope, 209–11
  integrity and, 230–35
  last Parliamentary antislavery battle of, 156–60
  as leader of Clapham Circle, 69–70, 82
  life purpose of, 33–34, 224–25
  Lincoln on, 243
  mentors of, 9, 27–28, 34–36, 70, 224–25
  Newton and, 30–32, 113, 120–21
  opposition, handling of, 212
  persistence and, 64, 80, 157, 172, 194, 213, 227–30
  Pitt and, 29, 30–32, 34, 63, 86, 116–17, 122, 152
  portrait of, 26f, 115f
  rededication to antislavery cause 1789-1808, 111–27
  resignation from Parliament, 156–60
  on responsibility, 207–9, 208n
  times of, cultural and political, 10–13
  vocation of, 33–35, 120, 205–6, 220, 224–25, 233–34
  worldview of, 188–92, 200–218, 230–31. *See also* Christianity
Wilberforce, William (uncle), 9
Wilberforce, William "Alderman," 8–9, 29
William and Mary, King and Queen of England, 79
The Wolf by the Ears: Thomas Jefferson and Slavery (Miller), 185–87
worldview
  defined, 14, 171–72
  of slavery, 38
  of T. J., 22, 40, 173–98, 218, 229–31. *See also* the Enlightenment
  of W. W., 188–92, 200–218, 230–31. *See also* Christianity
Wythe, George, 8, 16–27, 20f, 21, 42, 44, 46, 49, 189

Zong Case, 67

www.ingramcontent.com/pod-product-compliance
Lightning Source LLC
Chambersburg PA
CBHW050626300426
44112CB00012B/1672